D0402896

MVFOL

three famines

Also by Thomas Keneally

Fiction

The Place at Whitton

The Fear

Bring Larks and Heroes

Three Cheers for the Paraclete

The Survivor

A Dutiful Daughter

The Chant of Jimmie Blacksmith

Blood Red, Sister Rose

Gossip from the Forest

Season in Purgatory

A Victim of the Aurora

Passenger

Confederates

The Cut-rate Kingdom

Schindler's Ark

A Family Madness

The Playmaker

Towards Asmara

By the Line

Flying Hero Class

Woman of the Inner Sea

Jacko

A River Town

Bettany's Book

An Angel in Australia

The Tyrant's Novel

The Widow and Her Hero

The People's Train

Non-fiction

Outback

The Place Where Souls Are Born

Now and in Time to Be: Ireland
    and the Irish

Memoirs from a Young Republic

Homebush Boy: A Memoir

The Great Shame

American Scoundrel

Lincoln

The Commonwealth of Thieves

Searching for Schindler

Australians: Origins to Eureka

For Children

Ned Kelly and the City of Bees

Roos in Shoes

three famines

STARVATION AND POLITICS

Thomas Keneally

PUBLICAFFAIRS
New York

Copyright © 2011 by The Serpentine Publishing C. (Pty) Limited

Published in the United States by PublicAffairs™,
a Member of the Perseus Books Group
Previously published in 2010 in Australia by Knopf,
an imprint of Random House

Printed in the United States of America.

PublicAffairs books are available at special discounts for bulk purchases in
the U.S. by corporations, institutions, and other organizations. For more
information, please contact the Special Markets Department at the Perseus
Books Group, 2300 Chestnut Street, Suite 200, Philadelphia, PA 19103, call
(800) 810-4145, ext. 5000, or e-mail special.markets@perseusbooks.com.

Cataloging-in-Publication data is available at the Library of Congress
LCCN: 2011931075
Hardcover ISBN: 978-1-61039-065-1
Ebook ISBN: 978-1-61039-066-8
First Edition
10 9 8 7 6 5 4 3 2 1

CONTENTS

To the memory of Tim and Kate Keneally

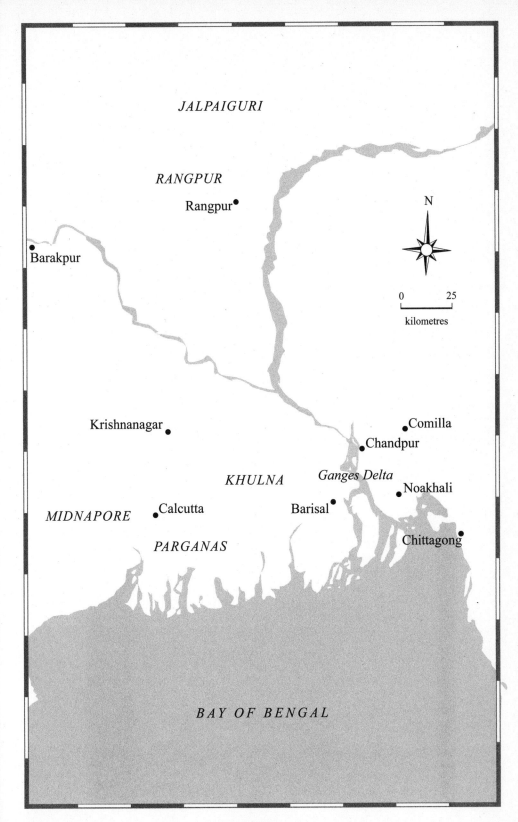

Bengal, 1945

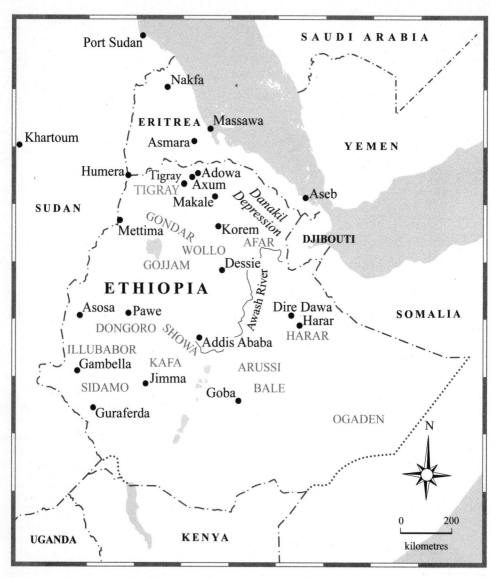

Ethiopia and Eritrea

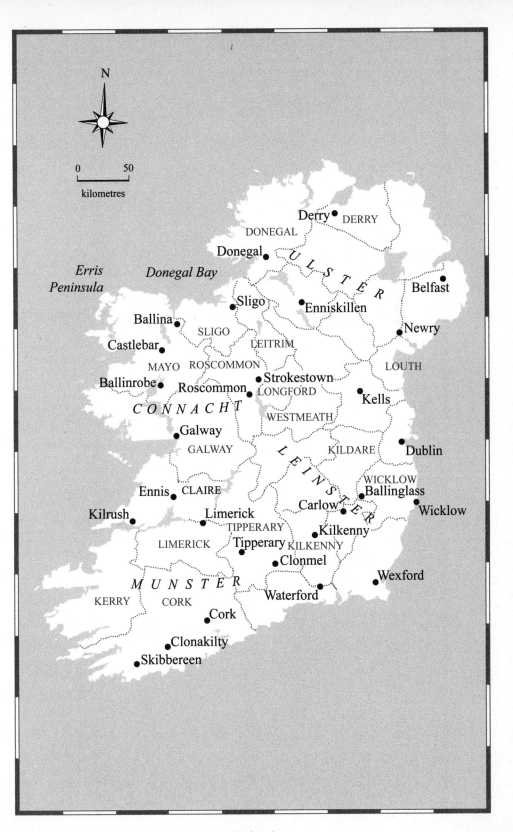

N

0   50
kilometres

Derry ● DERRY

DONEGAL

Donegal ●

Erris Peninsula

Donegal Bay

U L S T E R

Belfast ●

Sligo ●   ● Enniskillen

Newry ●

Ballina ●

SLIGO

LEITRIM

LOUTH

Castlebar ●

MAYO   ROSCOMMON

Ballinrobe ●   Roscommon ●   ● Strokestown

LONGFORD

Kells ●

C O N N A C H T

WESTMEATH

Galway ●

GALWAY

L E I N S T E R

KILDARE

Dublin ●

Ennis ●   CLAIRE

WICKLOW

Ballinglass ●

Carlow ●   ● Wicklow

Kilrush ●

Limerick ●

TIPPERARY

Kilkenny ●

LIMERICK   Tipperary ●   KILKENNY

M U N S T E R

Clonmel ●

Wexford ●

KERRY   CORK

Waterford ●

Cork ●

Clonakilty ●

Skibbereen ●

Ireland

INTRODUCTION

the Three Famines

In a world of cyclical and enduring historic and modern want, this account is in greatest part a comparative story of three terrible hungers. The first of these famines is *an Gorta Mór*, the great hunger of Ireland, the famine that began in 1845 and whose end-date is a matter of debate among historians. I have written about this famine before, but in terms of the history of Irish nationalism instead of as a famine that echoed and illustrated other famines. By comparing this renowned event with other outbreaks of starvation, I hope to tell its tale anew, and – while not avoiding the causes, actions and ideas that made it – narrate it stripped of its former nationalist rhetoric.

The second hunger is a more hidden famine than the other two, one I encountered first in the writings of Amartya Sen. Though less well-known and submerged by competing accidents of history, it was the even more deadly famine that struck Bengal in 1943–4. It was triggered by natural causes, but also by the impact of World War II on north-east India and by British–Indian government policies.

The third great hunger narrated here, that of the Ethiopians, had two phases separated in time – the early 1970s and then the early and mid 1980s. But, though presided over first by an emperor and then by a Stalinist dictator, they were interconnected to an extent that they could in some lights appear to be one continuing reality. I was moved to write about this famine by my own visits to Eritrea in the late 1980s and the evidence I saw that the tyrant Mengistu was spending massively on armaments rather than food and the means to distribute it.

In those people who suffered these famines; in those who denied the suffering or propounded theories to explain it, excuse it, and so see it as necessary; in those who – against the wishes of government – told the world what had happened and still was happening, or tried to address the suffering by giving aid, there is a remarkable continuity of impulses and reactions. So, though these famines are in obvious ways diverse from each other, they were also siblings to each other. It is as if they shared part of the same DNA, being as they are the result of a similar human fallibility, and of dogmatic and determined misinterpretation by governments and officials of both the victims and the events that had overtaken them.

In all famines there is a continuity of the features of the famished. Their hollowed and stark-eyed faces bring forth in witnesses the same sort of horrified descriptions, which become interchangeable; without any editing, one could be used to speak of any of the others.

Along with everything else, the sufferers lose not only accustomed food and seed crops and livestock, and clothing and all dignity, but also their particular culture. No matter how separated in time, they become members of the nation of the famished, who have more in common with each other than with the cultures starvation steals from them.

But, as narratives, there are also great differences between these disasters. One famine occurred in a country – Ireland – where there was certainly popular sedition but no full-scale military conflict to afflict the rural population. The bayonet and the rifle were part of the fatal mix, but they were not deployed anywhere near as actively in Ireland as weapons would be in Ethiopia.

The famine in Bengal was unwittingly, though not blame-lessly, instigated by the conditions of World War II. There was the imminent threat of the Japanese entering British-ruled India across the border from Burma, which they had captured with resounding military competence in 1942. This military pressure facing both the British government of India, and indeed the war cabinet in London, made it easier for those in authority to make choices that failed to meet, indeed worsened, the Bengali crisis.

But official and large-scale savaging and murder did not occur in Bengal and Ireland the way it would in Ethiopia in the mid 1980s, when, under the dictator Mengistu Haile Mariam the army slaughtered peasants, dissenters against the founding of collectives on the Stalinist model, escapees from detention and minority peoples unpopular with the central government. To identify this distinguishing factor does not, of course, deny the torment of the Irish or Bengalis. But in

Ethiopia, the violence undermined the growing of food and the survival of many people who were already under threat of extinction by hunger. In addition, in Ethiopia, a vicious war against rebels in the provinces was waged by Mengistu, regardless of its massive cost and its capacity to make the country's famine more intense.

This book, in telling its story, will argue that famine occurred in all cases not because of the loss of a single staple food, or because of natural disasters – drought or plant pestilence – in themselves. Whether applied to Irish families in the 1840s, Bengali families in the early 1940s, or Ethiopian families in the 1970s and 1980s, commentators have sometimes said that 'famine' is actually the wrong term to use. For the victims felt with some accuracy that the land itself produced enough food. It was the fact that the food became inaccessible to millions that produced the emergency. Jeremiah O'Donovan Rossa, for example, a nineteenth-century radical whose family left Ireland because of *an Gorta Mór*, argued that 'there was no famine in the land', but that food was taken out of Ireland to feed domestic needs on the British mainland. As the poet John O'Hagan wrote at the time:

Take it from us, every grain,
We were made for you to drain;
Black starvation let us feel,
England must not want a meal!

This is not to deny the however niggardly official aid instigated, sometimes against their own principles, by government, nor the private aid donated and distributed in a more generous spirit. Both forms of relief are believed to have saved perhaps hundreds of thousands of lives. Yet at the same time the Irish could complain that detachments of the British army and armed police were used to enforce thousands of evictions and to guard exports of food from Ireland.

In Ethiopia in the 1980s, the army operated as a vengeful force, destroying lives and imperilling the normal supplies of food. 'When we came back from the forest,' an Ethiopian refugee would later say, 'our wives were [already] in prison and we were accused of working with the rebels. They put us all in a big ditch as a prison and many died there. Many are still there.' Mengistu's army then burned down sixteen houses, shot people and raided corn and coffee. 'There was no hunger before this.'

Such testimonies are too numerous to have been totally fabricated. The famed Four Horsemen rode wild in Ethiopia.

The argument, therefore, that famine is due utterly to a natural disaster, or even to the previous sins of the victims themselves, is one that suits governments, who naturally wish to be exempted from all blame. Inevitable acts of God and deliberate previous wrongdoing by the famishing have brought on the calamity – so goes the assertion. Among other perceived faults of the starving: the Irish married too early, bred too many children and based their existence on one crop easily grown; the Bengalis were over-breeders, were caste-ridden and suspected of disloyalty to the Empire; the Ethiopians resisted relocation to collectives, were reluctant to plough without oxen and lacked a clear Marxist appreciation.

To show these ideas are fraudulent is one of the main purposes of this narrative; in all the cases narrated here, mindsets of governments, racial preconceptions and administrative incompetence were more lethal than the initiating blights, the loss of potatoes or rice or livestock or of the grain named teff.

1

Democracy and Starvation

IN HIS BOOK *Development as Freedom*, the winner of the 1998 Nobel Memorial Prize in Economic Sciences, Amartya Kumar Sen, wrote, 'No famine has taken place in the history of the world in a functioning democracy.'

How does this dictum apply to the Irish famine? Though at the time of the famine the term 'democrat' stood in most British minds for something close to the sense 'Communist' attained in the West in the 1950s, Britain considered itself the home of liberal institutions. The Reform Bill of 1832 had been a definite move in the direction of liberalism and progress. Just the same, after its exciting passage through the British Parliament, only men owning property worth £10 per annum qualified for the vote – that is, one in seven. And even there inequity existed: three dozen new seats had fewer than 300 voters, whereas the industrial cities had thousands. Despite a large movement for democracy and manhood suffrage, Britain probably did not qualify as 'a functioning democracy' in the modern sense in the mid 1840s, and perhaps especially because in Ireland itself, those who had the vote before the famine, if we surmise an adult male population of, say, 2 million (which allows for a population of 4 million children and of 8 million in total), came to a bit more than one in forty-four males (45,000 voters, all told).

So Ireland itself in the 1840s could not be described as a democracy or a successful polity at all. Like other famines, Ireland's grew from a prelude of poverty and shortage of nutrition, but the lack of direct democracy and franchise, common in that era anywhere on earth, had left millions unrepresented, voiceless and so captive to want, where any accident to their staple food could leave them hungering in the dust.

In India, government had always been paternal. There was an unspoken idea that good administration was a valid replacement for democracy. The cabinet in New Delhi, presided over by the viceroy, was appointed, as was the viceroy himself. In 1935, a new form of constitution (the Government of India Act) created a federal assembly, but of its 375 members, none were popularly elected. Two hundred and fifty members were to be put forward by the legislative assemblies of the provinces and 125 nominated by Indian princes. The 1935 act, however, also allowed provincial elections to be contested by purely Indian political parties, culminating in the election of Indian provincial legislatures. To the British this seemed a step in the direction of democracy, but in the view of nationalist leaders such as Gandhi, too slow and contemptuous a one. Many saw the new act as a device to divert

Indian political passion into local elections, into struggles for local eminence. The powers of the provincial governments, of which the government of Bengal was one, were limited to local administration under a British governor. He had the power to reject any law which in his or the viceroy's opinion was a threat to national security. He also had the power to suspend the local parliament and take over all government himself.

In Bengal, the business of enrolling voters was slow, and some millions of people who would be threatened by the Bengal famine either were not registered to vote at the first provincial elections in 1937, or lacked the competence or confidence to approach the polling booth. In these elections the two major parties were Congress, who ran candidates of high caste or social standing, and the Muslim League. Congress was in power in Bengal as the famine germinated, but the largely Muslim League government of Khawaja Nazimuddin took over in March 1943. The province was divided, the Muslims wary of trusting Congress, which they saw as the party of the Hindus.

In Ethiopia, the Derg had originally been elected by soldiers and policemen, and thereafter the election of leaders occurred not among the general population but among the Derg itself. Under Soviet urging, the Workers' Party was founded in late 1979 as a 'vanguard party' whose members would help shore up Mengistu's Ethiopian state. Theoretically, delegates to the Ethiopian Congress were elected from the various 'mass organisations' such as the All-Ethiopia Urban Dwellers' Association and the All-Ethiopia Peasants' Association. But, in turn, the input of most Ethiopian people into the election of these bodies was negligible, for the mass organisations were run by supporters of the Derg and party members. Few people likely to give trouble to the regime were elected delegates to these bodies, let alone to the congress of the Workers' Party. The nomination and election of delegates to the three congresses the Workers' Party held were therefore under the control of local party machines. Between 1200 and 1300 like-minded delegates from all the regions would attend these party congresses. But in general they spoke with one voice.

Thus the people who would perish in these three catastrophes had no input into the policies that would be applied to what they were undergoing.

Famine and the starvation process fascinate those of us who live in what is called the developed world. The fascination is sometimes perverse, to the extent that in the late twentieth century a term was minted for those who liked to observe its effects firsthand – 'disaster tourism'. To us the famine victim is remote, separated from normal, robust people by an impenetrable glass, and located far beyond our understanding of human experience. For, though we can find malnutrition on our streets and in our nursing homes, famine itself is seen as a phenomenon of the past. Starvation makes its appearance in the West most spectacularly in individual and political cases. Firstly, it does so in the mental disease anorexia nervosa, which occurs chiefly among young women who seek such fearful control over their bodies that they reduce themselves ultimately to the point of self-devouring starvation. Otherwise, starvation has manifested itself as a form of political protest and civil disobedience, a deliberately undertaken wasting of the body so that it becomes a graphic and potent statement of ideology or political meaning.

In the early twentieth century – sixty years after the failure of potatoes had put the English peasantry under pitiful pressure, subjected the Scots to the most acute want and coercive emigration, and come close to destroying the peasant population of Ireland – Emmeline Pankhurst's suffragettes went on hunger strikes in prison to shame the authorities and achieve equal suffrage for women. The government feared the potency of this individually chosen hunger by women. In all cases it ordered forced feeding, which was resisted by the hunger-striking young women. But largely, through occasional release and other stratagems of the authorities, the suffragettes survived their gestures.

In 1981, the Irish republican prisoner Bobby Sands, and a number of other prisoners in the H-Blocks in HM Prison Maze, Belfast, volunteered for a hunger strike. It was designed to lend moral weight to their demand for political status rather than the criminal status imposed on them by British law. Sands began his starving process first, in the hope his objective would be achieved before his comrades needed to start theirs. He died after sixty-six days.

Without questioning the courage of either the suffragettes or Bobby Sands, or the obviously disturbing impact their deaths had on those in power, I choose here to look at cases of unchosen hunger, unchosen necrosis, unchosen obliteration.

*

'The stomach is cruel,' said a Bengali victim in 1943. 'Unless you give it something to eat, it won't let you sleep.' But as the stomach howls, the body slowly devours its own substance. Starvation, for Bobby Sands equally as for the millions of its unwilling victims, is the ultimate stage of a long period of malnutrition.

The stages the body descends through while undergoing starvation are well described in medical literature. After a person lacks food for a few days, glucose, no longer absorbed from nourishment, begins to be supplied by invaluable glycogen stored in the liver, and from proteins and body fats. Body fat is broken down into fatty acids and some replacement glycerol, which the body transforms into a small amount of glucose. Amino acids are also processed into glucose. Fatty acids can for a time be used to maintain muscle, and so the glucose is used to sustain the brain, above all. Blood glucose levels, on which the organs and muscles depend for function, begin an inevitable drop. The decline becomes serious, though not yet irreversible.

Now, over ensuing days and weeks, the liver begins to transform fatty acids in the body into an increasing number of ketones – chemicals that assist the metabolism of healthy bodies, but that are now reaching unsafe levels. They too serve to run the brain. But the heart and the blood cannot readily use such an excess of ketones and thus begin to be damaged. Severe damage to the heart is one of the symptoms of the late stages of starvation.

The rate of the breakdown of proteins continues and so the body begins to look for protein in its own muscles and in their cells. Over time, the muscles waste pitifully, and the cells themselves, plundered of fatty acid, erode, death entering their very nucleus.

This wasting or self-devouring state is named marasmus and at this stage, because of the collapse of the blood's immune system, opportunistic diseases – malaria, shigella, dysentery or typhus, for example – can easily kill the victim. Deaths from the absolutely *final* phases of starvation make up as few as 10 per cent of the total deaths caused by famine.

Kwashiorkor, the swelling of the bellies of children, which we see in news footage from Africa, is a cruel accompaniment to starvation. The breakdown of muscle causes any remaining fat to accumulate in the belly. It is a condition not unknown in the West among alcoholics and, according to some estimates, 50 per cent of elderly Americans in nursing homes. It also occurs in victims of anorexia.

In the earlier stages of starving, hunger can diminish as the body attempts to negotiate what it hopes will be a short episode of want. But when, in days or perhaps a few weeks, it becomes apparent that the crisis will continue, a preoccupation with food becomes so intense that it has the power to overturn the starving person's normal morality and sense of self. The victim becomes a new person. The fastidious become slovenly; the kindly become aggressive; the moral are caught up in the great amorality of famine. Fraternity and love wither. Judgement vanishes and a hyperactive anxiety seizes the mind – it is this that in part drives people out onto the roads and gives them the nervous energy to seek nourishment. Perhaps because the brain is, at the same time, sustained yet confused by an unfamiliar proportion of ketones and glucose, emotional distress, profound depression and agitation overwhelm the victim. In some, a furious and disproportional shame at their condition will cause them to wall themselves in their houses and never re-emerge. Sexual desire dwindles. Sleep brings little comfort, for most starving cannot sleep properly. There are spasms of anger and hysteria, which mystify the aid-givers, should they turn up. Delusions and illusions overtake the mind – in many cases the starving become psychotic and sometimes do not even recognise food when at last they find it. Yet dreams of cannibalism also come to torment the mind.

Lieutenant Colonel K. S. Fitch, who saw many starving in military hospitals, wrote a medical history of the Bengal famine and gave a fascinating picture of the mystifying characteristics of the famished. The desperate cases would abscond from hospital to disappear into the uncertainty of the open countryside – 'a mass and individual urge to roam' – feeling driven by an inner need to go on doomed searches for food. In one destitute hospital, an emaciated man was seen sitting on a hospital bed with a dish of rice and curry in front of him, and crying out for sustenance. Starvation had conditioned him not to see the food before him. Fitch mentions decayed and septic teeth, coated tongues, and an irritable and morose childishness and unconsciousness of surroundings. The hungry would pass stools and urine wherever they were. 'The human destitute became closely akin to the starving pariah dogs seen in eastern bazaars.'

When starvation is well-advanced in a population, relief agencies must be careful with the food they provide to sufferers. World War II survivors of the concentration camps of

Europe and the prison camps of the Japanese often describe fellow prisoners, after liberation, enjoying unaccustomed access to as much food as they wanted, and then dying rapidly and unexpectedly. A sudden large intake of nourishment gives bacteria and viruses the minerals they need to rebound almost instantly and to attack the body, whose own immune system has barely begun to rebuild itself. And since the body's organs have not had time to accommodate themselves to an onslaught of plenty, they fail in their attempt to deal with it.

2

Short Commons

SEASONS OF NEED and marginal survival for millions generally precede a famine.

The Irish were familiar with a certain level of food shortage. Visitors to nineteenth-century Ireland, usually coming in the summertime, were struck by the obvious hunger that afflicted the peasantry as they waited for the next potato harvest. Travelling from Dublin to Carlow in midsummer 1835, Alexis de Tocqueville was shocked by the poverty he saw. 'The population looks very wretched. Many wear clothes with holes or much patched. Most of them bare-headed and barefoot . . . it is a frightening thing, I assure you, to see a whole population reduced to fasting like Trappists, and not being sure by fasting of surviving to the next harvest.' Summer visitors such as de Tocqueville travelled by main roads, and if the people on the highways presented such a picture, what must things have been like in remoter Ireland?

All this would explain the emotional and sometimes poetic anticipation of the harvest. When the blight came, an Irishman, remembering the days of plenty, wrote, 'A fond farewell to the white potatoes, it was good to be near them; always arriving in good humour, laughing at us at the head of the table. They were a help to the nurse, to the young and old, to weak and strong.'

Though they did not know it, the potato as the main item of diet for millions of the Irish protected them from scurvy, which occurred elsewhere in Europe, and from pellagra, the vitamin-deficiency disease endemic to those parts of the United States and Europe in which maize was the staple. Potatoes provided the Irish peasant with more than twice the protein of today's recommended level for active males, possessing nearly twice the energy value, three times the amount of calcium and three times the amount of iron. Sir William Petty, a famed statistician (or 'political arithmetician', as the term then went), said that 'six out of eight of all the Irish fed chiefly upon milk and potatoes'.

The potato had arrived in Spain from Central or South America, one of the less treasured items discovered by Spanish incursions, and reached Ireland in about 1590. There, it came to replace oatmeal as the main food. It was a popular food in Britain and Eastern Europe. By contrast, the French despised it as a stockfeed, and better-off Germans considered its consumption the mark of a peasant. But the potato was iconic in Ireland, and its obliteration in this garden and that created an enormous consternation.

An extraordinary variety of potato existed, and not all Irish were growing the same species. There is a welter of names – English Reds, Apples, White Eyes, Barbour's Wonders, Wicklow Banners, Coppers, Pink Eyes, Flat Spanish. On the edge of the famine, the poor were increasingly growing a potato called the Lumper, which was resistant to the disease named curl. Curl weakened the plant by attacking its leaves, but not the potato itself. Lumpers were not as succulent as Apples, but for the Irish small farmer and peasantry they were very reliable – as assured as the sun coming up.

The Irish ate their potatoes by their peat fires, the parents and older children sitting on stools, picking potatoes from a bowl and dipping them in a dish of salt. Such a meal was called 'dip at a stool'. If possible, as they ate they drank buttermilk.

The three million or so Irish most vulnerable to the famine lacked livestock, except that thousands of cabins were home not only to a family but to a pig, 'Paddy's pig', which would be sold in the spring or early summer so that the family could buy oatmeal and other food to tide them over till the next potato crop.

Similarly, Bengalis generally were poor in livestock. Their staple was rice, which was often parboiled while unmilled and still in its outer husk. This form of cooking happened to drive the B vitamins, thiamine, riboflavin and niacin, into the very centre of the grain, though the Bengali peasant knew nothing of the beneficence of this effect, any more than the Irish peasant did of the vitamins and minerals available in the potato.

The Bengalis were also fish-eaters. Most of the fish they ate were not from the Bay of Bengal but from the river systems. One of their favourites was the climbing perch, able to work its way across a paddy field, by the motion of its fins and gill covers, from one water course to another. Fishermen would sell the more succulent parts of the fish to better-off folk, and the poor ate fish heads and entrails.

Lentils were available to them, mainly through the markets, and would increase in price beyond the reach of threatened people once the famine began. Rice and fish are still the staples of Bengali life, but their fish, and the fish markets, have been diminished somewhat since the famine by overpopulation and accompanying pollution. Fish on their own – even had the starving had the energy to pursue them – were not plentiful enough to save the Bengalis.

In the highlands of Ethiopia, the equivalent of potatoes or rice was a grain named teff. It had aspects of convenience that had helped it become the staple crop of millions. Other crops often grown on the larger farms, or by landlords, included varieties of wheat, sorghum and a plant named zengada, a wild sorghum that grew in land races – that is, areas of unfarmed land that nonetheless could produce edible grains. Farmers might also grow white barley, maize, millet, peas, rapeseed and linseed. Barley was grown mainly as a stock feed. Durra, a form of wheat now considered a health food in the West, was also popular. Grown in the south-west of the country, around the city of Jimma, coffee was a major crop for trading and was enjoyed in the home as well, where the offer of strong coffee from beans roasted on a small fire was one of the major Ethiopian courtesies. Farmers throughout the country also grew chat, a mild narcotic whose leaves people chewed. Most of it was exported to Saudi Arabia and Sudan.

But the chief crop for a highland family's subsistence remained the four varieties of teff. Teff seeds were small, and so the seed crop did not take up much room in the farmhouse. It was easy for the farmwife to grind to a flour, from which the Ethiopians made their chief meal, the huge, thin pancake bread, injera – a fermented bread, bitter to any palate unfamiliar with it. Large circles of injera bread, spread on a low table or a large tray, are heaped with lentils and chickpeas, and each member of the family tears off a segment of the thin bread and scoops up the lentils and other food to form something like an open tortilla.

Ethiopian farmers look on teff with the same reverence the Irish displayed for the potato. They know that it is an ancient seed and a mercy of God. It is also high in calcium, phosphorus, iron, potassium, thiamine, amino acids and more.

The pastoral people in Ethiopia and Eritrea and the semi-nomadic people who lived in the eastern lowlands of Ethiopia near Somalia and the Red Sea, or in the western lowlands near the Sudanese border, owned camels, but above all the livestock they treasured were longhorn zebu cattle. Creatures so cherished by the pastoral Ethiopians look very scrawny and are often diseased, but they were beautiful and important in the eyes of their owners and produced milk, essential to their existence. Pastoralists also owned goats, which they used for meat and also for milk. They lived, and often still live, in *tuqals* – fold-up beehive shelters of grass and bark, easily loaded onto a camel if the livestock chose to move on to new pastures. As materially poor as they might seem to outsiders, to them their lives were the only desirable version. Yet they knew that some sudden affliction or some drastic failure of rain had the power to suspend and even destroy this.

The failure of potatoes, the lack of rice, the withering of fields of teff were the various instigators that created the conditions for these three great famines, even though for their true causes we must eventually look to other factors.

3

Nature's Triggers

FAMINE ALWAYS HAS an initiating spark or trigger, a natural disaster that may have a greater or lesser impact on the crops growing on farmers' land, and an event that tests the political will and wisdom of governments, the latter being more a potential cause of disaster than a trigger.

The triggers for the Ethiopian famines were the failure of one or both annual rains in 1973–4, and 1982 and 1985. Lack of rain was combined with the sudden appearance in the fields of army worms, a larval form of a moth, in reality a caterpillar rather than a worm, which is blown north on the wind from Kenya. In the past, army worms on their own had always been a blight, and Ethiopian farmers abhorred the sudden appearance of these insects among their crops. It was said, indeed it is still said, that they could devour a hectare of grain faster than a herd of 400 cattle. So their work impoverished overnight the owners of a hectare-and-a-half farm, the average size of land holding among the peasantry. Sometimes farmers planted peas among their grain crop as an insurance, since the army worms did not favour them. But peas occupied space the farmers often needed to give to their teff. In the 1970s and 1980s, the logistics of spraying crops, even if sufficient stocks of pesticide had been held in the country, continued to be beyond the capacities of both the emperor and the Derg.

Of people from Tigray in northern Ethiopia who fled to Somalia and Sudan in 1984 and were interviewed later, 30 per cent said army worms were as much of a problem to them as drought. One Tigrayan in Wad Kauli camp in the Sudan said, 'I decided to leave home because of the drought and our enemy [the Derg]. Insects and the lack of rain were equally important, but the government caused the famine too.'

Farmers with a family of six needed to produce 1500 kilos of food a year: 1200 for the family, the remaining 300 kilos being sold locally to buy other food, shoes, clothes and other needs. The crop did not need to decline much before the family had nothing to spend.

The rain failures threatened both the highland and lowland people. The highlanders feared their injera would vanish, and the lowland graziers suffered anxiety about the milk and meat of their quickly dying goats and the continued health of their cattle. The drying-out of waterholes and pasture in the lowlands and the consequent death or deterioration of their cattle, were watched with bewilderment and concern by the cattle-owning and grazing peoples of Ethiopia.

*

In 1769–70, a Bengal famine was estimated to have caused the death of 10 million out of 30 million inhabitants. Yet the province for the next two centuries was largely free from famine. Bengal is only 77,442 square miles, with a population of 60 million at the time of the 1943 famine. An administrative line divided West Bengal from East, and that would become the future border between India and Bangladesh. Bengal's twenty-six districts averaged over 2 million each in population and nearly 3000 square miles each in area.

Bengal is a country of waterways, but the main rivers that flow into the Bay of Bengal through broad deltas are the Hooghly, the Padma, the Brahmaputra-Jumuna and the Meghna. The annual rainfall is 85 inches, which sheets down between June and September on the south-east monsoon. During that season, the farmers and peasants survive in their huts and houses on mounds raised above the fields.

The trigger for the famine of the early 1940s was the arrival on the coastline of a number of cyclones during 1942, and of a November 1942 tidal wave, which flooded the region around the Ganges Delta, killing 15,000 people. Because of Bengal's small elevation above sea level, the tsunami rolled far inland, across the low farmlands and rice fields. It spread salt, which poisoned – just as they were about to be harvested – the crops of Muslim and Hindu farmers in one terrible act of God. A fungal disease named rice blast – which, like the potato blight, attacked the leaves, stalk and grain – struck the paddy fields as a result of the wave of saltwater, because the surge had swept the spores from infected parts of the country into as-yet-unaffected ones. The rice fungus reduced the average rice crop in the coastal areas and beyond by a third. There had already been the Bengali equivalent of a drought, arising from less than normal rainfall in the 1942 June to September monsoon season.

During a debate in the British Parliament, Secretary of State for India Leopold Amery raised the Malthusian concept that something must be done to outstrip the pressure of population, which, he said, was increasing at the rate of 300,000 per month. This left little of a surplus for the individual farmer or purchaser. When the Bengal Famine Inquiry Commission, established by the government in 1944, said that, of all the provinces of India, Bengal was pre-eminent, in that it had the largest number of mouths to feed, it also declared that the province produced the largest amount of cereals of any province, and it grew jute as well. But, for millions, the balance between viability and family disaster was a very narrow one.

The 1943 drought, unexpected but not unprecedented, even in modern times – since, for example, there had been others in 1925 and 1927 – had its own influence on all three of the annual harvests. The province's different seasonal crops had distinct names. The *aus* was a less important harvest sown in April and harvested in the monsoonal rain of August and September. It was a crop meant to see farmers and their families through a lean time in the autumn, and since it was eaten by poor people, among Hindus it was not considered appropriate for ceremonial purposes. Indeed, the *aus* is not a robust crop and needs to be parboiled to preserve it. The winter crop, *aman*, was sown in May or June in paddies that had begun to be flooded by the south-west monsoon, if it brought its normal rain to the fields. Harvested in November or December, the *aman* crop was intended to reach markets in the spring of the following year. It was of finer quality, and was the largest and most important crop from which the farmer took his family's food, with – ideally – some left over to be marketed. The *boro* crop was planted in the broad irrigated regions of Bengal in November and harvested the following February or March.

Over the entirety of Bengal, coastal and inland, the 1943 harvest was no more than 5 per cent less than the crop harvested in late 1941 and early 1942, despite the tidal wave and drought. In the areas most affected, it did put the families of farmers and artisans in immediate peril. None of that should have killed the millions whose deaths are attributed to it.

There were similar conditions of landowning between Bengal and Ireland, and Bengal and Ethiopia. The Famine Commission estimated that 7.5 million families depended on the cultivation of land. Of these, fewer than 2 million families held between two and five acres. That is, nearly three out of four families either lived on fewer than two acres or were landless. In good times, then, farming families were able to sell their surplus rice to pay rent and buy necessities in the market. But bad times were upon them.

In November 1943, in addition to the other problems the Damodar River broke its banks and flooded large areas in Burdwan district. Hundreds of villages were devastated by the water, and rice fields lay utterly drowned beneath floodwater. Cholera now broke out and allied itself with other famine diseases.

The seasonal rains elsewhere than Burdwan had fallen and caused no natural disaster, and a fair *aman* crop planted on larger farms, including land farmed by sharecroppers, seemed likely. But in the later view of the Famine Inquiry Commission, the chief harvesting month of November was probably the critical month of the Bengal famine, since prices were still rising. It was at this point that the death rate reached its highest level. The acute period of starvation was passing, but epidemics were killing millions of the malnourished throughout the countryside. The disease that took more than any other was malaria.

The trigger for the Irish famine was an agent nearly as voracious as army worms, a fungal spore named *phytophthora infestans*, which either travelled to Europe from America, where there had been a report of blight, on the prevailing westerly wind from the Atlantic; arrived in the holds of American ships; or both. Early in its European career it would afflict crops, particularly in Kent and the Isle of Wight, and elsewhere in England and then Scotland. But resultant want was not as acute in Scotland and England as in Ireland. The Scots, for example, though reduced to hunger, had better supplies of oatmeal and better fishing than the Irish.

At the time, people knew nothing of the blight's causation, and a Church of England clergyman, the Reverend J. M. Berkley, one of those clergymen whose undemanding work gave him room for natural research – which, in his case, led to an enormous understanding of moulds – and who described the blight as a 'vampire fungus', was not listened to.

Yet that is how it manifested itself in Ireland – one day the potato flowers were blooming and rejoicing the cottier's heart, then, overnight, everything had rotted. The mysterious fungus would within forty years be identified, and a treatment devised – copper sulphate. But *phytophthora infestans* is still with us, having built a resistance to sprays used against it throughout the twentieth century. It has at various stages attacked grape harvests, still infiltrates potato and tomato crops, and is now responsible for the failure of at least half of Russia's potato and tomato harvests. Most remarkably, it has also been considered by both the Russians and Americans as a potential instrument of biological warfare, a means of attacking the crops of the enemy.

The blight had led to a miserable Irish winter in 1845–6, but the people who planted their potato-seed crop in the spring of 1846 were full of hope for the late summer harvest. Then, after an early summer drought had in any case delayed the planting and growth of the tubers, continuous and heavy rainfall in late July and early August began to wash the spores of *phytophthora infestans* down to the tubers in the soil.

When, at the end of the summer of 1846, the potato flowers came out and gladdened the Irish, and indeed the government, an evil awakening of blight was about to occur. The fungus had survived the summer in the moist earth and now, amidst the rejoicing at the robustness of the crop, everything turned to mush as it had the year before, but in an even more widespread and fatal manner. The flower, the stalk, the tuber itself turned to putrescence. A famous Irish temperance campaigner, Father Matthew, a Capuchin monk who was travelling from Cork to Dublin in July, saw the plants 'in all the luxuriance of an abundant harvest. Returning on the 3rd inst [August] I beheld with sorrow one wide waste of putrefying vegetation.'

The summer of 1847 was spent in hope, but also in anxiety, and indeed in the autumn the crop was blighted again. In 1848 there was a remission from the blight after a less rainy summer, but because of the deaths, weakness or fevers of those who generally did the planting, as well as the fact that many people were labouring on the roads or had wandered to town looking for any form of relief, a much lesser number of potatoes had been sown in the previous spring. So the harvest in general was poor, the acreage under potatoes being barely more than 15 per cent of its 1845 level, with other crops down by 40 per cent. The blight returned in 1849. In 1850, too, it was back, though more local in its impact, and again less of a crop had been grown.

Thus, without intervention, one abnormal harvest could so diminish the number of people planting and harvesting that want could beget want, and food prices based on one shortage created by nature could be compounded by yet another created by the disruption of normal farming life.

4

God's Hand

PEASANT PEOPLES AND small farmers are generally believers. To many sufferers of want, famine has always been, among other things, a theological event. At the start of the outbreak they see God's will and God's anger as the cause of the failure of their food supply. Christ, through the filter of the writers of the Christian Gospels, also represents famine as a theological phenomenon, a sign of the end of the world. 'There shall be famines, and pestilences, and earthquakes in divers places.'

There is a comfort for people who face deadly shortages to see them as an unavoidable penance or a test of faith. For if God and the deities can punish with hunger, they can also be persuaded by fasting, prayer and sacrifice to bring an end to it. A survivor of the Irish famine remembered that 'several reasons are given as to the cause of the blight. Most people think it was a punishment from God for the careless manner in which they treated the crops for years previous when there was a very plentiful supply of potatoes.' Another remembered that, 'It looked like the hand of God.' Yet again, a Corkman's testimony to the Irish Folklore Commission declared that even after the Great Hunger ended, 'Old people said it was God's will to have the famine come. They abused fine food when they had it aplenty.'

And if it were not God's will, then it was the work of God's dark opposite. It was said that an old woman of Rossport in County Mayo, returning home, saw her potatoes rotting and cried, 'Oh, the Devil polluted all the potatoes last night. There is not a stalk standing.'

In 1943, Hindus and Muslims in Bengal were almost equal in population – 52 per cent were Muslim, 48 per cent Hindu. Hindus tended to live in the west of the province; the Muslims in the east. Both groups similarly saw the divine hand in what was developing. The Sunni tradition had a less formal hierarchy than the Shia, but now, in the red terracotta mosques of the villages, people were led in prayers to the Source of All Bounty by their most respected ministers. In the Hindu temples of the area, and in worship in their homes, the Hindus also sought to appease their deities and avatars. Inevitably these were more numerous than Allah. Brahma the Creator, Vishnu the Preserver and Shiva the Destroyer were propitiated. The more orthodox set of deities, the god Shiva and his female counterparts, Kali and Durga, were worshipped widely among the upper castes. Devotion to the engaging Lord Krishna, the flute-playing young deity, was popular among the lower. In each Hindu house stood a shrine where the god or goddess of the season was summoned by a small house bell and where small brass bowls of milk, water, ghee, salt and rice were placed in piety. Lakshmi, goddess of wealth and good fortune, received offerings in the home and the temple at harvest time especially, and so could not have been far from people's minds in 1943. In the waterlands of Bengal, imaginations must also have been drawn to Basanta Chandi, the goddess popular with women, who could conquer cholera and other diseases.

Some Ethiopian farmers in the 1970s and 1980s became desperate enough to revert to the animist practices of their ancestors, and gathered in the fields by night to enact the ancient rain-making rituals disapproved of by their Coptic priests. It was interesting that such rituals had remained, since Christianity had arrived in the fourth century by way of Egypt. The word 'copt' is said to have derived from the classical name of Egypt, *Aegyptus*, and its rituals are related to those of Orthodoxy and Roman Catholicism. Dawit Wolde Giorgis, a former officer in the Ethiopian army, who was in charge of Ethiopia's Relief and Rehabilitation Commission, set up in the aftermath of the 1973 drought, remembers that as the Ethiopian famine of 1984–5 struck, people had recourse to masses in the Coptic churches, doing penance for their sins in the hope that the curse might be lifted from them. He saw the same prayers uttered in the mosques – Sunni Islam arrived in Ethiopia via ninth-century exiles from Arabia in the east, and from trade and other influences from the Sudan in the west. Perhaps 30 per cent of Ethiopians were Muslim – many of them nomadic people, but town dwellers and farmers as well.

Religious observance might have edged some Ethiopians towards hunger already. In the Christian parts of the country, there were 293 days of the year when fasting was, according to the strict urgings of the Coptic calendar, to be observed.

Some days only meat and dairy products were prohibited, but others involved total abstention from food. Religion, as well as other factors, had made the Ethiopian highlander Christians an enduring race.

A sense of God's punishment for wantonness was common among those equally hardy Ethiopian Muslims, even the ones who were farmers rather than pastoralists. 'People had grown reckless. They used to compete at shooting bullets through their stack of harvest grain.' The practice was a boastful way of proving the plenty and density of the bagged grain. 'It was such arrogance which brought down God's wrath on them.' As an old woman in Wollo declared, 'When Allah is angry he does not need to cut a staff', that is, a stick to punish people with. A famine would serve.

There is little doubt that the priests and mullahs agreed with the people's devout acceptance of misfortune as God's will and punishment. The question arises of whether the clergy used the reaction of their threatened congregations to extract reward. In Ireland there were tales of priests and parsons who gave the bread from their own tables, and of others who built church improvements in the midst of the dying. Votive offerings are a part of all worship, and sometimes the faithful made a money offering to appease God and the gods in their anger. Much Hindu worship occurs in the home and at the domestic shrine, but the Hindu temples are busy at early-morning prayer time and at such an hour such an offering is normally made.

What is almost beyond dispute is that religious reassurance fortified people in the face of the trial. How early or late that reassurance was swept away by famine's reality we cannot say.

5

Coping

BEYOND PENANCE AND prayer, starving people have always adopted other and more palpable strategies, and these recourses are again similar, famine to famine.

Among the images of women that appeared during the Irish famine in the *Illustrated London News* is the memorable *Woman Begging at Clonakilty*. Clonakilty is a town in West Cork, a region where the famine was at its most intense. In this renowned engraving, the woman has in her right arm a skeletal baby corpse. In her left hand she holds a begging bowl. The woman in the illustration, with her dead baby in her arms, is described as begging for money to buy a coffin for her dead daughter.

Her utter helplessness, however, her torpid look, hides the truth that, like other women in all famines, she has been an actor in her own tragedy, fighting it by every stratagem she can think of. She has pursued all her options with all her energy on her way to this fatal state. Looking at her and her modern sisters, we feel a primal desire to believe that we could never let ourselves arrive at such a pass as this, that we would never become as passive as she seems to be. But there is another issue to raise. Even at these final stages of her hunger, is there any possibility that she is still actively pursuing her duty to survive? Apart from her obvious grief, is she using the small corpse as a begging aid? And should these two possibilities be mutually exclusive? In the extreme mental derangement that characterises famine victims, in the shrinkage of family feeling, which is one of the marks of starvation, both possibilities can operate together. And if she is begging for money for food as well as a child's coffin, then that is exactly what modern famine experts call 'a coping mechanism'.

The Red Cross and World Food Program estimate that the average healthy person needs 2010 calories of energy every day to do their normal tasks and resist disease. Yet one of the first coping mechanisms, from the cabins of Ireland to the huts of Bengal and the farmhouses and *tuqals* of Ethiopia, is to economise on the amount of food eaten daily in the family, thus reducing the intake necessary for good health. In East Africa, men and boys are fed first and the mother eats after them, having cut down on the food placed before the family. The appetite of the males often reduces even further what is left on the plate for women and girls. This is a form of customary practice, profoundly embedded though frowned on in the West, and sometimes condemned in tones that almost question the entitlement to relief of people who practise such cultural faux pas. But it is impossible to alter cultural habits in the span of a famine or even of a century.

Besides, it is likely that in the early stages of all famines – historic, recent and present – women in families have tended to take the greater portion of hunger on themselves.

The result of cutting down on food is, within a few days, a weakening of the immune system. As the family rations itself, keeping next year's seed crop sacredly reserved in a container safe from hungry gaze, it also finds its members have less strength. The farmer and his wife and children, even if they can hang onto their land and their seed crop, will lack as much vigour as they had last year for working hard on the next crop which, even if not attacked by blight, burned off by drought or eaten by locusts, will be less bountiful. Thus shortage begets shortage.

Another coping strategy in famines is the sale of family assets. In Ireland, it was a matter of selling clothes or fishing nets. Sadly, people bringing their goods to town to sell them on market day found the prices they got much lower than they had hoped: many other people were doing the same as them in a glutted market. In Bengal and Ethiopia, families sold radios or bicycles, which had often been bought before the emergency especially so that they could later be exchanged for food in harder seasons. People in Bengal exchanged their pots and pans, furniture and trinkets for the fistfuls of food that grain trading pawnbrokers paid them from pouches they carried about with them. Early in the famine, twenty cartloads of household utensils moved out of the port town of Barisal. One observer says the buyers were always 'aprowl' with their small rice bags and, if necessary, cash.

Bengalis sold the metal roofs of their huts. They sold their plough cattle to contractors supplying meat to the military forces. They mortgaged or sold their rice-producing land. As a result, over 250,000 Bengali families lost all the land they possessed.

In Ethiopia, women and children made long journeys to town to sell firewood or wild bush food they had gathered. But, again, since so many others did that, the prices they got were much lower than in normal times. Selling livestock in Ethiopia, especially the family ox, and the necessity of ploughing by hand were considered akin to the loss of self, a crisis for all the family. The health of the ox, or the ability to buy a replacement one, was crucial to a man's *amour-propre* as a functioning figure beneath God's sky; the number of cattle a man owned confirmed his self-worth. Sale or loss of livestock was a humiliation for millions of pastoral peoples, such as the numerous minority people called the Afar – according to legend the descendants of Ham, Noah's son. Their land was arid and included the Danakil Depression, a low-lying desert in the east of Ethiopia, one of the lowest and hottest places on earth, where some harvested salt. So among the pastoralists, the sale of animals was always considered a last option. An observer could tell how hard the Ethiopians were feeling hunger by the lines of their cherished cattle going to the towns for sale. The sickness or death of livestock could mean death for the family, in any case, because of the loss of the value of that cow and the loss of milk. *In extremis*, cattle could be slaughtered for scrawny meat. But that was the equivalent of a farmer and his family eating their seed for the next crop, devouring from within their family's status and health.

In both the Ethiopian famines of the 1970s and 1980s, the normal barter system broke down – no dealer wanted to exchange food for clothes or kitchen utensils. So, like the pastoralists, farmers had to sell the family livestock, mainly oxen and goats, for money. What they acquired that way quickly vanished – not only on foodstuffs, but sometimes also on water and fodder for any remaining animals.

They could resort to local money-lenders, and might have already done so before the famine. If the latter, they were now in a frightful state of thraldom to these men, who often charged 100 per cent interest. Even those who were not in debt, however, might now approach the money-lender, but find it hard to get a loan.

In Bengal, *zamindars*, that is, landlords, were the chief source of lendings. Their money-lending had always had an impact on the life of Indian communities throughout the subcontinent. Often *zamindars* were absentees, living in Calcutta and other cities, but lending money at high interest to local figures, who then made loans at further interest. The practices of money-lenders in Bengal provoked frequent protest and a nineteenth-century rebellion led by the *bargadars*, sharecroppers. But when famine came and at some stage the *bargadars* and the agricultural peasants, the village tinsmiths or barbers, went to the lender's house to plead for a loan, they found this minor grandee was more interested in demanding repayment of earlier loans than extending more money. In Bengal there also existed a culture of modest lending between families. In the crisis of 1943, those who had advanced money to their kinfolk began to call in their loans.

Some families cherished the hope that they could give their daughters in marriage to better-off families, who could afford to pay a dowry of money and animals. But this was even more unlikely in famine times.

In Ireland the money-lenders were called *gombeen* men, from the Irish word *gaimbin*, meaning interest money. The *gombeen* men were often general storekeepers, usually willing to gouge the hungry with fierce loan rates. But, like the money-lenders of Bengal and Ethiopia, they had little interest in lending to people who occupied or owned little or no land they could offer as security, and who might be dead before the loan could be paid.

After reducing food intake, selling family possessions and taking loans, a hungry people's next step in coping is to turn to food they would not normally eat, to the food they considered until now as food for their animals.

In Ireland, turnips had been a despised stockfeed plant. Some farmers in Kilkenny, a better-off eastern Irish county, who had lived well until the famine struck, now locked themselves away in secrecy to eat turnips. These more affluent people considered it shameful to devour turnip boxty (turnips turned into a form of flat cake or bread), or eat the mashed-turnip dish named champ. (Poorer folk, by contrast, tried to make a potato boxty out of their rotten tubers and ate it without any of the embarrassment the better-off turnip-eaters felt, but at much higher peril to their health.)

In Ethiopia, plants that grew on landraces, hybrids of wild and domesticated grains, were generally – like the Irish turnips – considered stockfeed, and so there was a similar reluctance to eat them. Ethiopians lay under even more serious food prohibitions, and observed the same food laws concerning animals as the Jews. Animals with uncloven hoofs, and uncloven hoofed animals that did not chew their cud, had always been prohibited, and only those properly slaughtered could be eaten. The traditional slaughter required the animal to be turned to the east, and the prayers, 'In the name of the Father, the Son and the Holy Ghost', or, 'In the name of Allah the Merciful', to be recited. It is unlikely that Ethiopians would have eaten prohibited animals during the famine since they were very rarely found in the country, but no doubt if other meat was encountered, the hungry would not have enquired whether it had been slaughtered according to the proper rituals.

In Bengal, food taboos concerned pigs and turtles for Muslims, and cattle for Hindus. Widows were required to be vegetarians, to avoid foods associated with lustiness – meat, fish, onions, garlic and spices. Again, hunger must have often overcome these prohibitions. Yet many Brahmin women, the members of the intellectual and priestly caste, rather than lower themselves to hunt for or accept food, wasted to death in their homes because they could not bring themselves to eat gruel prepared by either lower-caste or Muslim hands.

As well as unaccustomed or unsanctioned foods, emergency food growing wild – food that is not the product of agriculture or the pastoral life – was sought by the hungry. These were foods only sporadically eaten in times of plenty, and which could not be depended on as a staple.

*

If the farmers of the Ethiopian highlands found ploughing by hoe intolerable, was there some cultural reason why the Irish did not save themselves by fishing? They proved, after all, to be energetic scavengers. Some argue that a cultural resistance to fish-eating influenced the Irish, but the ruthless appetite human beings extend to other, less succulent, life forms in any famine makes that unlikely.

In Ireland there were, in fact, a number of fishermen in places such as the village of Teelin on the north-west end of Donegal Bay who survived on their fish haul, mainly by selling it to buy quantities of other food. Part of their fish they dried and salted, but their salting and smoking system was very primitive. In Galway and Mayo, further down the coast, many herring fishermen were too poor to buy salt to preserve a catch. An observer from the central relief committee of the Society of Friends, the Quakers, a group who became highly active in famine relief in Ireland, declared that the finest fishing ground was off Portulin, a small village on the remote Erris Peninsula abutting the Atlantic in north-east Mayo. But the only access to and from the place was along the most primitive trails over a high, boggy mountain. Fish would begin to rot in the process of fishermen negotiating this terrain.

The Quaker observer also mentioned that though the Portulin mornings were often fine, the weather would change in the afternoon. Wind would spring up and blow with such violence that the curraghs, wickerwork frames covered with hide or canvas and crewed by four or five men, would be overset or, dependent on the direction of the gale, likely to be destroyed on a coastline of fierce cliffs broken only by the small coves of Portulin and Portacloy.

As for the rest, there were a number of realities that inhibited fishing. Firstly, particularly in the west of Ireland, there were few heavy fishing boats able to load up with large catches – and even those were only twelve to fifteen tons. The curraghs – owned by poor coastal fishermen – were very manoeuvrable, but not big enough to allow the use of nets and far too flimsy to reach the outer grounds where the fish were. In that regard, though lashed by frequent gales, the coasts of Scotland were a little more forgiving. But if an Irish curragh crew managed to reach the outer grounds and a gale blew up from the east, the men would then have to try to reach Halifax in Nova Scotia – for to attempt to row back to the Irish coast would be impossible. Some witnesses describe men going out in any weather to find fish, but for lack of a catch they were often forced, like Bengali fishermen later, to trade their nets for food. So the relief from fishermen around the coast was small, and tended to help out small village communities or single families rather than the mass of Irish.

If the curraghs or coracles had been able to deploy nets, and brought them full of Atlantic salmon and cod to shore, one wonders how it would have been distributed to the starving inland people. There was no refrigeration, and – as was mentioned earlier – no extensive fish treatment or salting works. There were also landlord rights over some sections of coastal waters, and instances of the coastguard confiscating fish. Fish in the lakes and rivers of Ireland generally belonged to landlords, and though they were plentifully plundered by the hungry – at risk of transportation to Australia or imprisonment – it was on a personal and temporary level that the fine flesh of the salmon and trout relieved a family for a day or two.

Irish men, women and children travelled from the interior of the country to reach the beaches to scour the rockpools for limpets and fish for fluke in shallow waters. They collected all the seaweed they could find on the beaches – 'shore food', they called it. Carrageen moss and dulse (also called dillisk) were the most common of seaweeds to which the starving Irish had recourse. If prepared properly, carrageen had a neutral but not unpleasant taste, while dulse was said to have a taste of nuts and smokiness.

People who were coast-dwellers knew the rules for consuming seaweed better than those from the inland. Dulse could not be eaten cold, and some other species were not usually fit for consumption until after the first heavy frost in winter. (Coastal people also knew that some shellfish would kill them if eaten raw. For lack of such knowledge, the hungry beachcombers from the interior often suffered gastric illness or death.) Though nutritious and rich in iodine and vitamins, seaweeds lacked calories, and so did not give the eater much new energy.

Everywhere, Irish birds of all species were hunted down for food, and disappeared to the extent that a Wicklow landlord lamented that he never heard birdsong any more. People stole fish from landlords' streams where possible, and ate worms dug up from the bottom of the river. They sought a plant named charlock, known as field mustard. There was an inherited memory from eighteenth-century famines that it was a food for times of need – 'charlock of the fields, food of poor people'. Common wisdom said that charlock grew plentifully in graveyards. Once brought back to the Irish hearth, it could be chopped finely, boiled with oatmeal or made into a soup.

A further Irish emergency food was borage, a normally discarded plant pulled up from the midst of the landlord's corn, but rich in the fatty linoleic acid, and capable of inducing euphoria. Those who ate the weed acquired a yellow tint to their skin, but this was considered a minor price. Corn-weed, watercress and nettles, dock, sorrel and dandelion were widely used too. The Irish national symbol, the shamrock or wood sorrel, had declined in quantity as the primeval woods of Ireland were cleared for farming. Now there was not enough of it to be a famine food. But when ploughing was taking place anywhere, people followed the plough and hunted for remnants of the small flower or stalk, which grew from the underground pignut (*pratá cluracan*), a pleasant-tasting but very small root. They also sought out the roots of fern or dandelion, which they would boil, roast or crush to make a kind of bread. One Galway recipe combined sorrel, nettles and dockweeds with a spoonful of yellow meal. Children were sent to search the woods for nuts, and the bogs and mountains for berries. The fruit of holly, beech, crab apple and laurel, and the leaves and barks of trees, were stripped and devoured.

So the landscape was denuded of previously common plants and fruits. Indeed, the census of 1851 argued that grass itself was eaten by the starving, since dead bodies were found with it in their mouths. In Ethiopia 140 years later, grass would also be eaten – where it existed – as a near-final resort.

Blood from animals provided some nourishment to the

Irish. By dark, men would sneak up on young cattle, make a slit in a vein and collect the blood in a jar or pail to take home to their families. Before leaving the animal, they would seal the wound with a swatch of cow hair from the beast's tail, and with a pin. Cow's blood would be salted or fried or – if the family had further ingredients to hand – boiled with milk, meal, cabbage, wild mushrooms or wild herbs, and made into 'relish cakes'. An oral account tells of a man called Curnane bringing seven or eight cows to a starving family to allow them to draw blood, a quart from each cow. In many places, in fact, better-off people such as Curnane would take their cattle to a given site, where the ravening were permitted to draw blood.

We know a great deal less about the wild-food-collecting stratagems of the Bengalis, and there is a reason for that. The Irish and Ethiopian famines were visible history, but the Bengal famine seems submerged, specifically by World War II and its accompanying preoccupations. One of the reasons is that the area was closed off from journalists. For a long time, too, officials were more preoccupied with the threat of Japanese invasion than with the food crisis.

But we do know something of the plants sought out by the starving. As mentioned, among the Hindu population, Bengal Brahmin women sometimes chose death over undignified foraging. But others broke the taboos of their status to go out gathering famine foods their husbands had too much pride to collect. Whether Muslim or Hindu, people searched for *radhani*, or wild celery, and for the fruit of the *marula*, or elephant tree. This is a food much loved by elephants and claimed to have four times the vitamin C of an orange. Cobnuts (a form of hazelnut), wild mushrooms, rats and snakes and frogs were also hunted down.

Similarly, wild foods were gathered by Ethiopian farming families, including the many hundreds of thousands of them forcibly and disastrously resettled in unfamiliar regions to the west or south-west of the country. The Ethiopians scoured the countryside for wild dates and waterlily roots, and both farmers and the pastoral people stripped bare any berry trees they found. In the lowlands and the highlands of Ethiopia, there was a range of species of figs. A plant named *balanites aegyptiaca* gave edible yellow fruit, and roots that could be boiled up with cabbage to give the eater a good dose of vitamin A. Among pastoral people, the *yehub* nut tree produced fruit that tasted like almonds, and its leaves were so full of tannin they could be used to make tea. The less appetising waterberry or water pear was resorted to, and in desert regions, the baobab tree, called the bottle tree in English, grew large berries that could be mixed with milk. Black nightshade had a more ambiguous reputation. Its berries were generally eaten by children out herding the cattle or camels or goats, but its boiled-up leaves could be toxic and produce mental derangement and loss of eyesight. Ethiopian women of the kind who were seen on aid brochures (on their own way to becoming modern reproductions of the woman of Clonakilty) had knocked down termite mounds to find the grain that ants had stolen, or picked seeds out of the manure of animals.

But the fruits that made up the broad spectrum of wild

foods in Ethiopia and Bengal were – like Ireland's fish and seaweed and charlock – inadequate on their own to save life. Such sources were exhausted, in any case, by the time the starving had wasted away towards their final state.

That was when the most appalling foods were sought. The Irish had always found temporary relief from summer hunger, in the months when potatoes were not available, not only by selling their pigs but also by slaughtering the sheep that grazed mountain areas. But in the famine, they would resort in the end, and in competition with other starving people, to diseased cattle, to pigs infected with bovine cholera, to dogs who had eaten corpses, to dead horses, rats and carrion in general. That is, they became recklessly omnivorous, as would also be the case in Bengal and Ethiopia.

Emigration is a coping mechanism in many famines, though in others – in Bengal for instance – it took the form of an internal exodus. The poorest Bengalis, located mainly but not exclusively in West Bengal, were a vulnerable class who, stricken by lack of food, began, like the Muslim poor, to make for the cities. This exodus had occurred in Ireland too, as will be narrated later. Apart from the restlessness of the famished condition, perhaps there is a primal belief in the ravening mass of country people that the central authorities and their urban wealthy do not understand the depth of misery that prevails in the countryside. So the starving bring their visible suffering to town, where it might be seen and relieved.

Hindu and Muslim Bengali farmers made their march

to the larger towns of the region – Chittagong on the coast, Comilla nearer the Burmese border, Barisal to the west of Comilla, Krishnanagar, north of Calcutta, and, above all, Calcutta itself. In this internal immigration, the refugees from the country, once in the cities and disappointed by a lack of concrete help there, pleaded loudly and desperately at doorsteps and gates for the water in which the household servants had boiled rice, and competed for the muddy stalks of vegetables discarded in the streets. They fought over refuse in the dustbins and competed with the scrawny dogs of the city for shreds of meat. Rats and mice, dead or alive, were deemed a treasure of temporary protein.

For Ethiopian peasants and labourers and their families, there was, soon enough, that overriding urge to get to the cities. But this pilgrimage was thwarted, as those of so many Irish and Bengalis had been. Those who, at the end of all their other struggles, dragged themselves to the city of Addis Ababa in 1983–4 were not permitted to enter, and so were left to form a line for hundreds of miles in length along the roads leading to Mengistu's capital. The government kept them out of Addis by armed force, a denial method used in the 1970s by the emperor whom Mengistu had deposed.

Emigration or flight to the Sudan and to Somalia became an option for Ethiopian farming families, and the middle class also began to emigrate in unprecedented numbers, though in their case emigration was spurred not only by their having witnessed famine but also as a reaction to its accompanying politics, injustice and government-instigated terror. Until the famines of the 1970s and 1980s, the only travelling Ethiopians were those who had been sent overseas to be educated and to provide future bureaucrats and officials for the Ethiopian empire. Suddenly, however, Ethiopians could be found living in exile in the Sudan and Somalia and, ultimately, from Sweden and Alaska to Tierra del Fuego and Tasmania.

In traditionally honest communities, stealing seed and other food, or even stealing money, became common during famished times. In Ireland, the number of people committed for trial for theft rose from 20,000 in 1842–6 to 31,000 in 1847; 38,500 in 1848; and 42,000 in 1849. The statistics for other categories of crime remained level in the same period. One man sent to Australia for his crime was Michael Frawley, who was convicted of stealing money from the Board of Public Works, the body that supervised make-work relief. He claimed he committed his crime for the sake of his young and helpless family, for whom, he said, there was no room left in the workhouse. Michael Cullinan, also condemned to transportation, argued with some credibility that he had stolen a cow because his young family were hungry. But he was never shipped away because he died in prison of dysentery.

If given an opportunity, famished Bengalis thieved from government food depots without any sense that their acts were 'criminal', and sometimes under the blind eye of compassionate Indian police.

Attempted food theft became common in Ethiopia too. During the famines of the early 1970s and mid 1980s, people in Ethiopia who still possessed their seed crop tried to plant it in secret at night and to disguise the fact they had done so by spreading soil or straw, or employing other ruses, both to hide the fact that a crop had been planted, and to prevent people from digging up and stealing the seeds at night.

Under the pressure of coping, the ties between people, even within the same family, withered. Some separations, of course, were well-intentioned. In Ireland during *an Gorta Mór*, parents might send their children to the hated and punitive-looking workhouses instituted under the Irish Poor Relief Act of 1838. There, at least, some form of spartan succour was available, but of such a demeaning kind that many adult Irish were too proud to partake of it. Often the children would never see their parents again, and their parents knew this when they delivered them to the grim outer gate of the workhouse. Men who set out for the Bengali cities were often deluded enough to believe they would get work there and have their families join them later. Likewise, Ethiopian women and children were frequently sent by the fathers of their families to relief camps or towns, while the men searched for work rather than throw themselves on anyone's mercy.

But other separations did not have the quality of being designed for mutual good. In northern Ethiopia in the hungers of 1983–4, out of pure desperation families abandoned the elderly and weak, a pattern that had occurred in hungers of the past and would in those of the future. Vulnerable members of the family who seemed already too frail to walk towards relief, real or hoped-for, were frequently left behind to perish in the family house in the village.

In Bengal, among the families of sharecroppers, landless labourers, fishermen, weavers, barbers and potters, husbands abandoned wives and children were sold or left to die. Married men often expelled their widowed sisters from the house, and thus as good as condemned them to death by the roadside.

A frightful option taken in all famines is the maternal choice between feeding the child who might survive instead of the one who will not. An extreme Irish case of this preferential maternal love, reported by Mary Anne Hoare, a contemporary writer, was that of the woman who chose to neglect her 'miserable pallid infant' to suckle an eighteen-year-old son, a boy who worked on the road projects that were begun as famine relief. The family's survival depended on the boy, not on the infant, the latter almost certainly doomed whatever the mother did. For starvation induces a pragmatic desperation in its subjects, and this choice, too, is a coping mechanism. And as a crime it is minor compared to some of the other options historically taken with children.

These acts, morally repugnant to the well-fed, were often the only means left not only to soothe an unhinging hunger but, above all – a potent motivation in all famines – to make sure that some of the family came through. For the same reason, family groups chose to have less contact with local people to whom they had been close beforehand, and strangers were unwelcome. In the *clachans* of Ireland, the clusters of huts that developed on the so-called 'townlands' of the Irish countryside, it had been customary before the famine to ensure that no family would be permitted to wither away, and there was no blame or shame attached to taking the gifts of food given by other villagers. But now contact was unwelcome – it might have meant the necessity to give charity to friends, or to have them surprised by one's own somehow shameful deterioration, starvation being a great assault on one's sense of dignity and self-estimation.

A survivor of the Irish famine in north-west Donegal, at the Atlantic shore's limit of Ireland, mourned in the Irish tongue that even apart from starvation, such chosen isolation had other effects: 'Sport and pastimes disappeared. Poetry, music and dancing stopped. They lost and forgot them all and . . . these things never returned as they had been.'

To give an idea of the way the cohesion of a clan or a township is eroded by famine, it is opportune to go outside Ethiopia and look at a study of the Sudanese Relief and Rehabilitation Association (SRRA, an aid wing of the rebel Sudanese People's Liberation Army in southern Sudan). The research on the matter concerned voluntary cattle slaughter inside villages, and the way it peaked in 1998, during war-induced famines both in the vast, reedy Gogrial area south of Darfur and in Bahr el Ghazal province to the west of Gogrial. In southern Sudan generally, coping with famine had always been the task of village chiefs and councils. If a village family was in extreme danger of starvation, its menfolk were permitted to spear the cow of a wealthy neighbour. This was not viewed as 'charity' but as a customary transaction. But in the food crisis of 1998, landowners in southern Sudan began to fence in their cattle and prevent access to them. Fear, and the volatility of the region, where young militiamen with guns were the true rulers now, produced in chiefs and village worthies a desire to close in on themselves, to protect the family's resources and to ignore needs beyond that.

Short of selling one's flesh for food is the stratagem of selling a part. In May 1847 two girls came to a Clonmel barber and emerged bald, having exchanged their hair with him for two shillings and three pence.

But the sale of the entire body, even in such traditional societies, was another attempt at combating famine. In the Irish famine, there was near parity between male and female deaths, indicating that prostitution was not such a commonly adopted means of getting money and food. For where prostitution occurred widely, women – however socially ruined by what they did – survived better.

A famine play of 1945, *The Black Stranger* by Gerard Healy, raised the next-to-taboo issue of Irish women's prostitution in the famine, though the chief theme of the play is emigration. In a scene of the play, two sailors are overheard asserting that compliant women were always scarce in Ireland before, but that now they were 'cheap an' young an' plentiful'. A character named Bridie sells her body to buy cornmeal for a pregnant woman, and one of her companions declares, 'I'd do the same meself. What's a little thing like that, or the sins of the whole world, compared to the life of my baby.' Did Healy's play reflect the reality of the situation a hundred years before?

It is interesting that other works of literature and history on the famine did not raise the issue. But prostitution did occur. There was a rise in the number of younger women admitted to the Westmoreland Lock Hospital in Dublin, whose main brief was to treat prostitutes with sexually acquired diseases. For example, the number of women admitted there from the south-west (Munster) and the west (Connacht) rose eightfold during the famine. Arrests for prostitution in Dublin were a number of times higher during the famine years.

In Bengal there was a very nearly twofold difference in male deaths between the ages of ten and twenty as compared to females. Professor T.C. Das, who led a famous survey of Calcutta's homeless in 1943, was one who noted among the destitutes on Calcutta's streets the smaller number of girls as against boys in the age group of ten to fifteen years. This was due, he said, to 'the absorption of girls into city brothels'. A meeting of Calcutta women in January 1944 also addressed the existence of 'mass prostitution among village women'. By early 1944, the government of Bengal had expressed grave concern at reports received from 'various sources' that young destitute women were being recruited throughout Bengal by 'facile promises', and were then allocated to brothels or street prostitution. The consequence was not only a gender imbalance but a massive impact on the morale of the nation; a belief that Bengal after the famine would be threatened with social chaos. For the problem for those women who wanted to return to their villages once the emergency was over was that they would be considered unmarriageable outcasts, and this would be their destiny for life.

The practice of selling children into prostitution was

reported by a number of witnesses. In August 1943, *The Statesman* of Calcutta declared that the disappearance of young people into the prostitution business was a 'further evil'. They had been 'sucked or dragged down into the vice of a large city'. Their country innocence had been stripped away. In the spirit of that same derangement, in Ethiopia-bordering southern Sudan, where both the Sudanese army and southern rebels requisitioned animals and grain, children were sometimes sold into slavery to provide the majority of the family with cash for food, and girls were sent to the town to work as prostitutes – an option considered unthinkable in such a traditional society in normal times.

The exchange rate for a young woman prostitute in some areas of Bengal was said to be a rupee and a quarter, though a girl who was good-looking might attract four, five or even ten rupees. For parents who sold their children, it was often a crazily short-term solution to their needs, since rice cost a rupee a pound.

The issue of prostitution is readily addressed by the contemporary Bengali writers of the 1940s. Ela Sen's collection of short stories, *Darkening Days*, published in 1944, contains a tale in which one of two sisters' chances of using prostitution as an option is easier because of a nearby army base. A Calcutta woman pursues the same course in another story. As an observer, Ela Sen believed that about 30,000 from Calcutta's 125,000 destitute females went into brothels, one in four of them being very young girls. Sen declared that young and middle-aged women were won over by 'the chicanery of procurers' who smoothly promised food and shelter, which to the destitute meant paradise. She asserted that some women who unwittingly sold their daughters to the agents of brothels believed that they were to be taken into a decent institution where they would be fed. But often, Sen admits, the parents knew what they were subjecting the child to.

Bhabani Bhattacharya's renowned famine novel *He Who Rides a Tiger* is – like Sen's work – considered to be a reliable guide to the realities of Bengal in the famine years. He writes of a blacksmith who can find work only as a brothel agent, and discovers his own daughter in one of the Calcutta premises he visits. In Bhattacharya's other work, *So Many Hungers*, a mother who is chastised by another woman for having traded her daughter answers, 'You too will eat one day, for you have a daughter.'

T. G. Narayan, the Indian writer, also travelled throughout the famine-stricken area as the hunger took hold, and in a feeding camp met Aifaljan, a young woman of eighteen. Her story was representative – before the famine she had lived with her husband, Yakub, and their three-year-old son, Jamamuddin. In June 1943 their rice gave out. In the week that followed, they sold their hut, their utensils and every other material possession. They had nothing left to sell except their labour, for which there were no buyers. Jamamuddin, the son, died. His last cry was for rice, said his mother. Shortly after, Yakub divorced her and left to join the army. She had heard that the recently planted *aman* crop would prove to be a good one and hoped they needed workers in the field. Narayan wondered, would she get harvest work or end up in the hands of one of the slave traffickers?

In rural Ethiopia, as in much of Africa, girls – at some

time between the ages of five and ten – were circumcised. In many cases, this involved the cutting out of the vulva and sometimes of the clitoris by senior women, sometimes midwives, who did the work with razor blades or other implements. (Better-off parents had the operation performed in sterile conditions by health professionals.) Normally, the wound would be sutured with wooden splinters, but an opening was left to allow urination and menstruation to take place. This procedure was considered so important to the future virtue and marriageability of the child that it was sometimes ritually celebrated beyond the place of cutting by drum-beating and music and songs, which swamped the girl's screams. Her ankles bound together, the child might take a month to recover from the operation. The result at the age of marriage was that the husband should have the assurance of his wife's virginity, since it would be his erotic task gradually to open up the vagina. If a woman had been with other men, it was obvious to the husband or even to the elder women who might have examined her before marriage. Thus, famine prostitution resorted to by single women made it obvious that a woman was not fit for marriage, and again – as in Bengal but with even greater proof of her fall – she became untouchable and outcast.

Even further along in the starving crisis, the most baleful coping mechanism is cannibalism. There were a number of cases of cannibalism in Russia in the early 1920s, during the collectivisation-induced famine of 1919–23. In fact, dead bodies were sometimes traded and human flesh was trans-muted into meatballs, cutlets and minced meat. So many cases occurred in Leningrad during its 900-day siege by the Nazis in World War II that the Russian security forces formed a special squad to punish those guilty of it. But for people who would dig up the buried bodies of animals to eat, can-nibalism might not have seemed a huge further step.

In 1851, the Irish census stated that a stipendiary magis-trate in Galway City heard the case of a prisoner arrested for stealing food, who was discovered in his cabin with his fam-ily and a part-consumed corpse. With astounding tolerance, the magistrate found there were extenuating circumstances, since the man was subject to the mania that struck people in the late stages of starvation. Elsewhere in Ireland, a passion-ate observer wrote, 'Insane mothers began to eat their young children who died of famine before them; and still fleets of ships were sailing with every tide, carrying Irish cattle and corn to England.' Dawit Wolde Giorgis, the Ethiopian army officer who ran with questionable success his country's relief agency, had the same reaction when he saw cannibalism in an inadequate feeding centre in the Ethiopian highlands. These people were not to blame, he argued, as the Irish magistrate had nearly 130 years before. Starvation was not only a blight on the physical organism, but also on the brain. There was evidence that, under its influence, children were abandoned or suffocated by their mothers.

Because of the blankness of the Bengali record, we do not know if, or on what scale, famine cannibalism existed. But Bengal would have been unique if it had not happened there also.

6

Villains: Ireland

MOST FAMINES LEAVE behind in the survivors and their offspring the name of a supposed chief villain – the mal-administrator or tyrant, whom those who live and remember and pass on remembrance will forever after condemn and curse above all others. Particularly in the case of the Irish and Bengal famines, it could be argued that the disaster had many fathers, and even Mengistu, who is justifiably and overridingly the culprit for the Ethiopian famine, had the full-throated support of members of the ruling military, the Derg, and of his head of security, Legesse Asfaw, in all he did and did not do.

But to begin with Ireland: in a song often sung by Irish rugby fans, 'The Fields of Athenry', a young Irishman about to embark on a convict transport exchanges final words with his wife as 'the prison ship lies waiting in the bay', ready to bear him into exile in Australia. One of the verses points to the often-named great Satan of the Irish famine.

By a lonely prison wall
I heard a young maid calling,
'Michael they are taking you away,
For you stole Trevelyan's corn
That the young might see the morn.
Now the prison ship lies waiting in the bay.'

The corn referred to represents the grain that was shipped out of Ireland throughout the famine, popularly believed to have been sufficient to save the Irish. And Trevelyan is Charles Edward Trevelyan, who never visited Ireland during the crisis but who was, by way of his office at the Treasury in Whitehall, administrator of government relief to Ireland.

Certainly, there was an unyielding quality in the gifted Trevelyan, a man of nearly forty years when the famine struck. He was an evangelical Christian, and when he became convinced that certain events were in accord with the workings of Providence, he could not be moved from accepting those events. Similarly, at a secular level, his belief in the theory of political economy promoted by John Stuart Mill, a prophet of the uselessness of government intervention in famine, and others was immutable and to be embraced rigorously. These qualities were construed as virtues by his masters and many of his contemporaries, and that was the way he construed them himself.

Born in 1807, Trevelyan was the son of an Anglican archdeacon of Taunton in Somerset, and a child of a cultivated family of limited income but of broad intellectual and religious connections. In 1834, he became the devoted husband to Hannah Moore, the sister of Thomas Macaulay, the great historian, who was then a member of the Supreme Council of India. In his twenties, working as assistant to a commissioner of the East Indian Company in Delhi, Trevelyan helped to reform the Indian civil service and donated his own money to public works. He was anxious to clear barriers to trade – something that would be consistent with his behaviour in the Irish famine, when he saw trade, and not relief, as both sovereign and solution.

For nineteen years, from 1840 on, he was assistant secretary to the Treasury in Whitehall. It was in that role that he came to be responsible for what the British government devised for Irish relief and, to an extent, that he became an architect of the government's policy. This task was merely a prelude – in the eyes of Whitehall officials and Westminster politicians – to his ultimate governorship of Madras from 1859, and the distinction he would achieve as a cabinet member of the British government of India, positions he occupied without the slightest hint of venality. He was cast in a new mould; neither a man of inherited wealth nor a nabob on the make.

Like the family of the historian Macaulay, Trevelyan was a spiritual child of William Wilberforce, the evangelical reformer who had campaigned successfully for the abolition of slavery in Britain and its possessions. But the secular influences on him came from the political economists of the day. The impact of a passage from John Stuart Mill such as the following would have coloured his view of the world and of how to deal with its ills: 'In cases of actual scarcity,' wrote Mill, 'governments are often urged . . . to take measures of some sort for moderating the price of food.' There remained, however, said Mill, 'No mode of affecting it [price], unless by taking possession of all the food and serving it out in rations as in a besieged town.'

In the besieged town of Ireland, the rations were not going to be seized and served out. Adam Smith reinforced the concept: 'A famine has never arisen from any other cause but the violence of government attempting, by improper means, to remedy the inconvenience of a dearth.' Famines were matters in which governments should not try to intervene or attempt to achieve some sort of false justice in food markets. The best hope of salvation was to let the market do its mysterious and beneficent work. So, in the eyes of Trevelyan and his fellow thinkers, the famine resulting from the potato blight was a catastrophe that could not be substantially interfered with.

Another major influence on Trevelyan was the Reverend Thomas Malthus, a population theorist who declared a calamity in Ireland inevitable due to over-population. In his *Essay on the Principles of Population*, first published in 1798, Malthus forecast the unarguable cleansing in Ireland, though he moderated the idea in his *Principles of Political Economy* in 1836. But he had also famously written in an 1817 article: 'The land in Ireland is infinitely more peopled than in England; and to give full effect to the natural resources of the country, a great part of the population should be swept from the soil.' The Malthusian view served and enhanced the principles of political economy: resignation to what could not be prevented.

One of the reasons Malthus had an impact on Trevelyan,

and other officials and politicians, was the fact that in the immediate aftermath of the Napoleonic Wars, which ended in 1815, population growth in Britain as a whole had reached an unprecedented 11 per cent per annum, and poor relief expenditure – again in Britain as a whole – had risen to almost seven and a half million pounds per annum, compared with an annual expenditure of just over one million in 1776. Most of this expenditure, it should be said, was paid not by government but by a poor rate levied on land holders.

Combined with the two theories of inevitability, both the economic and the demographic, was the conviction that Providence had also provided for a great cleansing of Ireland. Certainly, the like-thinking cabinet of Lord John Russell, who became British prime minister in 1846, believed Trevelyan had done all he could to temper the sufferings of the Irish in the face of the severe but necessary workings of that divine dispensation. On 6 January 1847, Charles Trevelyan wrote, 'It is hard upon the poor people that they should be deprived of knowing that they are suffering from an affliction of God's providence.' Since God had ordained the famine 'to teach the Irish a lesson, that calamity must not be too much mitigated . . . the real evil with which we have to contend is not the physical evil of the Famine, but the moral evil of the selfish, perverse and turbulent character of the people.'

Trevelyan stuck to his views in various media – for example, in a famous letter to Lord Monteagle, a Whig politician, chancellor of the exchequer from 1835–9 and a progressive Irish landlord. Unlike many landlords, Monteagle – in between sittings of Parliament – actually lived on his land in the west of Ireland. On 9 December 1846, while a remarkably severe winter began to bring the first outbreak of famine disease to the Irish, sheltering, wild-eyed, by peat fires, Trevelyan wrote in reply to Monteagle's appeal on behalf of the peasantry: 'It forms no part of the functions of government to provide supplies of food or to increase the productive powers of the land. In the great institutions of the business of society, it falls to the share of government to protect the merchant and the agriculturalist in a free exercise of their respective employments . . . the cure has been applied by the direct stroke of an all wise providence in a manner as unexpected and un-thought as it is likely to be effectual. God grant that we may rightly perform our part, and not turn into a curse what was intended for a blessing.'

Again, Trevelyan was not alone in these views. The diarist (and racing aficionado and cricketer) Charles Greville said of the Irish in perhaps the darkest year of 1847 that they 'never were so well off on the whole as they had been in this year of famine. Nobody will pay rent, and the saving banks are overflowing.' Besides, they spent their money to buy guns with which to 'shoot the officers who were sent over to regulate the distribution of relief'. If a subtle intelligence such as Greville's thought such things, one can imagine the opinions of others.

There were more humane and instinctively compassionate voices in Britain. Charles Dickens later condemned Trevelyan's view. In *Bleak House* (its first instalment appearing in 1852), he would mock 'the gentle politico-economic principle that a surplus of population must and ought to starve'.

*

As well as his philosophic conditioning, Trevelyan brought to the famine some impressive, though not abnormal, prejudices against the Irish. First of all, the peasantry clung to Catholicism, with its debilitating irrationalities, its superstitions, its hostility to progress in thought, and the brake on inventiveness and adaptability it was seen to impose on people. Trevelyan believed the Irish too indolent to farm like civilised people, and in that regard the potato-growing term 'lazy row' seemed to confirm some of his prejudices. A lazy row or lazy bed was, in fact, quite a rational method, in which the potatoes were planted in a mound as a result of the planter shovelling out a row of sod and piling it on the planting mound after breaking any of its grass roots in the sod with a mallet. This was the best method for the Irish, who dug up the potatoes as they needed them and left the rest in the ground. It was true that growing potatoes did not require as much effort as growing oats, but the image of Irish laziness must be surely alleviated by that of the hundreds of thousands of Irish males who looked for harvest work during the summer, frequently travelling to England as deck cargo to do so.

For Trevelyan and many others, the devilish laziness of the race ran hand in hand with the unrest of the Irish in the face of God's will. This unrest manifested itself in 'rural outrages'. Landlords and their agents, and tithe proctors who collected tithes for the Established (non-Catholic) Church, were threatened by notices hammered to doors and trees demanding improved and more compassionate treatment. If their behaviour did not improve, they were subject to physical attack, sometimes being ambushed and killed.

The secret societies of peasants guilty of these assaults were called Ribbon Societies, and their members Ribbonmen, on the basis of their having early in their history worn ribbons during their assaults. These primitive acts of rebellion were seen as merely an index of the intractability, the unteachability, the malice of the Irish, rather than as an outfall from the grievous land situation under which most inhabitants of that fateful island lived.

A clinical psychologist, Deborah Peck, identifies the mental tendencies of those in power over the mass of the starving. The powerful perceive themselves to be loyal citizens, virtuous, industrious and thrifty, while the victims are disloyal, disreputable, lazy and improvident. The powerful, in their view, behave with sexual appropriateness; the victims are sexually profligate and, in their lust, breed recklessly. The powerful have rational religious beliefs. The victims' brains are perverted with multifarious superstitions. Trevelyan and others in power in Britain certainly accepted as givens these distinctions between themselves and the Irish.

In terms of sexual inappropriateness, the general belief had it that the Irish were guilty of early marriage and headlong child-begetting, and this perception was partially fuelled by the fact that the Irish considered they would always be able to feed themselves with potatoes and thus had no inhibitions about founding a family. Yet, as twentieth-century research would show, the average age for marriage among males in Ireland in 1840 was nearly 28 years (Trevelyan married, in England, at

27 years) and for women, 24.4 years – well above the averages for many other parts of Europe.

Trevelyan also blamed Irish landlords for their laziness and its influence on the backwardness of Irish society and agriculture. The Devon Commission, appointed to inquire into the state of law and the practice of land-holding in Ireland, having published its report in February 1845, just before the famine, attributed the apparent apathy of Irish proprietors to their lack of ready money. Many Irish landlords had inherited 'encumbered estates', estates on which their forebears had borrowed large sums in the golden days of the late eighteenth and early nineteenth centuries, when prices for agricultural goods were high – in part because Britain was at war with the French and, from 1812, with the Americans.

Trevelyan took up the theme of landlord incompetence and venality full-scale, blaming both landlords who lived on their estates and those who were absentees in England or the Continent for their major share of Irish backwardness.

The religiously devout Trevelyan considered murder a great wrong. It is sobering, then, to think that the deployment of convinced, virtuous intent – a belief in the most elevated philosophic principles of the day – and an intense belief in a providential deity, could be almost as destructive as the malignity of a dictator such as Mengistu Haile Mariam.

In the spring of 1848, following his declaration that the famine was finished – although it still had several years to run its course – Charles Trevelyan was granted a knighthood by Prime Minister Russell, a government sanction of all he had done, and a sign of the gulf between Irish and British perceptions of what was still happening. Indeed, his ultimate reputation would be that of reformer of the British civil service, as governor of Madras at the time of the Indian Mutiny, and as minister of finance in the British government of India. He devoted his later years to charity and work on army reform, and died in 1886.

The British prime minister at the time of the famine's birth, Sir Robert Peel, bears only a fraction of the scale of blame attached to Trevelyan's name.

When the potato blight had first struck in the autumn of 1845, destroying a considerable and often irreplaceable part of people's food supply, the gifted Tory prime minister (called by the Irish 'Orange Peel' because of his initial opposition to Catholic emancipation – the granting of full civil rights to Catholics) was moved by pragmatism rather than by belief in steely and immutable principles.

'There is such a tendency,' said Prime Minister Peel, 'to exaggeration and inaccuracy in Irish reports that delay in acting on them is always desirable.'

His basis for saying so was that he had served under Prime Minister Lord Liverpool as Irish chief secretary in 1811–17, residing in Dublin, and then as home secretary of Great Britain in 1822, and in both those years there were food shortages in Ireland because of poor potato crops. An equally poor grain harvest reduced the amount of flour milled and drove up its price beyond the reach of the poor. In Mayo in 1822, discarded fish heads from the east coast, the Irish Sea, had been shipped in, and the Mayo starving ate them and the bodies of occasional porpoises washed ashore. But Peel and his cabinet believed these conditions in the always-hungry west of Ireland were far from being a general famine.

So, during late 1845, when the blight did not strike everywhere, Peel was wary, but at least he sought daily reports from the London-appointed executive who served under Ireland's lord lieutenant, and he set up a scientific commission consisting of a Scots chemist, Dr Lyon Playfair, and an English botanist, Dr John Lindley, and sent them to Ireland to report on the situation. They toured stricken parts of what were normally the more prosperous eastern counties – Dublin, Westmeath to the near north, Louth to the coastal north of Dublin, Meath, which was north-west of the capital, and Kildare to the south-west. In a private letter to Peel, Dr Lindley said the situation was 'melancholy' and argued that reports of the situation were not exaggerated but understated. Yet Peel was still locked in his earlier experience and believed what he believed. Indeed, in all three of these famines, scepticism – willed or chosen – would prove fatal.

In Ireland, the Irish political leader Daniel O'Connell had a more reliable view of what was happening. He was a Catholic landlord, member of the House of Commons in Westminster and leader of the Irish Party, whose object was the repeal of the union with Britain. He had received news of 'the visitation' – the blight – from repeal branches throughout the country. Hence, in late October 1845, he went with a delegation to visit Lord Lieutenant Heytesbury in Dublin Castle. (Later the following year O'Connell would say memorably that this was 'a death-dealing famine'.) But for now, he pleaded for a suspension of the export of the annual grain harvest, which, he claimed, was close to 1.6 million tons. He asked in particular for a prohibition on distilling and brewing using grain. While Heytesbury thought the demand about the harvest premature, he did counsel Peel to open Irish ports to the importation of foreign grain – an option that was contrary to British government protection policies. He also sought permission to stop the use of grain in distilling. His advice and requests were ignored.

However, in the bitter winter of 1845–6, when the starving had begun, Peel decided to make an urgent purchase through a London brokerage of £100,000 worth of Indian corn or maize from the United States. He intended to keep it a secret so that the grain prices in the markets of Britain and Ireland were not influenced downwards. He did dare hope, however, that once the secret was out and the corn began to be sold at cost to the Irish, it would bring down high grain prices in a reasonable way.

Indian maize was harsher than the corn grown in England and Ireland, and was unaccustomed foodstuff to the citizens of the British Isles. Thus it had the advantage that the Irish would eat it only if they needed it. The Indian maize, or 'yellow male' as the Irish called it, probably saved lives, even if the Irish cursed it. Improperly ground, it generated another name based on its influence on the gastric system: 'Peel's brimstone'.

Peel's interference in the market did not sit so well with believers in political economy, and aggrieved many among his Tories. But it was part of a broader plan. From October 1845 onwards, Peel struggled with his party to abolish the Corn Laws. These import tariffs had been originally introduced after the Napoleonic Wars to compensate British farmers for the post-war fall in prices, and had kept grain prices throughout Britain high. Peel argued that not only Ireland, but the condition of England as well, required the repeal of the Corn Laws. He did so as a proponent of enlightened Toryism. He told his party that he foresaw an English revolution and the shadow of the scaffold falling over the privileged if grain prices were not reduced.

The resistance in Parliament was immense. As the Duke of Wellington, one of Peel's party, said, 'Rotten potatoes have done it all. They put Peel in his damned fright.' The Corn Laws were in fact repealed, but Peel's government was so divided by the process that it fell in June 1846. Yet, in reality, the reduction in the duty that supported grain-growers was abolished only gradually, which did not much help the poor of Britain in general, let alone the ordinary Irish. When – to the astonishment of the populace – the potato crop failed again in the autumn of 1846, there was still a duty of four shillings per quarter on corn.

Now the talented Lord John Russell was prime minister, and under his administration the famine would take on its full, deadly exorbitance. Trevelyan's new master was of a pragmatic mind, rather as Peel had been. He was intelligent, sometimes strangely shy, and he had been a notable champion of the Reform Bill of 1832, without which it was believed Britain's unrest, inequalities and ridiculous electoral system would have dragged it down into chaos. As prime minister, he was surrounded in Parliament by free-trade radicals of the kind who had been subject to the same influences, and believed the same principles, as Trevelyan. Charles Wood,

Trevelyan's immediate superior as chancellor of the exchequer in Russell's government, subscribed absolutely to the principles Trevelyan brought to famine relief. Yet his name – like Russell's – is barely known to Irish nationalists and to laymen interested in the famine. It did not appear in aggrieved folksongs, nor was it repeated bitterly to the young at Irish hearthsides, nor is it nowadays tunefully denounced in pubs before Irish international rugby test matches.

Russell was ultimately responsible for subsequent government policies on Ireland, and Wood approved of them. But it was Trevelyan, as the man in charge of government's mercy to Ireland, who became an infamous figure to Irish nationalists, who hated political economy and believed it could not be applied to their country, and who then, in turn, informed popular feeling.

7

Villains and Heroes: Bengal

THE VILLAINS IN the case of the Bengal famine are far more diffuse. As Charles Trevelyan did, the Marquess of Linlithgow, Victor Alexander John Hope, viceroy of India and thus head of British administration in India, has an especially poor name. But it has not remained a byword in India, the way Trevelyan's has in Ireland. Nor were his actions backed by as clearly perceived a set of principles as those that Trevelyan followed. Linlithgow was not the man of ideas that Trevelyan had been. His talents were described by one British official as 'pedestrian'. His behaviour was an amalgam of incomprehension, administrative failure and a sense of racial superiority. Unlike Trevelyan, he was no scholar.

Instead, Linlithgow was a Scots banker – 'tall, strongly-built and staunch,' said *Time* magazine in 1936; a lean giant of a man, six feet seven inches tall. He was born of a notable Tory family and his godmother was Queen Victoria. He had been a lord of the Admiralty and involved in government bodies dealing with the distribution and pricing of agricultural produce. He had turned down the governor-generalship of Australia. (His father had been Australia's first and not very successful governor-general, Lord Hopetoun.) He accepted the supreme position in India in 1936. His imagination and empathy were not, however, of any great stature. He was not a friend of and had no warm feelings for Mahatma Gandhi, as his predecessor Lord Halifax had. Nor did he aspire to such intimacy. He would write, 'If India is to be really capable of holding its own in the future without direct British control from outside, I'm not sure that it will not need an increasing infusion of stronger Nordic blood, whether by settlement or inter-marriage or otherwise.'

His personal life was as unblemished as Trevelyan's had been and he went on to be a particularly fond grandparent. He kept a pet turtle named Jonas, to whom he fed worms. Nor was he venal or corrupt. He was perhaps an incarnation of a type about whom Gandhi had written in 1922. After defining British occupation as a criminal endeavour, Gandhi declared: 'Englishmen and their Indian associates involved in the administration of the country do not seem to understand they are engaged in the crime I have attempted to describe. I am satisfied that many Englishmen and Indian officials honestly believe that they are administering one of the best systems devised in the world and that India is making steady but slow progress.'

Linlithgow was appointed as viceroy to make sure the new Indian constitution of 1935, by which provincial legislatures would be run by Indians under a British provincial governor, was decreed and began functioning properly. In February 1940, when the war in Europe had already begun, even if it was rather quiescent, Gandhi wrote to Linlithgow, in answer to the viceroy's 'dreary, prosaic' assurance that Britain had an ultimate 'dominion status' in mind for India, that, 'The vital difference between the [Indian] Congress and the Viceroy's offer consists in the fact that the Viceroy's offer contemplates final determination by the British government whereas the Congress contemplates the contrary.' Nor did the left wing of the Congress party treasure this promised 'dominion status', which would still leave India loyal to the crown of Great Britain.

Gandhi argued that there should be no British troops in India, nor (once the Japanese entered the war) any Americans, until India was free. The Allies should withdraw and India could make a peace with Japan and become free and neutral. It was an unlikely scenario – Japan was not disposed to stop advancing. But many Indians agreed with it. For a time, the British considered deporting Gandhi.

By May 1942, the news that disturbed Linlithgow did not concern any omen of famine in Bengal, but the disastrous loss of the city of Rangoon and all of Burma, one of India's eastern neighbours. There was now an apparently imminent Japanese invasion of Bengal, and of Assam to the north of Bengal. A shared, though lesser, consideration of Britons and Indians was that Burma had been exporting food into India, and now would not be doing so.

By this time, a number of British warships had been destroyed off the Bay of Bengal by the ships of Admiral Nagumo, the leader of the Japanese attack on Pearl Harbor, and approaches to the province of Bengal were largely controlled by the enemy. The fall of Burma, in the context of the earlier losses of Singapore and Hong Kong, preoccupied Linlithgow and the cabinet of the government of India. They considered that the Indian political leaders, especially the forceful Mahatma Gandhi, the more moderate Jawaharlal Nehru and – indeed – the entire Indian National Congress party, did not seem to appreciate that there was a war in progress and that their British benefactors needed the unstinting loyalty of all Indians at this time of acute crisis. The British refused to discuss India's future status with them until the war ended. The Indian leadership wanted to discuss it now, and in return they would promise to sanction India's participation in the war, instead of resisting it with all their influence. Nehru at least said that the thought of fascism dominating any part of the world was repulsive to him. But, with some success, he did his best to soothe and court American opinion.

To Linlithgow, as to London, this was a form of treachery second only to the collaboration of the Japanese with the Germans. The United States disagreed radically with the British over India. President Roosevelt himself believed the British position was inherently self-contradictory – Britain was supposedly fighting for freedom and independence, while refusing to extend such benefits to the Indians. He wished it was otherwise, so that everyone in India would be galvanised to resist the Japanese. Vice-president Henry Wallace recorded in his diary that the president had 'a very profound concern about India and a definite belief that England has not handled India properly'. Liberal American newspapers and magazines all hoped that the problem between the British and the Indians would be resolved positively through negotiations. The *New Republic* thought that negotiations between Britain and India, even in the midst of the war, might well 'shape the destinies of white men as well as brown, black as well as yellow, for generations to come'. Even the soft-edged *Saturday Evening Post* thought it would be better if the British had left India years before. The manager of American Express in Calcutta declared that the British had the capacity to alienate even those Indians who were loyal. Nonetheless, while Roosevelt approved of Indian independence, there was much American criticism for the apparent willingness of Indian leaders to stand in the way of the war effort, particularly after the Quit India movement began.

The war cabinet in London had sent one of its members, Sir Stafford Cripps, to try to settle the Indian question. But once more he could offer independence only as a condition of cooperation in the war, and when the war itself ended. The mission was, of course, a failure and led to serious results.

The Indian National Congress had been founded in 1885, and gradually became at least the Hindu organ of the struggle for Indian independence. As a member, Gandhi in particular had moved it away from its original character as an English-speaking, Indian middle-class body to appeal to a broader language and wider social membership base. On 8 August 1942, a 'Quit India' resolution – a call for a campaign of civil disobedience to make the British yield up Indian independence immediately – was being discussed by the Congress leadership at the Gowalia Tank Maidan, a park in central Bombay, when a crowd of supporters invaded the dusty reaches of the parkland and passed the motion. Jawaharlal Nehru, future prime minister of India, and other senior members of Congress, had doubts about the wisdom of the Quit India motion, and Mohammad Ali Jinnah, the leader of the Muslim League, considered the Congress's approval of Quit India a great blunder, an undue forcing of the pace at a time when the Empire was at great peril and so distracted by the war.

Linlithgow viewed all this with bewilderment, and the war cabinet in London with enhanced, if not outright, fury. Linlithgow, against the wishes of a number of Indian members of his executive council, ordered the arrest of the Congress leaders, including Gandhi and Nehru. The depth of passions is demonstrated by the case of one Indian arrestee's young daughter, who yelled at the arresting soldiers that they were rocks on the road to freedom and suckers of Indian blood. She remembered, 'After that, we children used to go out and throw date seeds covered in dried mud at British soldiers when we saw them in the street.'

Some British and Indian army officers and men responded brutally to Quit India advocates, especially to Indian women taking part in demonstrations. One activist claims that a woman demonstrator in Delhi was raped 'not by one officer but by officer after officer, including the British officers'. The authorities in some regions had advocates of Quit India publicly whipped. If missionaries, especially American missionaries, supported Quit India, they faced expulsion from the country.

American attitudes may well have bolstered what in this case would prove to be the fatal stubbornness of Churchill over Bengal. Another result, however, would be that as the Bengali famine began in 1943, the council of the Congress Party were in prison, and could not react to the disaster as they might have, had they been free. So the famine ran the risk of being overshadowed not only by a great crisis for the British at the war front on the borders of Bengal, but by Indian politics. Because of their arrests, the Indian leadership was not available to protest at, or visit the sites of, the famine. The Bengal famine, rich in destruction as it was, never held a position in Indian history that the Irish famine did in Irish history, or the Ethiopian famines have come to occupy for the Ethiopians.

Linlithgow himself, subject to the advice of his experts, permitted provincial governments to retain all the food they produced within their boundaries and refuse to export it to other parts of India. The ruling of November 1941 by Linlithgow's executive council, over which he sat as chairman and chief executive, meant that no food came from other provinces into Bengal, even though troops were consuming a great amount of that province's food. In December, Linlithgow and his council introduced maximum prices of wheat, but this simply made grain dealers retain their wheat in their warehouses, waiting for a better price. In May 1942, a Foodgrains Control Order fixed prices at a level that ensured, without meaning to, further hoarding and ultimate profiteering.

Neither was Linlithgow solely responsible for other

decisions and events, such as the British government and army's 1942 Rice Denial Scheme – their buying-up of Bengali rice to ensure that any advancing Japanese would not be able to use it. In its policy of rice denial, the government forcibly purchased 40,000 tons of grain and trucked it away to feed the army. Though not as much rice was acquired as the authorities hoped, or people in Bengal feared, the psychological impact was far larger than the amount taken away. Its effect on the Bengali imagination was the equivalent of the Irish sense of grain being transported by road and canal for shipping out of the country to England. Since people believed the government and army would take more still, it led to the sometimes panicked, sometimes deliberate, hoarding of rice for future sale, and thus to a huge ramping-up of the price of rice for the labourers and craftsmen who tried to buy it at their village shops.

It is likely that such policies as these derived from London instead of New Delhi, from the war cabinet itself. And the governor of Bengal, Sir Jack Herbert, agreed to the denial policies without briefing the Bengali provincial cabinet. He assured the Bengal provincial legislature that the government did not intend to burn houses or remove household grain. The Bengal chief minister wrote to Herbert, 'In a matter of such vital importance, affecting the question of the foodstuffs of the people, you should have called an emergency meeting of the Cabinet . . . but you did nothing of the kind.' Herbert had not done so because he knew the removal of surplus grain would, in itself, drive up prices of food in the *mofussil* – the countryside. He did not want to face any political opposition to the policies until he had to.

Like Trevelyan, as the famine developed, Linlithgow was not open to the proposition that things were as bad as people on the ground in Bengal said. So he refused to invoke the 'famine codes', provisions published in a manual early in the century, designed to bring special systems of relief into play. He had persuaded himself that the problem was in part a matter of inefficiency of distribution by the Bengali provincial government, a new and inexperienced government, and not a concern of the British government of India. He also consoled the secretary for India in Whitehall that the situation in Bengal 'does not constitute a grave menace to the peace and tranquillity of Bengal . . . for sufferers are entirely submissive'.

Under him, in 1942 the government of India sent out the order for the confiscation of thousands of Bengal's boats, so essential to trade and fishing, along the region's numberless waterways, lest the Japanese get the use of them. On 1 May 1942, the process of the removal of boats began in southern coastal districts, in which the transport of goods and people was almost entirely by water. The 'denial line' ran from Barakpur above Calcutta in the west across to Chandpur in present-day Bangladesh, close to the Burmese border. By the end of November, 60,000 boats were gone and only about one third of the normal number were left on the area's waterways. From November onwards, when military and civic nerves had become less tremulous, many boats were returned to their owners. But they had been stored at 'reception stations' and had often been damaged. Their absence had made it harder to move grain, driving up its price.

The government also ordered the moving of 350,000

families, to clear the ground for military operations. They were trucked out of East Bengal by an administration they hated, and found temporary homes with family members and in barracks further to the west. In military terms, the edicts were quite understandable. In their effect, they would further ensure the coming misery in Bengal. The roads and railways were unable to do the work the country boats had done. In many cases, once a truck reached rivers such as the Padma (of which the Ganges is a tributary), the Mahanadi, Godavari and Krishna, it had to be unloaded and somehow got across the water for reloading on a further truck.

Had there been enough early political will, these problems would not necessarily have foreshadowed a disaster for Bengal's people. In spite of all adverse conditions, everything needed to feed the army was supplied and distributed at the famine's height in the second half of 1943 – itself an indication that a similar distribution to Bengal's civilians could have been possible. There were suggestions on top of all else that a scarcity of food in the *mofussil* was at least welcomed by the military for recruiting purposes. It certainly spurred enlistment into the ranks of the nearly two-and-a-half-million-strong Indian army, whose members served in the British forces. The Military Labour Corps, which recruited women as well as men to work on military installations and emplacements, gave a chance of survival to a certain number of starving women, but they were often used or abused by soldiers, and some were afflicted by venereal disease.

*

The idea that there was an imminent food crisis continued to evade Linlithgow. On 26 January 1943 he wrote to London, to Secretary of State for India Leopold Amery, reporting that he had ordered Bengal it 'simply *must*' send more rice out of Bengal for Ceylon, where there was a shortage. In reality, it was not nearly as acute as that of Bengal. But the export had to take place 'even if Bengal itself went short'. Linlithgow told Amery that he was not unsympathetic to Bengal, but that nonetheless he might be able to 'screw a little out of [the Bengali premier]'. He thought the Bengal food situation could be treated with guarded optimism – there were recent improvements in India generally and an excellent prospect of the *rabi* (also known as the *boro*) harvest in the spring. In any case, he felt he had done everything he could by writing in June 1943 to the war cabinet asking for imports of food grain from other parts of the Empire.

By the end of his vice-regency, in June 1943, the nervously exhausted Linlithgow had at last become convinced of the urgency of the Indian situation. Yet his advice to London, after beginning bravely, was cynical. He told Leopold Amery: 'A firm promise of 100,000 tons of barley and the possibility of a small additional quantity of wheat will go nowhere in meeting our essential demands.' So he asked for 300,000 tons of food grain, especially wheat. He said that these shipments were needed to feed the army, but that he would declare in public that the imported wheat would be made available for the general population as well. His telegram concluded: 'The propaganda value of this would be great indeed.' In the meantime, he warned the cabinet: 'I can't be responsible for [the] continuing stability of India now, or her capacity to serve as a base against Japan next year unless we have appropriate help in prospect'.

Later, he and other members of the British government would work out a complicated explanation of the famine, blaming it on the fact that Bengalis had eaten the 'carry-over' – that is, stored remnant – of the crop before the famine struck. This, he announced, was a major cause of the shortage of food in Bengal. Reserves having been consumed, people were hungering. The results of eating the carry-over would, said Linlithgow, persist for some time. The Famine Inquiry Commission reported that one cause of the famine was 'a shortage in the stock of old rice carried forward from 1942 to 1943', but it gave no evidence to prove its argument, and this might even have been an unconscious symptom of the tendency of authority to blame famines on their victims. The 1945 report of the Commission did not, at least, as heavily invoke Malthus's ideas of inevitable culling as others did, nor was Malthus turned to for justification of what had happened, as he had been in the narrower geographic confines of the Irish disaster.

In Linlithgow's place, the government of Great Britain appointed a soldier, Field Marshal Archibald Wavell, who was also to act as commander-in-chief for India. He would, arriving however late on the scene, address the famine frontally.

Though Lord Linlithgow would not visit Calcutta, the acting governor of Bengal, Sir T. Rutherford, had the courage to walk its streets and then to reconnoitre some of the *mofussil* before Wavell arrived. On 19 September 1943, Rutherford wrote, 'I have wandered around Calcutta after nightfall and scenes are pretty ghastly. I have also done a long mufti tour through 24 Parganas District . . . I envisage a large death toll throughout the Province from starvation following on previous malnutrition coupled with endemic malaria . . . Though famine is not officially declared, the conditions are those of famine.'

On 28 September, he visited the Midnapore and saw corpses being torn to pieces by dogs and vultures. He believed that the majority of the starving were the beggars and elderly until now maintained by private charity. But he thought that the large sales of metal, household vessels, ornaments and land were ominous signs. The peasants faced dizzying fluctuations in the policies of governments – price-fixing adopted and then abandoned and then adopted again. The Bengali government's response to the Japanese advance was to call on people to keep a two-month supply of food grains in their homes. Worry about what was to happen meant that those who could manage it accumulated a six-month supply and so reduced the amount of rice in the stores. Then a US army air transport command and 6000 Chinese nationalist troops who had escaped Burma also had to be fed, which created a further drain on the local food supply in north-east Bengal and in Assam.

The question arises: was Churchill, a man of considerable compassion, nonetheless a villain in the story of Bengal? By the time of the famine's onset, Churchill had been British prime minister for three years and was absorbed by the European war, to which he and Roosevelt had decided to give priority. Yet Churchill knew that British survival as an empire, and much of Britain's wealth, depended on saving India from the Japanese. He was also convinced that India owed Britain a debt for providing its civilised administration. Quit India made the Indians, in many British eyes, less worthy of help when the food crisis came. Though many thousands of Indians were serving with Indo-British forces, Churchill felt there were countervailing examples of Indian ingratitude.

In a speech at a dinner in London in October 1943 to farewell Field Marshal Archibald Wavell to India, Churchill declared, 'I must say, I am in a state of subdued resentment about the way in which the world has failed to recognise the great achievements of Britain in India . . . Famines have passed away – until the horrors of war and the dislocations of war have given us a taste of them again – and pestilence has gone. Vast works of construction have enabled shortages in one part of the country to be equalised by the plenty in another, and disease has been diminished – with what results; with the incredible result . . . that in ten years the population of India under the blighting rule of Britain [*laughter*] has increased by 50 million – 50 million.' Yet he was ambiguous about this population increase. As Trevelyan had with the Irish, he condemned the Indians for 'breeding like rabbits'. India's population was then 400 million and Bengal's 60 million.

Responding to the demands of the European war, Churchill and his cabinet directed inadequate shipping in

India's direction. Frederick Lindemann, Viscount Cherwell, the son of an Alsatian businessman and – like Churchill – an Anglo-American mother, was often his adviser on such matters as shipping priorities and India. During World War I, Lindemann's loyalty was to Britain, and he took part in the scientific testing of aircraft, defining the physics of an aircraft's spin and the method to get out of it. In the mid 1930s, while a professor of physics at Oxford, he became close to Churchill on the basis that both men were passionately opposed to any appeasement of Hitler. Churchill called him 'the scientific lobe of my brain'.

Like Churchill (and, again, like Trevelyan in the case of Ireland), Lindemann believed the Bengal situation was exaggerated, a statistical invention, a creation of the Bengali imagination. He also believed he had the figures to prove wrong those who were proclaiming a Bengali emergency. In fact, he claimed that the Bengal famine could be managed by reforming the food distribution system.

Later, in London to meet the cabinet Food Committee, Archibald Wavell would write in his journal that Churchill's secretary of war, his minister for war and Viscount Cherwell spent all their time saying that the Indians should not be as they were and suggesting that a number of wealthy and famous Indians should be hanged. Wavell described Viscount Cherwell as having been introduced into discussions to present 'fatuous calculations' about harvests and yields. Wavell could make no impression on 'Dr Berlin', as Lindemann's associates had nicknamed him.

Not all Britons accepted the British government's view of the Bengali food emergency. Many thought that the government had failed. Leading British churchmen, headed by the Archbishop of Canterbury, called for daily prayers for India's starving. A thousand delegates of British women's organisations passed a resolution calling for the removal of Leopold Amery as secretary of state for India. Labour member Frederick Pethick-Lawrence, who succeeded Amery in 1945, would call the British government's handling of the Bengal food crisis 'a dishonourable failure'.

Churchill and Lindemann had further and more notable reasons than Quit India to accuse the Indians of ingratitude, and so to be unimpressed by their cries for help. There was the issue of the extraordinary Indian Subhas Chandra Bose. Born in 1897, Bose was a charismatic Bengali of Hindu stock. He was one of the Indian elite who had passed examinations to qualify for entry into the Indian civil service. He had twice been elected president of Congress. Today he is considered a great Indian hero, celebrated as Kalki, the final manifestation or avatar of the god Vishnu, and of Shivaji. Calcutta's airport and Bombay's Bose Marine Drive have been named after him. Any follies of the man have been forgotten in modern India, and he is seen as a prophet of Indian independence.

In his lifetime he was given the honorific title of 'Netaji' by Indians, which means 'great leader'. And such was his aura by the early 1940s that when the Japanese bombed Calcutta in December 1942, many enthusiastic Indians attributed it to Bose.

Bose attempted to collaborate with the Nazis, a fact that

was appalling to the British and to a great number of Indians, but obviously did not outrage all Indian opinion. Bose had gone to Germany in 1941 and tried, without much success, to create a 'free Indian government' in Berlin and to raise an 'Indian legion' under the aegis of the Nazis. It was Bose's hope that the Germans would get beyond the Volga and Stalingrad to reach Tajikistan and Uzbekistan and, through Afghanistan, would enter north-west India. There, it was assumed, the local population would join them in fighting the British. Bose's fantastic expectations were not approved of by Gandhi, despite his earlier statements about the British and Americans leaving, nor by the other great Congress leader Jawaharlal Nehru. The leader of the Muslim League, Mohammad Ali Jinnah, thought that it was crazy to swap one imperial master for yet another and worse one.

By 1942, the Japanese were hammering on the door. After a private meeting with Hitler, Bose left the German port of Kiel for Japan by U-boat. In Napoleonic style, he left his 3500 Indian soldiers to the German army, in which they became the 950th Regiment. In July 1943, he travelled through Japanese-captured Asia to recruit an Indian National Army from prisoners of war.

Asia proved far richer pickings for Bose than Germany had been. Many Indian POWs, and some Indian nationals throughout the Japanese-conquered areas, were willing to join his army and fight with the Japanese in the invasion of Bengal and Assam from bases in Japanese-conquered Burma. Some of the POWs in Japanese prisons in Singapore were motivated by the general incompetence of the British leadership in the face of Japanese military competence throughout south-east

Asia. The Indian POWs of the Japanese in Burma, thousands having been caught on the wrong side of the Sittang River, did not have the fondest memories of the battles they had lost under British command. Of the British army's Indian regiments who had been surrounded and captured by Japanese, 35,000 remained loyal, but more than a third of the Indian POWs from Burma agreed to go over to the Japanese under Bose's command.

Under the Japanese, Bose was Indian head of state and prime minister and war minister of a government in exile, as well as supreme commander of the Indian National Army. Members of his army fought on with the Japanese until the end of the war, despite the Japanese tendency to use the Indians for coolie work. Bose had offered Burmese rice to victims of the famine in Bengal by way of a broadcast through German radio on 14 August 1943. In return, he required British acceptance of his Indian Independence League, and for Britons to give an undertaking that any food he sent would not be used to feed the military or be exported from India. Naturally enough, the cabinet found the first of these demands unacceptable and no deal was done. Bose himself would be killed in a plane crash in Taiwan – on the way to Japan – in the last days of the war in 1945.

By then, 3 to 5 million Bengali deaths from famine had occurred.

Linlithgow's successor as viceroy, Field Marshal Archibald Wavell, was a cultivated soldier and held, as well as his viceregal post, the military role of commander-in-chief for India. Unlike most generals, Archibald Wavell had published his own anthology of poems, entitled *Other Men's Flowers*, and a biography of the World War I commander Sir Edmund Allenby, a work that showed sensitivity for colonised people, the Egyptians and the Arabs in particular. He had himself lost an eye in that conflict. Married to a rather distracted woman named Eugenie, he may have been a non-practising homosexual. He enjoyed the company of his homosexual aide, Major Peter Coates, and in London stayed at the house of one of Coates's boyfriends, the politician Henry 'Chips' Channon, a residence archly described by the British diplomat Harold Nicolson as a mixture of 'baroque and rococo and what-ho and oh-no-no'.

Wavell knew from experience a military emergency when he saw one – he had been involved in a number of them. At the beginning of the war he had led a small and highly successful force in North Africa and conquered an Italian army that outnumbered it many times over. He had angered Churchill by reminding him that a huge death toll was not a sign of military success. But then he had been ordered to halt his advance into Libya and send troops to Greece. With his forces strung out between Greece and North Africa, those remaining in North Africa were surprised by the German General Rommel's Afrika Korps' counter-attack of April 1941. Greece was a debacle, and the withdrawal to Crete no better. Then, as commander-in-chief in south-east Asia, he presided over the collapse of Singapore, Burma and the Dutch East Indies (Indonesia).

Churchill did not blame Wavell for any of these disasters,

which were due sometimes to the folly and incompetence of generals under his command and often to the overwhelming numbers of the Japanese army. The prime minister still thought him one of the best generals of his era, though he also irascibly once said of him that he should be running a country golf course.

Wavell had come close to being appointed governor-general of Australia, a post that would have sidelined him for the rest of this historic phase. He seized the posting to India with some gratitude. In the months leading up to Lord Linlithgow's retirement, he waited in London and spent each morning reading documents at the India office, developing a plan. He intended to tell Gandhi and Nehru, as well as others, including Mohammad Jinnah, that the British wanted self-government for India as early as possible. Then he proposed to leave them in a room with access to a secretariat of experts on matters such as constitutional and international law, so they could reach a constitutional answer to India's problems, which he would then do his best to implement. Wavell's argument was that though this was unorthodox, orthodox methods had already failed. Churchill and his cabinet were appalled at his plans. One leading bureaucrat said that Wavell gave no impression of being the strong ruler that a great soldier might be expected to be.

While Wavell was sitting in deliberations with the prime minister, India Secretary Leopold Amery pushed a note across the table that said that Churchill knew as much about India as George III did about the American colonies. From this and other signs, Wavell decided that the cabinet was 'not honest in its expressed desire to make progress in India'. It would be left for peacetime, another prime minister and another vice-roy to negotiate Indian independence.

On the matter of Bengal, Churchill told Wavell that more food for India could not be provided without taking it from Egypt and the Middle East, where a reserve was being accumulated for other areas of battle and for the ultimate liberation of Greece and the Balkans. Wavell wrote in his journal, 'Apparently it is more important to save the Greeks and the liberated countries from starvation than the Indians.' He knew there were special arrangements for feeding workers in essential industries, but he pointed out that practically the whole of India outside the rural districts was somehow engaged in the war effort, and that it was impossible to sort one particular individual from another 'and feed only those actually fighting or making munitions or working in particular railways, as PM has suggested'.

In the week ending 9 October 1943, just under 2000 deaths were recorded in Calcutta, and 1600 the week before. The removal of corpses from the street became a municipal preoccupation. K. Santhanam, a former member of the Legislative Assembly and a journalist, believed 100,000 were dying of starvation in Bengal each week. By contrast, Leopold Amery in London said that between 15 August and 16 October a total of about 8000 had died in Calcutta from causes directly or indirectly connected to malnutrition.

Within a week of taking office in New Delhi on 20 October 1943, Wavell rushed to Calcutta and saw the dying in the streets outside the gates of houses and the glass fronts of restaurants and bakeries. He intended to galvanise the entire government apparatus to tackle what he significantly called the 'man-made' crisis. Then he toured the *mofussil* itself, in particular the nearer western regions, Midnapore and Parganas. What he saw there – corpses scythed down at the height of their hunger by cholera or smallpox, and lying in the roads and ditches – disturbed him profoundly. It was a sight Linlithgow had never deigned nor dared to see. Wavell decided to use the army to aid the civil administration and introduced rationing in all areas in Bengal, including Calcutta. Air-raid wardens throughout the towns of Bengal were now put to the task of carrying bodies from houses and the streets, and burning them in pyres or burying them in mass graves.

Wavell's most powerful and highly unpopular cable after this journey was addressed to Leopold Amery and Churchill. 'Bengal famine is one of the greatest disasters that has befallen any people under British rule and is dangerous to our reputation here both among Indians and foreigners in India.' His urgency was motivated in part by the desire to save Britain from the world's censure, and to ensure no collapse of morale in the British Indian army. Indeed one of the chief terms of his appointment was that he should solve the crisis in Bengal, since it was beginning to get in the way of the war. And in that spirit he also cabled, 'There is now a military as well as a charity problem, since army must have a stable base.' But humanity and compassion were also at play, and he whipped up the inefficient government of Bengal to recognise and react to the scale of the event.

To the new viceroy, one of the minor villains of the famine

may have been Bengal's chief minister, Khawaja Nazimuddin, whom the viceroy thought 'straight but incapable', and exactly the sort of man of whom the corrupt take advantage. And one of the corrupt in question, Wavell believed, was Nazimuddin's minister for civil supplies, Huseyn Shaheed Suhrawardy, a former Oxford graduate, one of the founders of the Muslim League and a future prime minister of Pakistan. Suhrawardy, it was claimed, siphoned money from every project that was undertaken to ease the famine, and awarded to his associates contracts for warehousing, the sale of grain to governments, and transportation.

With some justice, Suhrawardy himself blamed the black marketeers and hoarders for the tragedy, and claimed that he had worked around the clock setting up food distribution centres and gruel kitchens all over the city. He argued that he had threatened the grain hoarders and black marketeers – mainly Hindus, he was careful to point out – with confiscation of their produce. This caused rice to appear in the shops of Calcutta sooner than it would have otherwise. Suhrawardy also declared himself to have gone to New Delhi many times begging for rice shipments to Bengal, but found, he said, that Hindus did not want to send rice to a region they saw as largely Muslim.

To Suhrawardy, the famine was entirely a sectarian tragedy.

Wavell's motives for having the destitutes of Calcutta's streets gradually removed to army holding camps from November of that year are not clear. It was a movement that the hungry invaders of the city themselves resisted. But he also involved the army in food and medical relief. He supervised personally the running of kitchens for the famine victims still crowded into Calcutta, and brought in as many government agencies as he could to deal with the crisis. The fact that the army itself proved a creaky and inadequate agency of relief was not his fault.

Above all, he was willing to remain grossly unpopular with his masters by peppering them with cables and memoranda about the famine. Churchill would send a mocking cable to Wavell asking why, if food was so scarce, Gandhi hadn't died yet? Unchastened, throughout the months of February and March 1944, Wavell continued to ask for assurances of substantial imports of grain. One of his cables declared that the attempt by His Majesty's government to prove on the basis of defective statistics that India could do without the help demanded would be regarded in India, by both British and Indian opinion, 'as utterly indefensible'. He considered his own resignation. 'They must', he wrote to London, 'either trust the opinion of the man they have appointed to advise them on Indian affairs or replace him.' No document so eloquently proves the moral courage and strength of character of Wavell.

Requests from Wavell in New Delhi for food imports into India continued, and finally, in March 1944, the British government offered 400,000 tons of wheat in exchange for 150,000 tons of rice. In contrast, the food stocks of the UK, with a population of about 50 million, rose by about 10 million tons in the second half of 1943. Secretary of State for India Leopold Amery backed up Wavell as far as he could, but nonetheless was instructed by the war cabinet to suggest that Wavell announce the import of the 400,000 tons without referring to the 150,000 tons to be sent to Britain in exchange. Wavell wrote in his journal, 'I shall do nothing so dishonest and stupid. And I shall not let HMG think that they have solved India's problems for 1944 by 250,000 tons when I have told them all along ten million is the minimum.' And then again, 'I think I have to resign to bring the situation home to them. They refuse to approach the Americans for shipping.' Wavell tried to work through the newly founded United Nations Relief and Rehabilitation Authority (UNRRA), without success. Eventually he himself approached Roosevelt, asking for US shipping to bring grain to India. To Churchill, this was nearly as bad as collaboration with an enemy. In June, Wavell did manage to extract another 200,000 tons from the war cabinet, though this was still far short of what he believed was needed. When the respected prime minister of Canada, William Mackenzie King, offered a shipment of wheat as a gift from Canada, the offer was delayed – for lack of available shipping, Churchill said. Australia had a surplus of 4 million tons of wheat and large supplies of meat, and said they were willing to send both to India, but, again because of the lack of shipping, the offer was turned down. Churchill finally requested US assistance in mid 1944, but by then Roosevelt had also committed the mass of his shipping to the European conflict.

Once the emergency, both the military and humanitarian, ended, Wavell was not above the stratagems of other viceroys, particularly playing off Hindu against Muslim. But his behaviour regarding the famine was professional and humane, even though circumstances – his late arrival on the scene and the failures of others – prevented him from saving millions of Bengalis.

We cannot know how many died in the famine. Frequently, too, there was no relative left to report a death. In 1943, Amery put the number of deaths at 700,000. The Famine Inquiry Commission estimated 1.5 million, which was believed to be too low. India's home minister in the early years of independence, Sardar Vallabhbhai Patel, put the number at 3 million. Others, such as the writer Kali Ghose, mentioned 3.5 million to 4.5 million. Many experts mention 5 million, but the Communist Party of India nominated more than two times that number.

8

Villains: Ethiopia

IT IS POSSIBLE to attach the ripest and least ambiguous blame for any modern Ethiopian famine first, in the early 1970s, to Emperor Haile Selassie of Ethiopia, and then, even more notably, to his successor, the military officer Major (later Colonel) Mengistu Haile Mariam in the 1980s. The emperor and the tyrant, both for the sake of their imperium and of planned events to celebrate it, denied the existence of famine in their country even as they lived within its reach, when any limo-borne deviation from their daily travels would have proved its clamorous and multifarious existence. In both cases, their denial involved all the organs of state and all permitted media. As for foreign journalists, strategies were devised to keep them in the capital and away from the dying fields, no matter how close those might have been, for as long as possible.

The slight-built, serene Haile Selassie came to maturity

with the belief that famine was an inevitable phenomenon in the empire and an inevitable accompaniment to the imperial processes by which Ethiopia was ruled. Selassie was born in July 1892 in eastern Ethiopia near the city of Harar. His birth name was Tafari Makonnen, to which the honorific Ras, 'prince', was added. Hence, Ras Tafari, from which derived the name of the sect that still venerates him. He spent his youth at the imperial court of Addis Ababa observing his relative, the Emperor Menelik II. Menelik, who ruled until 1913, had defeated Italian incursions in such famous battles as Adowa on the northern border of Ethiopia, and kept his country of so many nationalities together by force. He also had his own prodigious famine, on a scale worth examining.

Indeed from the reign of Menelik II to that of Haile Selassie, food policy in Ethiopia was based on attempts to starve regions that harboured grudging subjects or were in open rebellion. Ethiopia teemed with nationalities – Amharic, Oromo, Tigrayan, Ogadenian, Sidamo, Afar and eighty or so others. Though many Amharics were poor, it was from this Christian tribe that Menelik and later Haile Selassie rose. In Addis, the Amharic supplied the governmental elite. The Amharic language in Ethiopia was considered the equivalent of Mandarin in China, and it remains so to this day. Under Haile Selassie, the Eritreans suffered the same imposition and told of people's hands being lopped off for failure to speak the imperial tongue.

The great struggle of Amharic imperial governments was to keep Ethiopia together by brutality and the application of want as an act of discipline. Under pressure from the great powers – the British, the French and the Germans – in

1889 Menelik had yielded up the northernmost province, Eritrea – the equivalent of Scotland or Ireland in the British empire – to the Italians. But when it was won back in World War II, following the defeat of the Italians, it, like the rest of the country, was made ruthlessly to cohere.

Menelik's famine, the famine of 1888, was known as the *Kefu Qän* – the Evil Days. It had in fact begun even before Menelik took the throne by force from his predecessor, Johannes IV. The stimulus for the famine was a curious variation on the usual Ethiopian tragedy of drought. In March 1888, Johannes had gone north and besieged an Italian garrison at Sa'ati on the Eritrean coast. When the Italians surrendered, the emperor captured a great deal of military and other material, including a herd of cattle. The cattle, imported by the Italians from India and southern Russia, carried bovine cholera or rinderpest, endemic to the steppes of central Asia. Ethiopian livestock had not been exposed to it at all.

As Johannes marched south again, he spread the disease through his empire – an empire soon to be Menelik's. First of all, the disease struck Tigray in the north and then moved onwards to the south. The highlands, with their plentiful farming population, were hard hit, but so were the pastoral peoples. An Ethiopian, Asmil Giorgis, observed that the extermination of the cattle spread from the Red Sea port of Massawa to Kafa (in the extreme south), and from Harab (in the Sudan borderlands) to Harar in the east. As oxen died, Ethiopian farmers found themselves deprived of their ploughing oxen. To add to the disaster, rains failed to fall, and whatever harvest appeared was attacked by plagues of locusts and army worms. In the lowlands, when their cattle dropped dead, pastoralists were immediately deprived of their family wealth and food. There were no relief agencies at all to help, and no organised government relief. Internal conflicts, and the Ethiopian war against Italy and the Sudan, continued with conscription of young men for the army, and this led to the plunder of village granaries by soldiers.

It is believed that an astounding number, a third of the Ethiopian population, died over the four years from 1888 to 1892. It suited Menelik's chroniclers to depict the famine as yet another example of a people struck by natural causes, unabetted by political and social factors, and responded to mercifully by a compassionate emperor. But, as in pre-famine Ireland, the underlying conditions of land tenure in which the Ethiopian peasant lived in 1888 left him and his family in a state where hunger was a familiar companion. Under the landholding system named *gult*, the tenant had to pay 75 per cent of his produce to his landlord. He was required to provide free labour for the landlord's farm – as the possessors of Irish potato plots were; free transport of the landlord's crops; firewood for his fuel; and, on demand, unpaid labour as a domestic cook, a guard or a builder of granaries. The peasant was utterly concerned with subsistence and was unable to absorb the shock of any emergency, any inroad on any aspect of his subsistence.

The regions of Tigray, Gondar and Gojjam – that is, the entire north – were struck by the failure of the harvest in November 1888. This was the major harvest of the year, dependent on the mid-year rains called the *kremt* or *meher* – the same rains that would fail to turn up in the early 1970s under Emperor Haile Selassie and in 1983 under the tyrant Mengistu.

The scenes of the *Kefu Qän* go largely unrecorded in Europe, except for the occasional account of European witnesses. In October 1890, the Italian government representative in Showa in central Ethiopia declared that people were resorting to cannibalism. Ferdinando Martini, an Italian who later became governor of Eritrea, left a picture of what the famine was like, describing how, in the countryside: 'We are accosted for help, and from their deathbeds suddenly rise a mob of skeletons whose bones can be seen under the taut skin as in the mummified skeleton of St Bernard. They cry, *meskin, meskin* (help, help). I stumble on young boys searching in the excrement of camels to find a grain of durra.' Parents sold their children as slaves to the Arab traders rather than see them starve. Bandits roamed the countryside, taking the already depleted possessions of ordinary people. Lions, leopards, jackals and hyenas became so confident in the incapacity of humans to resist them that they prowled the villages and even the larger cities to feast on the victims. In some villages they would attack the living who, lacking the strength to defend themselves, were dragged screaming into the night. The usual famine diseases – smallpox, typhoid fever, dysentery, cholera and influenza – bore away the weakened.

As nine out of every ten cattle in the country perished and seed withered in the ground, refugees headed for the coast or the cities, convinced – like others in the past and future – that there would be grain there. But the Italians in Asmara, the capital of Eritrea, were so appalled by the numbers of refugees that they closed the gates. Other victims made for Entoto, Menelik's capital near the present site of Addis Ababa.

Amharic accounts of the famine, including those of Menelik's official chronicler, tell us that Menelik responded like a genial and responsible leader. He gave out food from his own granaries, forbade the consumption of meat in his palaces, distributed healthy cattle, had rudimentary shelters built for the starving and hoed in the fields to show the peasantry that it was not beneath an emperor to labour without oxen. The difference was, of course, that he did not have to hoe all day, nor did he eat at a table where the food dwindled and then disappeared.

Menelik's successor, the Emperor Joshua, was never crowned, and was disliked for his rumoured conversion to Islam and his sympathy during World War I with the Central Powers Germany and Austria-Hungary, who urged him to attack British Sudan and Italian Eritrea. He was deposed in favour of Menelik's widow, who elevated Ras Tafari to the role of crown prince, heir to the throne and regent. Ras Tafari, the future Haile Selassie, was a small scrap of a man with piercing eyes, who now set about courting the West, to whom he would become a darling. As I write, there are still Europeans and Americans alive who were charmed by him and cannot tolerate a word against him. He had the cachet, too, of being, ultimately, emperor of the only African country not in any permanent way conquered by the European empires.

In 1923, the true power in Addis, he abolished slavery,

and newspapers began to operate, most of them heavily in favour of the crown prince. He toured Europe and negotiated the entry of Ethiopia into the League of Nations. He met the Pope and Mussolini, visited the great capitals and received an honorary doctorate from Cambridge University. The impression he gave – that under him Ethiopia was a rational empire – would remain in place for decades after his fall.

After the death of Menelik's widow in 1930, Haile Selassie became Emperor, Lord of Lords, Conquering Lion of the Tribe of Judah, Elect of God, King of Kings. He improved the streets and buildings of Addis, and introduced electric light for his coronation and that of his wife, the Empress Menen.

The Italian invasion of Ethiopia in 1935, when Caproni bombers blasted villages and machine guns slaughtered the antiquely armed Ethiopian army, drove Haile Selassie into exile in Europe, where he became the African favourite of all opponents of fascism. He returned to Ethiopia in 1940 by grace of British forces, which had cleared the country of the Italian army. After the war, he helped to found the Organisation of African Unity (OAU) and persuaded other African states that its headquarters should be placed in Addis – the capital of the only uncolonised nation in Africa.

And yet, internally, his state was run like a medieval kingdom, with accompanying poverty and chronic hunger. After he fell from power, Polish journalist Ryszard Kapuściński visited a number of the emperor's old officials who were in hiding, desolated and demented by the loss of their status. These deposed men spoke graphically about the way the emperor had governed. Whether he was at home in the palace of Menelik in Addis, or touring the provinces, exacting from them food for his entourage and setting up tented cities to accommodate his court, the emperor maintained government by devoting to all major aspects of the state an hour at a time. He presided, for example, over an Hour of the Ministers, an Hour of Assignments, an Hour of Development, an International Hour, an Army-Police Hour, and so on. The Hour of Development, in a country where most public facilities, and thus food distribution, remained primitive, occurred between four and five in the afternoon. In a special black tent, the Hour of Justice was held. In an even more medieval pattern, there were the Hour of the Cashbox and the Hour of Informants, at which people would denounce ministers of state and other officials, and an Hour of the Supreme Court of Final Appeal. At the end of the latter hour, those who by clamour or main force did not manage to get the emperor's attention for their final appeal, went away unheard. The hours, along with his setting of some ministers to spy on others, and a full-fledged secret security force, allowed him to rule by dividing a cabinet that lived in fear of his anger and judgement. Satisfactory governance did not exist, and the focus of cabinet was on Addis Ababa or whatever site the emperor's court happened to be.

Selassie crushed a number of regional rebellions and dealt with minor famines by ignoring them – the one in Tigray in 1963, and in Wollo in 1966. When, in the early 1970s, UNICEF tried to bring the attention of the government to the drought and crop failure in Wollo and Tigray, the vice minister of planning told them, 'If we have to describe the situation in the way you have in order to generate international assistance, then we don't want that assistance. The embarrassment to the government isn't worth it. Is that perfectly clear?'

The 1972–3 famine, of which the emperor attempted to achieve wilful ignorance, struck in particular the two northern provinces, Tigray and Wollo. The famine began with the failure of the main rains in mid 1972. Nor did the *belg*, springtime rains, come in early 1973. The lack of *kremt* rains in mid 1972 caused an almost immediate disaster in the pastoral lowlands towards the Sudanese border to the west, and over in the grazing grounds of the east, bordering Somalia. But it was the lack of *belg* rains in early 1973 that had a devastating, if slower, effect in the farming highlands.

Amartya Sen calculates, however, that in 1972–3 there was only a 7 per cent decline in the harvest from normal output. Seven per cent should not have produced famine. There was no sudden and precipitate lack of food output in Ethiopia, certainly not enough to justify the emperor's famine. Yet by December 1972, the Ethiopian Red Cross was trying to succour a thousand refugees from Wollo who had arrived outside Addis Ababa but whom the officials of the court did not want to see inside the capital. In this time of want, the Ethiopian peasants undertook a long march towards the cities, just as the Irish and Bengalis had done – the impulse served as a sort of 'symbolic performance'; a remonstrance, as one commentator has called it.

The emperor ordered that roadblocks be set up to stop

more peasants from marching on the capital. He changed the itinerary of a visit to Wollo in November 1972 to avoid meeting a crowd of 20,000 people who were gathering to beg for his mercy. It was a priority for the emperor and his officials that there should be no food demonstrations inside Addis, and he always made sure there was food for sale at an acceptable price in his city, in the hope of keeping its citizens ignorant of outside events. Nonetheless, there was political activity involving university students who, in the imperial court's eyes, should have been more grateful for their education. They had already embarrassed the emperor by responding to a 1970 cholera epidemic in the country-side by taking preventive health education into the villages. Now, in 1973, they tried to hold an exhibition of famine pictures taken in Wollo and Tigray, but it was broken up by the police. In the Wollo capital of Dessie, school students protested against the famine. A number were arrested, and six students were shot down by the police and army. And when foreign correspondents asked to go to the northern provinces to observe the famine, the emperor refused to permit them, arguing that the region was subject to bandit attacks and the roads were unsafe.

The famine was a state secret. For the emperor, military mat-ters were far more pressing. As Mengistu would after him, the emperor was wasting a great deal of money fighting Eri-trean rebels. But by January 1974 a large part of his army was in mutiny. A general on an inspection in Ogaden, near the southern border of Somalia, was arrested by the soldiers, who forced him to eat the same fare that they were served. There was plotting among the officers in Harar. A division in Eritrea mutinied, apparently over the issue that in the Ethiopian army only dead officers were buried, while privates and NCOs were left to the air, the animals, the birds. (I saw the phenomenon from the Eritrean side of the trenches in 1989, where other ranks of Ethiopian soldiers lay in the open, unburied by the thousand, mummified under a ferocious sun.) As of the famine among his subjects, Selassie declared in a newspaper article, 'Rich and poor have always existed and always will. Why? Because there are those who work . . . and those that prefer to do nothing . . . each individual is responsible for his misfortunes, his fate.'

In the autumn of 1973, as the emperor fretted about his army, Jonathan Dimbleby, a BBC journalist who had always seemed to be an admirer of the emperor, somehow got into Wollo province with a camera crew. His footage of the starving of the northern highlands was, in his ultimate documentary *The Unknown Famine*, intercut with footage of the emperor presiding at banquets. The documentary attracted the world's attention. Pirated copies were smuggled into Ethiopia, and now Haile Selassie was forced to let relief agencies into the country to feed the people of Tigray, Wollo and Harar.

The first, often informal, relief camps that were set up were mainly a result of initiatives by provincial authorities in the north and north-west. Among those in sharpest need were professional beggars, labourers who hired themselves out by the day – generally in the towns – servants, water carriers, beer sellers and prostitutes. Weavers and craftsmen were also hit hard. Wives and children either stayed with relatives or came to town to beg for a living, or sought shelter in the relief camps. These first camps were primitive. Famine diarrhoea filled the laneways with human waste, which tainted the water supply.

In the US Senate, Senator Ted Kennedy criticised the Nixon administration's tardiness in sending aid. 'Is not the real reason for our slow response that we did not want to blow the whistle on the Ethiopian government? . . . As a result a lot of people starved to death.' By the time foreign relief started arriving, many of the inhabitants were either dead or had gone elsewhere. Some migrant workers went off looking for work in the Setit Humera cash-cropping region near the border with Sudan, and in the cotton plantations of the Awash River in the southern part of the Tigray province.

Landowners were better off at first sight, since they did not have to pay rent. But many of those who owned small areas and few livestock had, by now, lost them. There were cases when government collectors were confiscating halfway-dead cattle for tax.

Like the Irish peasant producing potatoes for consumption rather than for sale, many Ethiopian farmers with small holdings ate the food grown by the family without buying any in the market. In Ethiopia, as in Ireland, what mattered for the poorer cultivators was the fall in what their family could grow, rather than any decline in the total food grown and harvested in their region as a whole. A number of farmers had run out of seed when a second planting became necessary after a false start to the *kremt* rains the year before. Some landowners finally sold their land. But there was a fall in the price of land because so many were trying to sell, and a similar fall in the market price of livestock. Neither those who owned or tenanted much land, nor even the very poor, moved from home easily, but now they did. Many of them had become indebted to the large landowners and thus were tied to them to the death, which for many came from starvation and its effects.

As the famine moved southwards, more camps needed to be set up in those regions as well.

During the emperor's famine, among those most severely struck by want were the Afar nomads. Their cattle, camels and goats grazed, in particular, in the north-east of the country, between the highlands and the coast. There had been drought in 1972, but their chief troubles became very serious as soon as the *belg* rains failed in 1973 and their livestock began to die.

The Afar community were affected not only by the drought in north-eastern Ethiopia but also by the loss of grazing land owing to the expansion of commercial agriculture, particularly in the Awash Valley to their south. The land involved was the best of the grazing land ancestrally used by the Afar. When this smaller area close to the river was made unavailable for dry-season grazing, a much larger area away from the river was turned to desert because the Afar cattle overgrazed it. The nomads of the great southern triangular plateau, the Ogaden, and those of the Issa desert, were also under pressure. Their problems began to build in 1973, a year later than for the farmers of Wollo. The wet season had been late and short. Though the grain the Afar and Issa went to town to buy had risen by 15 per cent, the price of cattle had generally fallen to a third of the normal rate, which meant that in real terms grain had risen to three times the norm. The loss of grain in the family diet was significant, since the body takes in calories from grain far more quickly than it does from milk and meat.

During this southern famine of 1974, the death rate of nomad children increased threefold. Between November 1973 and December 1974, Ethiopia received foreign relief aid donations of 137,000 tonnes to see them to the next good harvest. Wollo and Tigray received 70 per cent of this, despite the fact that their problems were nearly over, and Harar and the Ogaden, where famine was at its height, received only 8 per cent.

Famine in the Ogaden region was not responded to well by either the Ethiopian authorities or international agencies. One might ask whether this was a result of operational difficulties or whether the Coptic Christian starving were more attractive to the world than the Muslims of Ogaden. The question does sometimes arise – are some destitute people in famines considered more entitled to food than others? That certainly was the case at the level of the emperor and his officials. The Ogadenians were troublesome citizens who seemed, at times, to have more kinship with the Somalis, whose ethnicity they shared. But was it true at an international level as well? There has always been the argument that it is very hard to get truckloads of emergency relief down the badly built roads to remoter provinces. For aid organisations this was certainly a test in the case of Ogaden, but also, and perhaps above all, a matter of the government's lack of willingness and cooperation. For the emperor did not find it impossible to truck a considerable part of his army into the Ogaden.

The problem of roads cannot be an explanation for the famine, because one of the best roads in Ethiopia ran north from Addis Ababa through Wollo province to Asmara. Yet Wollo was an epicentre of the famine. Here at least, however, many travellers were flagged down and asked for food, thus giving greater visibility to the hunger in Wollo. The main foreign relief camps were set up near this highway because that is where most imperilled people in the area were now presenting themselves. And yet here, despite all the relief efforts, 30–40,000 people perished. The numbers who died in the less-observed and accounted-for regions is not known. And, as previously mentioned, there were a huge number of refugees – as many as 200,000 – who fled into Somalia and a lesser number into the Sudan. These, too, could be counted among Ethiopia's losses.

Outraged by the famine and the emperor's mismanage-ment, in September 1974, officers and soldiers took over the radio station in Addis and announced that a committee of the armed forces and the police would act on behalf of the emperor in leading a movement for a new Ethiopia. The Derg, the coordinating committee made up of army, navy, air force and police, and including lowly sergeant-majors and prison guards, was formed in the conviction that the emperor could no longer rule an Ethiopia where the army was in rebellion and the cities full of unrest. Generals were, by and large, not trusted enough to belong to the Derg. Most of its 120 members were 'simple soldiers' who brought no ideology to their task.

In its mistrust of most senior officers, the Ethiopian army had become very like the Russian army on the eve of the October Revolution, and city intellectuals did their best to press the glories of Marxism upon the Derg, just as the Bolsheviks did on the soldiers' and sailors' soviets of 1917. In late August, as a test, the Derg began to nationalise transport and breweries, as well as the emperor's own corporation, the Haile Selassie trust.

One of the Derg's leaders was a largely unknown, handsome young officer named Mengistu Haile Mariam, who now began to argue most strongly for the emperor's total removal. Ruling Ethiopia under the emperor's aegis was not working, said Mengistu, and violated the spirit of the revolution. Mengistu was characteristic of the Derg, in that he was not an intellectual and probably believed at the time of the revolution that his objective was mere reform. As an officer, he had secured a position in a foreign training program at Fort Leavenworth, Kansas, and he studied English in classes provided by the University of Maryland. He was in his mid thirties at the time the emperor was deposed, and had been serving as a major in the Third Division in Harar when the Ethiopian revolution began. Major Mengistu's origins were mysterious – he was variously said to have been born of a princess and an NCO, or of a private soldier and a serving maid. Fantasists even depicted him as an illegitimate relative of the emperor, taking vengeance for his exclusion from the court.

Now, to focus the support of the people, Mengistu ran Jonathan Dimbleby's documentary, with its scenes of the emperor living high, attending a profligate wedding and feeding his dogs from a silver platter with better meat than the peasants saw in a season. The emperor himself was forced to watch the documentary and, according to report, was overcome with tears by the shame of it. He was deposed on 12 September 1974. A sub-committee of the Derg, chaired by Mengistu, now began to argue for his total elimination. In late August 1975, he was strangled at the Menelik Palace and his body buried in a toilet floor, a punishment for the 200,000 people who had died in his famine. The rumour was that Mengistu himself applied the garrotte to the old man's neck, in which case the assassination was carried out by a man whose own famine record would ultimately make the emperor's seem modest.

In the brief season of exhilaration at the fall of the emperor, the Relief and Rehabilitation Commission (RRC) was set up to deal with future want. In early 1975, the feudal land system was abolished for good. As in Russia, peasants seized the land of their masters, and this often led to local warfare between the landlords and farmers. Mengistu Haile Mariam was the strong presence behind all these changes.

By the end of 1974, Mengistu had become vice-chairman of the Derg, at a time when other parties were contributing to the committee's ideas and competing for power. One such group was the All-Ethiopia Socialist Movement, led by an intellectual named Haile Fida, who was in fact considered the architect of land reform. The young tyrant-in-training Mengistu hated intellectuals such as Fida, rather as Stalin had hated Marxist intellectuals and ultimately expunged them.

In 1975, the Derg initiated a movement named Zemecha, which involved sending 60,000 high-school and university students into the provinces to spread literacy among the peasants and to prepare them for land reform. Dawit Wolde Giorgis said that Mengistu and many of the Derg were pleased to get the troublesome students out of town and to place them at a distance in the countryside.

Only a short time after the emperor was deposed, Mengistu and another major competed for chairmanship of the council of the Derg. For once, the soldiers who made up the body asserted themselves and, ambiguous about both candidates, called on Mengistu's superior, Aman Andom, a general they trusted, to take control. Andom was an Eritrean, and could see no sense in continuing the emperor's wasteful and increasingly intense war against the northern province of Eritrea, formerly an Italian colony. The war had been initiated by the emperor's abolition of Eritrea's legislature, originally put in place to appease Eritrean desires for self-government. Eritrean hostility was also sparked by the savagery of the Ethiopian army in that province. The Eritrean Parliament should be reinstated, said Andom, and a policy of conciliating the Eritreans should be put in place. But Mengistu was even more determined than the emperor had been to crush the Eritrean revolt, and the result would be disastrous during the coming famine. It was an endeavour on which Mengistu would spend the substance of Ethiopia, making effective famine relief from the state – had he acknowledged the existence of famine when it came – even less likely.

Mengistu sent armoured cars and hundreds of troops to attack Andom's house. It was a murderous and bloody affair. Andom and twenty-two other officers who wanted peace with Eritrea were killed. Mengistu took the opportunity to kill, as well, fifty-nine royal officials who had been imprisoned in cells beneath the gardens of the Palace of Menelik.

Though the confused and disoriented Derg were by now dominated by Mengistu's personality, they found the courage to invite not Mengistu but another general, Teferi Banti, to become their chairman. Yet under Mengistu's influence, a river of blood similar to that which flowed in Stalin's purges became the accustomed reality of the Derg, no matter that it was headed by someone else. Nineteen others who were seen as soft on Eritrea were also assassinated in mid 1976. The governor of Eritrea was then executed. Hundreds of intellectuals were imprisoned. Within a week of the executions, two other young officers, frank opponents of Mengistu, tried to escape from Ethiopia, but were caught and shot down. Political rivals from outside the Derg were also put to the sword, but those within it were not safe either. In early 1977, in the Palace of Menelik, a regular meeting of the steering committee of the Derg was in progress. Suddenly Mengistu and his supporters got up and left the chamber. Mengistu's bodyguards, led by his chief assassin, Legesse Asfaw, entered with machine guns and forced the seven leaders of the Derg, including Banti, down into the cellar. There, Mengistu appeared again and, with Asfaw, shot down the men.

In November 1977, Colonel Atnafu Abate, a Derg moderate, presented himself at the Palace of Menelik for a conference and he, his bodyguards, drivers and assistants were assassinated downstairs in the palace cellar, which one member of the Derg called 'the revolution's shooting gallery'.

A by-product of all this slaughter was that Mengistu was killing off a number of independent thinkers who might have helped their fellow countrymen when the famine struck.

To get to absolute power, by 1978 Mengistu had taken an extraordinary toll of prominent figures: three heads of state – that is, the emperor and two chairmen of the Derg – and eight members of the original 120-strong Derg. Having acceded to the chairmanship and to total power, Mengistu expressed a particular admiration for Stalin – for his surgical ruthlessness towards counter-revolutionaries. He had emulated him and continued to do so. Stalin's criminality in permitting up to 10 million Ukrainians and Russians to die of famine in the early 1930s must also have been, implicitly, admirable to Mengistu, given that it had swept counter-revolutionaries off the map.

By the late 1970s, Mengistu's behaviour had predictably grown psychotic. He lived in the splendid palace the emperor had occupied, surrounded by servants in livery. The torture chambers and prison beneath the palace and its garden remained in operation, while Mengistu played tennis at ground level and afterwards ordered the assassination in the street of imprudent opponents.

He now began to distribute weapons to the Urban Dwellers' Associations, known as the *kebeles*. They were made up of Derg supporters, local bullies and sometimes former criminals. His cry to the *kebeles* was, 'We shall beat back white terror with red terror!' or 'Death to counter-revolutionaries!' At a public rally, he suddenly produced two bottles of what appeared to be blood and smashed them to the ground on either side of him, to reinforce his proposition, borrowed from Lenin, that the revolution needed to be fed with the blood of traitors.

The period from 1977–8 would be known as the Red Terror. Members of the Derg, and Mengistu himself, presented to the *kebeles* lists of suspect people for execution or imprisonment. Operatives of the East German Stasi gave the *kebeles* advice on tracking down the enemies of the regime. On the most remote suspicion, young men and women were shot dead in the street, and the *kebeles*, sometimes delivering the dead to the door of the family home, demanded payment for the lethal bullet. Other citizens were summarily executed and their bodies left where they lay. University students and professors were particularly vulnerable. In 1978, high-school students became the target, and 5000 of them were said to have been executed in one week. A Swedish observer saw some thousands of bodies of the young lying on the roads leading from the capital, which, like those felled by the Evil Days, were eaten by hyenas.

In prisons run by the secret police of Legesse Asfaw, guards augmented the torment of prisoners by using a nylon rope called 'Mengistu's necktie' to kill or torment. The bastinado, an excruciating caning of the soles of the feet, was also a common implement of torture and crippled thousands of Ethiopians.

Again, through his sundry assassinations, Mengistu was eliminating men and women who could have reacted with some efficacy to the coming famine.

Taking advantage of the disorder, Somali dictator Mohamed Siad Barre invaded Ethiopia in July 1977. The Somalis had been supported by the Soviet Union and Cuba, which Mengistu and the Derg now began to court, Mengistu abandoning for good the emperor's old alliance with the United States. The Soviet and Cuban military abandoned the Somalis, began to equip the Ethiopian army heavily with Soviet arms, and took part in driving the Somalis out of Ethiopia. It was Mengistu's intention to deploy the tremendous amount of Russian *matériel* he had acquired into the subduing of rebel Eritrea and Tigray. Mengistu's military association with Russia would have a fatal impact on the Ethiopian people. The falling-out with the West was acrimonious and accompanied by much vituperation on Mengistu's part.

In the meantime, 'land reforms' were reducing the peasantry to a level of grain vulnerability they had not previously felt. Soon after the revolution, the Derg transferred all land to regional Peasant Associations, which would decide how much land a peasant would get for his own use. Though seven million peasant families in Ethiopia were granted land by their associations, the average grant was one-and-a-half hectares. A large amount of a farmer's time was devoted to communal labour on the food, which the association sold at a low rate to the state's Agricultural Marketing Corporation (AMC). This communal, compulsory labour frequently did not leave farmers enough time to produce adequate food for their own survival. Their food production was also intruded upon by compulsory political classes, in which for some hours a day cadres instructed them on Marxist thinking.

Gradually the peasants lost faith in Mengistu and their Peasant Association leaders. They saw that the associations were well supplied with seed, at least until the famine started, but that the committee members cornered it for their own communal or individual use. The individual landholder now earned so little that he could not afford the price of fertiliser.

The AMC did exactly what Haile Selassie had done: its agents bought grain from five provinces to supply three cities: Addis Ababa, the capital; Dire Dawa, the major city in the east; and Asmara, the capital of Eritrea. The five provinces were Showa, the province in which Addis Ababa sat; Arussi, to the south; Gojjam and Wollega, to the west; and Gondar, to the north. It was not, however, for the sake of the Eritreans that Asmara was supplied, but for the sake of the army and bureaucrats stationed there. Just as the emperor had, Mengistu knew that in a primitive society keeping the cities happy would tend to keep him in power.

After the AMC had had its share of a declining farm output, the farmer was allowed to sell his produce on the local market, but found he could not afford cloth, sugar, salt and soap, even where these were available. Such was the system Mengistu had created to replace feudalism, and such was the system operating, even before the initiator of the famine – drought – struck the landscape.

The failure of the *kremt* rains in mid 1982, and of both the spring *belg* and high summer *meher* rains in 1983, provided more than enough tension. But by then Mengistu's attention was monomaniacally fixed upon the celebration of the tenth anniversary of the revolution in 1984. At the apogee of the famine, he would ultimately spend $100 million upon the festivities.

When the northern provinces of Wollo and Tigray were afflicted by the failure of rains and then by famine, Mengistu seized on the pretext that their farming areas were environmentally degraded, as was in fact the case, to move thousands of northerners to the south, by force, in a massive program of resettlement. These people, particularly the Tigrayans, had in any case always been rebellious, and Mengistu's motives were mixed, both ideological and military. The resettlement areas, with their inefficiencies, inequities, brutalities and lack of facilities and food, would bring about the deaths of a million people.

In the same way, Mengistu's policy of villagisation, which ran parallel to resettlement, gathered together peasants into central villages and towns, often hours' walk from their individual holdings. Those who resisted were asked, 'Why should people have a right to be fed when they don't listen to what we tell them is best?' Villagisation would also make it less possible for peasants to grow a survival crop from which they could retain a small amount that could be sold for cash so they could buy soap or kerosene or other essentials.

As the anniversary of the revolution approached, people

were being driven onto the roads by hunger or had begun to die of famine diseases. In Addis Ababa, meanwhile, red flags decorated pillars and lamp posts, and images of Mengistu, Marx and Lenin were everywhere. Signs declared, 'The oppressed masses will be victorious!' 'Marxist Leninism is our guideline!' One slogan half admitted that there were problems out in the countryside: 'Temporary natural setbacks will not deter us from our final objective of building Communism!' Highways were constructed from the airport to Addis, and conference halls and a statue of Lenin went up in the middle of the city. A ten-year economic plan was put in place, based on a 680-page document, which did not mention famine. Mengistu insisted, when speaking to Dawit Wolde Giorgis, head of the RRC since 1983, that the drought and famine were mere temporary setbacks. He refused to leave the city and visit the countryside, where, on the 300-kilometre road between Addis and the city of Dessie to the east, he would have seen starving and half-naked people trying to sell their ancestral ornaments handcrafted from silver. Bureaucrats and foreigners drove out of town and bargained with the starving, but Mengistu refused to know anything of this trade outside his door. The drought, he said, had hit many African countries, and thus it was a pan-African event. Yet, though there was drought elsewhere, it was not causing the pain this one was and it was not 'pan-African'. Given his politics, he could not use the term 'act of God', but the implication was that the matter could be left to nature to resolve.

The response from the West was slow, given Mengistu had as strong an antipathy for Western NGOs and relief agencies as the emperor had shown. When they did arrive and begin their work, he did what he could both to thwart and control it, again diverting supplies to the cities and to his army. His expenditure on MIG jets, Antonov bombers, T-55 tanks and cannonry of all calibre remained an even greater scandal than his anniversary celebrations, but any relief organisation who complained about his bullying or fooling of agencies was expelled. Indeed, it has been an accusation directed at NGOs ever since that because Ethiopia in the mid 1980s was the chief arena for famine, many wanted to keep a foothold there and thus became complicit in Mengistu's corruption, misdirection of aid and neglect.

9

Whistleblowers

GIVEN THE CAPACITY and the determination of governments to believe that the news of a famine outbreak is exaggerated, immeasurable lives must have been saved by those who tried to outflank government by alerting the world at large to the scale and gravity of events.

In the Irish case, the correspondents of the *Illustrated London News*, by letting the world know about the Irish famine and thus evoking relief, had a powerful but gradual impact on British and international opinion. The first reference to the famine in the *Illustrated London News* was on 18 October 1845, but its correspondents had covered earlier, related Irish events too, such as the 1842 season of need caused by local shortages, which affected labourers and the weavers in the north and resulted in attacks on potato stores by the hungry.

Each *Illustrated London News* story throughout the 1840s was accompanied by engravings of artists who travelled through Ireland with the correspondents. One of these engravings was the picture of the woman begging at Clonakilty, mentioned earlier. The equally famous engraving of Bridget O'Donnell, a hollow-cheeked, withered, but still handsome, famished young woman dressed in rags of cloth, with her arms cast around her two equally thin and ragged daughters is – if the term can be tolerated – a classic image of *an Gorta Mór*. While the government invoked the workings of Providence and of the great economic machine, the correspondents and artists of the *Illustrated London News* brought the British public's attention to the individual village, the individual sufferer, the individual corpse – whose name they often gave. It was their words and these images created from sketches made in the field by artists that riveted public attention, and that rivet us even now. Through those engravings, we see the deserted and roofless *clachan*, or communal village, the famished children digging futilely for potatoes, the evicted family in a ditch. Much of the credit for reporting the famine so graphically must go to the magazine's founder and manager Henry Ingram, a printer who had made a fortune out of selling a patent medicine named Parr's Life Pills and a man in his thirties when, in 1842, the *News* first appeared and he fulfilled his true ambition to own a magazine.

The *Illustrated London News* was probably considered populist and vulgar by the high priests and mediators of both Providence and rationalisation, but it is likely to have influenced the Society of Friends to take up their Irish endeavours and possibly gave impetus to the founding of the British Association by various British merchants and other businessmen in January 1847 'for the relief of extreme distress in remote parishes in Ireland and Scotland'.

The *Illustrated London News* reported at great length from the epicentres of the famine – Skibbereen, Clonakilty and similar West Cork towns and their hinterlands. There were certainly other papers reporting the famine, including *The Vindicator* in Belfast, which covered the general famine but paid a lot of attention to Ulster. 'The distress in Ballymacarrett [just outside Belfast] was the first cry of want that unhinged the fine philosophy that would starve the poor for the honour of the rich,' *The Vindicator* said on 22 April 1846.

In *The Nation*, the organ of the radical nationalist Young Ireland movement, Miss Elgee, a bourgeois Irish Protestant nationalist from Dublin, and the future mother of Oscar Wilde, wrote excoriating verse under the name *Speranza*.

> 'There's a proud array of soldiers – what do they round your door?'
> 'They guard our masters' granaries from the thin hands of the poor.'
> 'Pale mothers, wherefore weeping?' 'Would to God that we were dead –
> Our children swoon before us and we cannot give them bread.'

John Mitchel, the son of a Unitarian Presbyterian from Newry on the border of the north, and a member of Young Ireland, rendered a radical by what he saw on his Irish travels, wrote a great deal for *The Nation*. In the early summer of 1847, he journeyed through Connacht, where he and his companions came on a village in which they had been hospitably received two years earlier.

> But why do we not see the smoke curling from those lowly chimneys? And surely we ought by this time to scent the well-known aroma of the turf-fires? . . . What reeking breath of hell is this oppressing the air? . . . Had we forgotten that this was the Famine Year? And we are here in the midst of those thousand Golgothas that border our Ireland with a ring of death from Cork Harbour all round to Lough Foyle . . . Yet we go forward, though with sick hearts and swimming eyes, to examine the Place of Skulls nearer. There is a horrible silence: grass grows before the doors; we fear to look into any door, though they are all open or off the hinges; for we fear to see yellow chapless skeletons grinning there . . . we walk amidst the houses of the dead and out of the other side of the cluster, and there is not one where we dare to enter. We stop before the threshold of our host of two years ago, put our head, with eyes shut, inside the door-jamb, and say with shaking voice, 'God save all here!' The strong man and the fair, dark-haired woman and the little ones, with their liquid Gaelic accents that melted into music for us two years ago; they shrunk and withered together until their voices dwindled to rueful gibbering, and they hardly knew one another's faces.

But neither Speranza nor John Mitchel nor *The Nation* nor *The Vindicator* were likely to be read by the British. On the other hand, the *Illustrated London News*, with its massive middle-class readership, was considered by the majority of British readers an undoubted source of reliable news, and its images endowed the British public with a great portion of their sense of the broader world.

Some of the early reports of the *Illustrated London News* were highly dispassionate, but one of the earliest impassioned, intimate and graphic reports that there were 'stern and striking realities of the sufferings of the people' which should evoke 'the sympathy of every well-regulated mind' was from Cork and Tipperary in the south and south-west, namely the towns of Youghal and Dungarvan, where there had been food riots and 'turn-outs for wages', that is, demands for public employment. The reports said that the artist whose engravings appeared in the story was treated roughly while he was sketching in the street, and was asked that he promise mothers that their children, then engaged on public works, would be given wages higher than the five or six pence per labouring child, because it was insufficient to buy Indian meal.

The article mentions a boy called Flemming, who took part in a food protest and was shot in the knee and died slowly. Over fifty men were arrested by the authorities, and the *Illustrated London News* quoted an Irish correspondent as saying, 'Never have I witnessed any scene so effecting as the meeting of the prisoners and their poor hungry wives and children.'

But at this stage the famine was just beginning, and in the New Year, on 16 January 1846, the *Illustrated London News* reported an increase in famine deaths. Buckley of Ballyderrane and Sullivan of Oyster Haven, first names not given, died with that suddenness that had begun to strike down famished men and women. Buckley dropped dead on the public works after a journey of 'three miles before day'. His wife said that she and the rest of her family lived thirty-six hours on wild weeds 'to spare a bit of the cake for him'.

On 30 January an engraving appeared of a funeral at Skibbereen, a young corpse flung on a primitive dray accompanied by men in rags, one of them beating a bony horse. The accompanying story went as far as to challenge and even mock the remarks of the lord lieutenant governor of Ireland, Lord Clarendon (lord lieutenant governor was a post under the Crown, equivalent to that of the viceroy in India), on the terrible state of agriculture in Ireland. Clarendon declared that there was a problem, in that the Irish peasants 'now prefer working on the roads, like convicts in a penal colony', as if out of a perverse desire to avoid irregular and ill-paid day-labouring on farms. For the instruction of British readers, the correspondent wrote, 'If one pound of meal per day keeps these people upon the roads to break stones, a higher rate of wages than is usually offered to them by those who hire labour . . . might draw them from the roads and the pound of meal', that is, from the ration of corn permitted every day and paid for out of the money earned on the roads. But 'the large farmers and gentry' offered labourers only three pence or four pence a day, without any allowance of food. This wage of four pence could buy them even less food than they would get in the workhouse, said the *Illustrated London News*.

The same article alerted the British middle class to the fact that the peasantry was full of fear because of the prosecutions proceeding for rural 'outrages' in Ireland – the government had the means to place informers throughout the country and to reward them for results. 'Even though innocent of insurrectionary sympathies, they fear an accusation.' A man one of the correspondents spoke to near a railway line in Cork trembled when he was asked questions, for fear the *Illustrated London News* reporter was an informer, or a policeman in disguise.

The *Illustrated London News* trusted the information it was given in the field by a Cork physician named Dr Donovan, who was a respected and energetic medical practitioner and relentless reporter of the famine. It reprinted a report of Dr Donovan's from the *Cork Southern Reporter* of 23 January 1847.

> The following is a statement of what I saw yesterday evening on the lands of Taureen. In a cabbage garden I saw . . . the bodies of Kate Barry and her two children very lightly covered with earth, the hands and legs of her large body entirely exposed, the flesh completely eaten off by the dogs, the skin and hair of the head lying within a couple of yards of the skull, which when I first drew my eyes on it, I thought to be part of a horse's tail . . . I need make no comment on this but ask, *Are we living in a portion of the United Kingdom?*

As evictions became more common through 1847 and 1848, the *Illustrated London News* took up this issue as well, producing an illustration on 16 December 1848, just in time for Christmas, of the unroofing of a cottage by force and the eviction of the family. In this engraving, sheriffs and constables and hired toughs (themselves in need of pay) look on, while the evicted father and his daughter plead with the

mounted bailiff, who retains the writ of eviction in his right
hand against his saddle. A further engraving shows the father,
mother and daughter 'after the ejectment', living in a shelter
made of hay, a wagon wheel and other oddments. The father's
head lies on his forearm. 'Those who laboured to bring those
tracts [of farmland] to the condition of what they are, capable of raising produce of any description,' said the *News*, 'are
hunted like wolves, or they perish without a murmur. The
tongue refuses to utter their most deplorable, their unheard
of sufferings.'

Such illustrated news brought the reality of the famine
to many respectable British hearths in a manner few other
media could achieve, and many were stirred to compassion.

A British newspaperman named Ian Stephens, who had lived
in India for a considerable time and respected Indian culture,
was the editor of the Calcutta English-language newspaper
The Statesman of Calcutta, an organ that predictably enough
had been a strong supporter of the British war effort in the
East. It was Stephens who broke ranks to talk about what
the government in Delhi was unwilling to. After the Bengal
famine, he would write eloquently about the fact that it had
not made an appropriate impact on the public or the civil
authorities, and attributed some of the reason to the nature
of starvation itself:

Death by famine lacks drama. Bloody death, the deaths
of many by slaughter, as in riots or bombings, is in itself

blood-bestirring; it excites you, prints indelible images on the mind. But death by famine, a vast slow dispirited noiseless apathy, offers none of that. Horrid though it may be to say, multitudinous death from this cause regarded without emotion as a spectacle, is, until the crows get at it, the rats and kites and dogs and vultures, very dull.

The Statesman's first editorial on the famine appeared on 22 August 1943, and Stephens had, from the point of view of the authorities, the gall to publish pictures of famine victims in the streets of Calcutta in the same edition. He was breaking no secret – the destitutes were there to be seen – but, as he said, human sensibility could get very much accustomed to them. He wanted to deliver the most permanent of records, and no doubt he wanted to influence Linlithgow in the dying days of his position as viceroy. He believed he was demonstrating the problem in the most potent manner, in a form in which both friends and enemies of Britain might read it.

The late emergence of a public stance by the press was very much influenced by the prior demands of war and of British loyalty, but also by the threat that the chief press adviser might close the newspaper down. Stephens would later say that the chief press adviser's activities involved doing everything his office could to prevent the word of famine getting out. Cables from India to Britain were vetted to make sure words such as 'famine', 'corpse', 'starvation' were erased. At New Delhi's instruction, the Bengal government ceased reporting daily deaths by starvation. Stephen's bravery was all the more remarkable against such a background, and given the fact that the previous editor of *The Statesman* had been removed by the authorities for ignoring their strictures.

The *Amrita Bazar Patrika*, a nationalist newspaper published in Bengali throughout the region, but also in English in Calcutta, more predictably, but with no less bravery, also published famine photographs, in the teeth of the chief press adviser's warning that the newspaper was 'very near the borderline and might get into trouble'.

One of the photographs Stephens published was the Bengali equivalent of the *Woman Begging at Clonakilty*: a woman who has come to the city from the *mofussil* and now sits, head in hands, beside an infant wrapped in rags from which a skeletal arm appears. The infant's small face resembles that of a withered, elderly man, and the infant may be alive or dead, but if he or she is alive, death is obviously imminent. In another, a woman squats on her haunches by her two dead children. In a further photograph, two older children, ribs protruding, nurse a boy on what looks like rush matting set on the pavement. There were many photographs of huge-eyed children (for the eyes of the starving do not reduce when all else does) and one of a man collapsed on a road in a gutter with one foot still lying on the pavement. They are precisely the kind of scenes the *Illustrated London News* published from Ireland, and in their raggedness and the withering of their last shreds of muscle, the Bengalis in these pictures share such a terminal state of humanity that they lose national particularity and could equally be figures from Ireland and Ethiopia.

*

The reality was that Bengal became a closed region to journalists, both as an arena of war and a site of famine. But former member of the Bengal legislature K. Santhanam, reporting for the *Hindustan Times*, toured the famine area and ultimately wrote a book on the famine entitled *The Cry of Distress*. He visited first the north-east area of Bengal at Loharjang, usually a prosperous area. He found it much changed. Most of the children were skeletons, the destitutes were hollowed out and in despair and the middle class were now feeling the hardship acutely. One of the organisers of a relief committee in the area, whose family owned some land, had borrowed 1200 rupees from the Provident Fund, and it had gone into trying to buy highly priced rice on the black market. He belonged to the sort of people who could permit themselves to beg, and whose borrowing power was exhausted. In many cases, farmers had already sold their land and were thus trying to take in a harvest that would belong utterly to the landlord or the hoarder.

Crossing the river at Loharjang, Santhanam saw women and children squatting or lying pell-mell in slush in the narrow streets. The nakedness of the corpses in the street shocked him and he saw a mother trying to protect her child's naked body from a biting wind with part of the rag she was wearing.

Temporary 'destitute houses' – something like the Irish workhouses – were created by the authorities, Santhanam reported. In Comilla (in present-day Bangladesh), on the eastern side of Bengal and quite close to the Burmese border, the destitutes were locked up inside buildings by the Red Turbans, the police, and cried out to him, saying they would rather die in the streets. In Chandpur, a little to the west but still in modern-day Bangladesh, he witnessed the handout of inadequate *khichri* or gruel, and the tendency of some to choose death over a begging destitution. Santhanam declared that he thought the gruel so inadequate that it lengthened life only at the cost of inflicting a more drawn-out suffering. 'The smell of the *khichri* was thus repulsive, the colour blackish, the whole substance was almost as liquid as water itself; it was not pleasing or soothing for the stomach either; it produced a feeling of nausea (apart from the nausea caused by fasting).' It did not contain, he said, even half the calories required for survival.

Yet, while the famine did its work, there were few Santhanams to record it.

Under Mengistu, as under Emperor Haile Selassie, there was no halfway free press, and no editor such as Ian Stephens to alert the outside world. Dawit Wolde Giorgis, as head of the RRC, was under pressure to depict the famine as a result of the failure of the *belg* rains in 1983 rather than as government supineness. In May 1984, the RRC used the widespread failure of these short *belg* rains as a pretext for claiming catastrophic drought. The RRC claimed that the highlands of Wollo, Bale and Showa were the major *belg*-production areas and that the fall of the *belg* accounted for at least half the annual production of these areas. *Belg* crops, however, produced only a small proportion of the food grown in the north.

The 1984 drought was thus made the absolute cause of the famine. It proved an excellent scapegoat. Its effects were visually and statistically dramatic – production in Wollo was only 28 per cent of the 1983 level. Giorgis did not mention that perhaps the main cause of the famine could be the campaign of the Ethiopian army and air force against the Tigrayan People's Liberation Front in North Wollo from 1980–5. The TPLF sought to focus the Tigrayan people's anger at the continuing Amharic supremacy of Addis, which they believed had gone undiminished, but with a newer, even more savage face. The zone of severe famine coincided with the war zone and the phases of the developing famine corresponded with the major military actions.

Giorgis, however, continued to claim that he was, in effect, the chief bearer of the news of an act of God – drought resulting in hunger, whereas, according to one commentator and Africa expert, Alex de Waal, the famine was a war crime. Giorgis would argue that he had tried to persuade Mengistu to acknowledge the famine, and had pleaded with members of the Derg to recognise the imminent danger. He found that they believed sufficiently in the famine, though they did not say so explicitly, to send him around the world – of course, in the most luxurious travelling conditions – to visit sceptical governments and agencies in Europe and North America, and to alert them to the coming threat to Ethiopia. Thus Mengistu was grudgingly willing to acknowledge at an international level a crisis he was determined not to recognise at home. Giorgis admits that on his travels he lied about the policy and political objectives of the Derg, in particular about their purchase of military equipment, in the hope that the flow of aid already being planned would not be diminished. Giorgis had the uncomfortable problem of explaining away not only his master's attitude, but – as time passed – Mengistu's expensive plans for the anniversary of the revolution and his unrepentant and increased purchase of weaponry. He was also asked what the Soviet Union and Eastern Europe were doing for Ethiopia, apart from selling them weapons and providing military advisers. The Eastern bloc was, in fact, giving no aid.

If Giorgis later claimed, after his defection to the West in late 1985, to have been a whistleblower within his own country and the world at large, he did not achieve a great success. In the West, as a representative of the Derg he was not trusted, and even now many people from East Africa claim that his dissent from Mengistu's policies was not as robust as he would say later in his memoirs. But that he energetically carried qualified news of the coming Ethiopian disaster to the nations of the West is undeniable.

It was, as in the 1972 famine, British television that really alerted the West to the catastrophe. By late October 1984, BBC News broadcast images it had taken outside the town of Korem in Tigray. It was, said the brave commentator Michael Buerk, a former print journalist then in his late thirties, a famine on 'a biblical scale', that is, a consuming, apocalyptic famine, with a child or an adult in Korem dying every twenty minutes. The night following the first report a similar story was run, involving footage from Makale, a little north of Korem and the capital of Tigray. A documentary named *Seeds of Despair* had appeared before Michael Buerk's reporting. The journalists who filmed these reports had been able somehow to find their way out of town by night and talk their way through roadblocks.

Western Europe and North America were galvanised by the images from northern Ethiopia. As the whole world began to see the footage, and a tide of private aid began to flow, 400,000 bottles of whisky were being shipped from Britain to Addis Ababa for the tenth anniversary of the revolution.

10

Famine Diseases

Throughout all famines, there are parallels between the diseases that opportunistically strike the malnourished. Dysentery and diarrhoea, often caused by people eating unfamiliar food, whether wild or supplied as relief, strike hundreds of thousands in a way that is not necessarily as fatal at first as it will be later in the hunger process. Through the process of dehydration, dysentery generally kills children before adults. (The elderly, by contrast, are generally borne away by pneumonia.)

In Ireland, dysentery and diarrhoea showed themselves from the beginning in gastroenteric symptoms caused by eating diseased potatoes. Dr Daniel Donovan of Skibereen in County Cork found 'starvation dysentery' almost universal among the destitute, and though it was resistant to treatment, treat it he tried. Donovan said that the sufferer's face was ghost-like and the voice a low whine, very similar to what he called the 'cholera whine'. The smell from the waste was almost intolerable, like that of 'putrid flesh in hot weather'. He said that the patient, though he retained his faculties to the end, died without a struggle.

As the food supply declined, one of the other earliest diseases to appear was scurvy, caused by a deficiency of vitamin C. Since scurvy is now seen as a disease easily cured by fresh vegetables and fruit, it is hard to imagine a world in which it was one of the most dreaded diseases. It had a terrible impact on the system: disorientation, depression, agony of the joints, loss of teeth and such ultimate failure of organs that the skin turned purple. Dark purple blotches progressed up the leg to the middle of the thigh, so in the nineteenth century, scurvy was sometimes named Black Leg. In the last phase there was a relentless spate of retching, which eventually exhausted the heart. The Poor Law Commission in Dublin was so worried about scurvy that it sent a directive to those who were running soup kitchens, asking them to try to include well-cooked vegetables in the meals issued inside the walls of the workhouses. Sadly, vegetables too well cooked lack vitamin C as well.

Hunger edema, which the Irish called dropsy, was common in all three famines in this book. Since the starving body consumes its glucose, fat and protein, and has eroded the muscles, the body can no longer operate efficiently. Neither the heart nor the kidneys are any longer functioning normally, and death soon results from heart failure. Edema was not so commonly filmed in Ethiopia because it was such a contradictory condition – a skeletal upper body combined with fat legs. Famine edema was nonetheless visible in some of the children pictured in photographs published in 1943 by the brave English editor of the Calcutta newspaper *The Statesman*, and in 1943–4 became a common feature of destitutes who crowded into the city.

The incidence of the famine-induced eye disease named xerophthalmia, unknown in Ireland when potatoes were the daily diet, was investigated by William Wilde, the Dublin physician (and father of Oscar). Working with a colleague, he found that 94 per cent of the cases of this terrible, blinding disease were to be found among children. He recommended doses of cod-liver oil, pre-dating by seventy years the discovery that cod-liver oil was rich in vitamin A, for lack of which the disease had struck. In Ethiopia in its worst form, said witnesses, xerophthalmia caused blindness in thousands of children and, also in the worst cases, could cause the eye to break open into an ulcer.

Pollution of streams and wells by dead bodies and by sufferers from dysentery and diarrhoea grew worse in Ireland as more and more people turned up in towns looking for food. The same happened in modern times in Ethiopia – people turning to towns almost by instinct and there contributing to lethal outbreaks of cholera, the bacterium named *Vibrio cholera*. Cholera was sometimes transmitted to the Irish by their eating shellfish, which had ingested infected water, but most of those who died of it perished from drinking contaminated water sources. The infection caused copious diarrhoea, dehydrated the body, and so brought death.

People were also afflicted by the water-borne bacterium *Salmonella typhi*, which causes typhoid fever. Though in Ireland and Bengal the starving and the fevered were attacked by dogs and pigs, sometimes before they were dead, these carnivores could not pay society the benefit of removing the corpse in its entirety. During the Ethiopian famines, however, hyenas played a sanitary role in devouring bodies and diminishing the risk of infecting nearby water, even though it was sometimes the weak but still living who were consumed by them. An Ethiopian aphorism declares that a hyena can take you apart faster than God can put you together. These fast and ruthless devourers of all organic material seemed themselves to be immune from any diseases the dead might carry.

In the Ethiopian highlands especially, because of the cold nights in which people huddled outdoors, often in mere tatters of clothing, the great killer was pneumonia.

In Ethiopia and Bengal, malaria was one of the opportunist diseases of starvation, particularly – though not always – of children under five years. In the Ethiopian case, the disease was spread by armed conflict, and moved northwards into Eritrea, where it had never been seen before. In the Eritrean highlands during the war between the Eritrean People's Liberation Front and the forces of Mengistu, I met an American doctor from Columbia University as we both sat on rocks waiting for the last light to fade and the generators to begin working in the camouflaged Eritrean mountain hospital of Orotta. The doctor told me he was an epidemiologist and was studying the spread of cerebral malaria, a complication of malaria brought about by the same parasite as normal malaria. Cerebral malaria drove the body's temperature so high that the victim died of exhaustion brought on by frequent and long-lasting seizures. Previously unknown in the northern highlands, the disease had been brought up here by Mengistu's conscripts, some of them from the far south provinces of Bale and Sidamo near the Kenyan border. Cerebral malaria was then picked up from the blood of Mengistu's southern conscripts by the northern mosquitoes and democratically transmitted by them – blood meal by blood meal – into the bodies of soldiers and civilians on both sides of the trench line. As always, it attacked with particular force the malnourished.

Malaria was also a massive killer in the Bengal famine. When, in late 1944, supplies of the new synthetic drugs mepacrine and quinacrine reached Bengal, the black marketeers, in an attempt to maintain the high cost of quinine, spread rumours about the damage these medications could do.

For inoculations, the undermanned medical staff, whether military or civilian, intercepted peasants on the roads to markets. For fear of foreign elements being introduced into their bodies, these people were resistant to the idea. Sometimes they would let themselves be immunised, but refused to subject their wives to it. Public meetings were held to explain the reason for the needles, but they never entirely overcame the people's prejudice against them.

There were two other dangerous diseases at work in Bengal. Beriberi, a disease known to Westerners mainly from accounts of the experiences of prisoners of the Japanese during World War II, was common. (The name is said to come from the Sinhalese, *I cannot, I cannot*.) Beriberi was in fact a disease not unknown in happier years, as the white rice staple of Bengal was already low in thiamine, a lack of which brought on the malady. Again, lethargy and fatigue mark this illness, as gradually the cardiovascular, nervous, muscular and gastrointestinal systems give way. Beriberi felled its quotient of the starving ill who lay littered along the streets and river-banks of Bengal, in the outdoors to which the frenzy to find food had driven them.

Shigella, a disease named after the scientist who identified its bacterium in 1897, Kiyoshi Shiga, was common in the Bengali and Ethiopian famines, caught by eating infected food or from contact with human carriers, who might be as yet unaffected by it. Shigella commences as other fevers do, but then begins to release toxins, which are carried by the blood to all parts of the body, producing acute pain throughout. The temperature of the person can rise to 43°C. Shigella bacteria also kill off the first layer of cells in the intestine and produce a number of small lesions in the large intestine, so that there is anal bleeding and diarrhoea. The real danger is that of dehydration, which, if not checked, will cause the patient to go into shock and die. People would often appear to get over shigella, only to drop dead a few days later. The same amazed observations of recurrent illness were true of both Ireland in the late 1840s and Bengal and Ethiopia in the 1980s. A solution of glucose and salt in water can be given to be absorbed by the damaged gut until it has time to heal itself, but this simple remedy was not available to the victims in the famine fields of Bengal and Ethiopia.

Khichri, the Bengal gruel provided during the famine, also contributed to health problems in the eyes of Bengali people. It was popularly believed that those who ate it fell victim to dropsy, beriberi and other diseases, including dysentery and diarrhoea. Or perhaps it was its lack of nutrition that allowed these symptoms to arise.

*

Through Field Marshal Archie Wavell's involvement in the British army in relief, Lieutenant Colonel K. S. Fitch was the doctor in charge of treatment for famine symptoms in a section of Bengal, and dealt with 1400 victims. In physical terms, the figures Dr Fitch kept on them were, apart from the tropical diseases, an echo of the illnesses contracted in the Irish workhouses a hundred years before. More than 35 per cent of the people whose treatment Fitch supervised suffered from dysentery, nearly one in three from edema, one in four from scabies. Then there were tropical ulcers. The ulcers, nicknamed 'Naga sores', were due to malnutrition and low resistance to the parasite that caused them, and were particularly hard to treat, penetrating to the bone. More than half of Fitch's patients were thus afflicted with various famine fevers, even apart from malaria. Since Fitch's numbers for various diseases added up to more than 100 per cent of patients, it was obvious that many people showed the symptoms of two or even more perilous conditions at the same time.

The Reverend Henry Brennan, the parish priest of Kilglass in County Roscommon, wrote to the *Freeman's Journal* in Dublin on 14 July 1847: 'Sir – there is not in Ireland any parish where fever and destitution prevail to so fearful an extent as here . . . by this time fever has made its way into almost every home . . . In some parts the fields are bleached with the bones of the dead which were previously picked by dogs.'

What is at first sight remarkable about Father Brennan's account is that, as with Lieutenant Colonel Fitch, its chief emphasis is not on starvation as such, but on disease.

*

Fever struck very soon after the onset of the Irish famine and people called it 'famine fever'. Thomas Burke of Roscommon wrote, perhaps clumsily but with great force, to his emigrant sister in Australia, 'They are dying like the choler [cholera-smitten] pigs as fast as they can bury them. And the dogs eating them some buried in mats others in their clothes.' As early as 17 December 1846, a Mr N. M. Cummins, a justice of the peace, wrote to the Duke of Wellington that, in his locality, famine and thus famine fever were already raging. Again, there was an emphasis on disease rather than starvation. Cummins entered a hovel and saw six 'ghastly skeletons' huddled in a corner on straw beneath a horse cloth, their naked legs protruding. 'They were in fever – four children, a woman, and what once had been a man.' Within a minute of emerging he was surrounded, he said, by two hundred such spectres. 'A mother, herself in fever, was seen the same day to drag up the corpse of her child, a girl about 12, perfectly naked; and leave it half-covered with stones.'

By fever, the Reverend Henry Brennan and Justice of the Peace Cummins meant either famine fever (typhus) or relapsing fever. The Irish, whose clothes were often in tatters, huddled together in mutual filth, and the fetching and boiling of water to wash clothing and destroy lice became as far beyond them as they would later be for the famine-weakened Bengalis and Ethiopians. As a result, clothing became infested by lice.

Typhus is caused by a microorganism, which would be named rickettsia, appropriately to honour Howard Taylor Ricketts, who first identified the bacterium. Such were his energetic researches that he contracted the disease himself and died of it in 1915 – in itself a proof of how infectious the organism was. This disease was generally released in the clothing of the starving through the faeces of the louse, which impregnated unwashed rags and which, on touch, produced a sort of dust that even priests who gave the last rites to sufferers, or anyone who handled their corpses, were vulnerable to. It could be similarly caught from a louse bite that was scratched, or even by the crushing of a louse. In fact, in Ireland, doctors, priests, parsons, members of relief committees who supervised outdoor relief, Poor Law officials, kindly middle-class visitors to the workhouses and relief workers in general all proved highly susceptible to the infection. A Doctor Carroll of Waterford actually claimed that typhus fever mortality increased in ratio of the rank and respectability of the individuals attacked.

Wherever it appeared, typhus caused fever, the appearance of drunkenness and a rash. The small blood vessels were particularly affected by rickettsia and the skin turned dark, so that in Donegal they called it *firbrhas dubh*, 'black fever'. A characteristic of famine fever was the way it replaced the odour that people gave off in healthier times with something more repellent. The smell of fever patients was described by a doctor in West Cork as 'a cadaverous suffocating odour' with a 'peculiar mousy smell which was always the harbinger of death'. Wherever people huddled together, as they did in the Ethiopian highlands and in Bengal, typhus must have been present too.

Fever brought a shadow over families. The families of sufferers were often wary enough to vacate the house. Some saw this isolation of the stricken as a form of sensible quarantine.

In Ireland, once or twice a day people would feed the individual inside by tying a can of water and some hot gruel in a container to the end of a long pole. When there were no more tugs on the pole, the peasants would pull down the house on top of the corpse and burn it – a mimicry of the evictions and subsequent unroofing of houses by landlords, and a totally unaccustomed method of disposing of the body of a beloved.

In Ireland *Firbrhas buidhe*, 'yellow fever', cut down a lesser but significant swathe than famine fever or typhus. It was a puzzling disease, which doctors called relapsing fever, and it was also carried by lice, but involved an organism much longer than the bacterium of typhus. Relapsing fever came from the louse's body, and was let loose if the insect was crushed or damaged. Interestingly, it is a fever not generally mentioned in the famines of Bengal and Ethiopia. A violent fever struck the victim for perhaps five days, when the patient recovered and was able to walk about. Perhaps a week later, the illness struck again, in very sudden and increased intensity, often jaundicing the victim (hence 'yellow fever') before felling him, as witnesses to the disease declared, virtually in mid-stride.

Famine fever and relapsing fever were spread in the close quarters of the workhouses of Ireland. The Irish had despised the workhouses before the famine, looking at them as hostile in architecture and intent, and fatal to individual dignity in their punitive atmosphere and the lean relief they gave. But now the poor came crowding in through their gates, and thus the workhouse became a huge petri dish of bacteria. The practice of fitting out new arrivals with the clothing of those who had just died spread infection exponentially.

Fever wards – the populace called them 'fever sheds' – were erected, into which those suffering from typhus and relapsing fever were placed. But they were never adequate – famine and relapsing fevers always outran their capacity.

Another focus of fever during the famine days was the gaols, which were overcrowded with those who had committed thefts and what the authorities called 'rural outrages' – attacks on the property, agents and person of landlords.

In Dublin early in the nineteenth century, a number of philanthropic souls, including the Quaker Samuel Bewley, whose teahouse still operates in Dublin, and the brewer Arthur Guinness, acquired an orchard on the south-western outskirts of Dublin to build a fever hospital. Its 220-bed capacity was now overwhelmed. Similarly, the Cork Street Fever Hospital was swamped by people who had moved, in the universal famine manner, from the countryside to the city looking for relief.

Unlike the physicians of Bengal and Ethiopia, many Irish doctors blamed the outbreak of fever on bad air and miasmas. But Dominic John Corrigan, a Dublin physician who was an early expert on heart disease, perceived that famine was the common element in all fever outbreaks, and argued the direct connection between the two. He was much contradicted by others, who pointed out that fever often existed in times of plenty. In Bengal and Ethiopia, people had the advantage that medical practitioners saw an unarguably clear causative connection between famine and disease. But in those cases the problem was how to get medical attention.

In an Ethiopian resettlement or collective farm site at Guraferda in Kafa province, in the far south-west of the country, resettled newcomers were attacked by Central African diseases they had never encountered before, and died for lack of medical attention. Among all else, they contracted a killing disease derived from the effects of the tsetse fly, the carrier of so-called 'sleeping sickness', to which the northerners had never been exposed, along with malaria, which was far less common in the highlands than it was in Guraferda. The bite of the tsetse fly causes a red swelling at the site of the bite, which is quickly followed by anxiety, mood swings, fever, sleeping by day and insomnia by night, but ultimately – through the deterioration of the central nervous system – coma and death. When Mengistu heard about this regional disaster and received a report of the high death rate, he declared that the minister of agriculture had misinformed him. He then abandoned the Guraferda resettlement project.

Not as much attention has been given to the psychiatric results of famine. As he wrote in his medical history of the Bengal famine, Lieutenant Colonel Fitch was mystified by some of the reactions of the starving. They often refused to eat anything but rice and some spices and fish. They rejected food grains such as wheat or millet or maize. Westerners in Calcutta would leave their residences or flats and give the starving on the pavements 'eatables such as plum cake'. British soldiers in outposts in the *mofussil* would try to share their rations with the villagers, but to very little effect. It was as if they were blind to any food but that familiar to them, and sometimes even to that.

*

A final question must be asked: what are the effects on those who were carried in the wombs of starving mothers during famine?

A team of epidemiologists from the United States made a seven-year study of those born in the western Netherlands during the so-called Hunger Winter of 1944–5. They found that mortality in those born during famine was higher in both the first and second years of life. And famine foetuses might have also in some cases suffered a loss of brain cells. Even so, the researchers found no sign of lower mental ability once the children who were conceived and born in the famine reached mature age. And those carried in the womb of famished mothers, but born after the famine ended, suffered no effect in body size, whether in height or weight.

This Dutch study also showed that during famines the rate of conception is reduced. Amenorrhoea, a lack of menstruation, is widespread in all famines. The first research into amenorrhoea was carried out by Polish epidemiologist Johann von Jakowski in the hunger of the German winter and spring of 1916–17, caused by the blockade of the German coast by the Royal Navy, and called by Germans 'the winter of rutabagas'. Amenorrhoea also occurred in Nazi-occupied Western and Eastern Europe in World War II, and in particular in the concentration camps. A Hungarian expert estimated that 99 per cent of women prisoners suffered it, and there were reports of the same phenomenon in East Bengal and Ethiopia during their respective famines. The body returned to normal once however marginal meals were able to be eaten.

If bacteria were sentient, they would look upon famine fields as arenas of near-miraculous chance, an opportunity for a vicious dance across grand reaches of humans, whose resistance to invasion has fatally withered.

11

Evictions, Movements and Emigration in Bengal and Ireland

REGARDING MASS EVICTIONS and migrations, especially by comparison with Ethiopia, where so many journalists and aid agencies worked, Bengal was, once again, the hidden famine. The Bengali famine did not create an exodus of people out of the accursed country, as did Mengistu's Ethiopian famine. From the summer of 1943 until November that year, when the round-up of starving street people by the military and police began, the greatest movement was towards Calcutta and other Bengali cities. A swell of people travelled without tickets on the railways, sitting atop the roofs of rolling stock, clinging to doors and windows in prodigious and apparently impossible numbers, or riding the rattlers beneath the carriages or freight trucks. Massive crowds of skeletal people waited at every station trains pulled into. Destitute women were raped at night while lying on the roads without strength to resist.

The writer Bhabani Bhattacharya witnessed the flight of people from the *mofussil* and describes the refugees who tried to hang from any railing or window frame of trains going west. As cane-wielding Red Turbans attempted to force them to the ground, they cried, 'Give us a ride to the great city. Food enough in the great city [for us], and even the dogs and cats . . .'

Once the hopeful destitutes reached the city in their fragments of clothing and settled in its streets, many respectable people, almost in self-protection, began to believe that if Calcutta could be cleared of the destitutes, the famine would have been dealt with. For in famine, irrationality strikes not only the starving but the witnesses as well. So even the spaces taken on the pavements by the destitute and starving from the *mofussil* were not secure to them. When the victims died on the streets, the delay in collection of bodies and the onset of putrefaction increased the feeling among the citizenry that something must be done. As to how many arrived in Calcutta alone, the Famine Inquiry Commission puts the number at 100,000, but many accuse them in some significant matters of underestimating. In any case, the picture is muddied by the fact that some destitutes spent their nights in outer suburbs and villages and travelled on the outside of trains, hanging from any purchase or perched on the roofs, back into Calcutta by day.

We do not know how many of the destitutes were *bargadars*, the sharecroppers who gave half their produce to the person they worked the land for. This man might not be the *zamindar*, the overall landlord, but – in a pattern that existed in Ireland as well – one of a sequence of middlemen, *ryots*, the more prosperous farmers who themselves held land under the landlord and paid tribute to him. Without wasting excessive sympathy on him, sometimes the *zamindar* himself was under economic pressure, since the tax he paid the government was not reduced in the event of drought or famine, even though his sharecroppers could not produce now, and thus even the middlemen, from whom the sharecroppers leased land, became less able to pay their rent. In Bengal, therefore, there was not the same obvious and overriding impulse in landlords to evict and force tenants off their land. Some *bargadars* were driven out and became landless. But at least Bengali *zamindars* wanted to keep the pattern of land-use as it was, whereas the Irish landlords wanted to turn it upside down.

In September 1943, the Bengal government decided to move the destitutes off the streets of Calcutta and truck them to poorhouses and destitute camps around the city, as a first step in their journey back home. The clean-out began in November. The city was now full of scenes in which employees and police struggled to lift the weak off the road and into trucks, and found the destitutes resisting with their last resources of strength. The arrival of police trucks in the streets of Calcutta caused the hungry to flee. Among the victims, there was great fear of government camps, a belief that sinister things would be done there. Rumours about the malign intentions of government had spread among the hungry, who had been taught by their experience to believe the worst. Fazlul Huq, a Bengali politician, would say that the ultimate removals of the destitute were done with 'rough handling and callousness'. The ultimate report of the Famine Inquiry

Commission said that the round-up was achieved with 'some force' and 'unpleasant scenes of coercion'.

In these compulsory round-ups, families were separated. When the authorities replaced police trucks with civilian vehicles and the police with volunteers, the transportation went more smoothly. But even when placed in the camps, which were often based around old army barracks, the famished would wander away, again seeking food, and among the most restless of those detained in camps were the children collected from the streets. 'The wandering habit among children,' a witness said, 'was difficult to stop.' Their brains had been deranged by starvation. 'Children – skin and bone – had got used to eating like dogs. You tried to give them a decent meal, but they would break away and start wandering and eat filth.' Special famine rooms for children had to be set up to deal with this impulse to move in any direction. It took two weeks of detention and adequate food, now extended to the destitutes by the Bengal government as a means of keeping them in the camps, to break the wandering impulse.

When the army took over relief at Wavell's command that November, after a less than distinguished start by the civil authorities, some destitutes were repatriated to the countryside by army transport without having to confront the detention centres. Instincts told them this was to be preferred over custody. About the procedures in the detention centres little is known, but gradually the desperate were cleared from Calcutta.

*

Evictions and subsequent emigration were not only part of the mythology of the Irish famine, but also of its bitter reality. The government in Westminster always intended that Irish landlords should be made to support by taxes the overwhelming bulk of relief handed to the Irish, and given that less and less rent was being paid by the peasantry, and by small and even larger farmers, a program of rigorous action would be undertaken by many Irish landowners. It was fuelled in part by a belief common to many landlords that their tenants were grudging payers of rent, and by the economic reality that some – certainly not all – of the evictors laboured under the necessity of paying off mortgages raised on their estates, and on the grand houses and castles built by their forebears in more profitable times.

Evictions were already well started by the spring of 1846. In East Galway, in the village of Ballinglass on the Galway–Roscommon border, a Mrs Gerrard had evicted for unpaid rent more than sixty tenants – 300 people, based on the average Irish family size. The eviction was carried out by a detachment of the 49th Regiment and numerous constables. That night the ejected families slept in hastily put-together shelters – their neighbours had been warned on pain of eviction against taking them in. Subsequently, they lived either in *scalps*, burrows roofed over with boughs and turf, or in *scalpeens*, holes dug in the ruins of a 'tumbled' (the remains of a) house. But Mrs Gerrard's men or the police drove the evictees out of these too and onto the roads. There, many chose to die in the open, given that they had every excuse for giving up their souls.

A notorious evictor early in the famine was elegant military man and member of Parliament the Earl of Lucan, George Bingham, who owned over 60,000 acres in the Castlebar and Ballinrobe areas in County Mayo in the west. He was largely an absentee landlord, wild Mayo being admittedly a barbarous place for a man of the world to live. He declared as part of his motivation for the evictions that he 'would not breed paupers to pay priests'. He evicted 2000 tenants from one parish in Ballinrobe alone, and tumbled – that is, smashed in – their houses.

During the summer of 1846 and into the late winter of 1847, Lucan's ejections added to the burden of the local Board of Guardians, the worthies whose role it was to administer the workhouses. After his eviction of 2000 tenants, the Mayo *Telegraph* complained of 'the shoals of peasantry' crowding into the Castlebar workhouse. 'We afterwards, at the dead hour of the night, saw hundreds of these victims of landlordism and Gregory-ism sinking on our flagways.' (Gregory-ism referred to a law requiring tenants to give up their land if they wanted to enter the workhouse.) Some of the evicted people on the stones of the streets had green foam dripping from their mouths, as if they had eaten grass. But the Castlebar union workhouse, which had previously taken 6–700 persons, would be closed by order of the chairman of the Board of Guardians – that is, by Lucan himself – in October 1846. To keep it going, said the Earl of Lucan, he would need to increase the poor rate which landowners had to pay, and that would be beyond their resources. After the workhouse closure, nearly a hundred people died outside its gate.

His feelings in this matter are interesting. He considered himself a gentleman, engaged in a salutary exercise, transcending the sentimental, the fraudulent and false com-passion, which ignored the way the world was trending. In that spirit, he would attract the opprobrium of Parlia-ment, because his evictions were illegal – these tenants had paid their rent. To Lucan's intense chagrin, the House of Commons and the House of Lords, having from the beginning criticised his actions, went on asking questions about him afterwards. Not only were people now unable to get into the abandoned Castlebar workhouse, those already inside remained utterly neglected both in terms of medical care and food. When they died, their bodies were removed to an outbuilding called the Dead House, where, since there were no coffins, they putrefied away. But, in furiously defending himself in the House of Lords on 16 February 1847, Lucan placed part of the blame for the closing of the Castlebar workhouse on a recalcitrant fuel con-tractor who had failed to deliver a contracted-for amount of peat and wood.

Lucan had ordered his evictions by way of his land agents, and did not need himself to deal with the messy business of enforcement and harsh orders and keening. He was not squeamish or by any means a compassionate man, but he would have described himself as a realist, and would certainly not be the only landlord to describe himself as such.

No official records of total evictions in a given year were kept until 1849. But in 1846, on estimation, 3500 families were turned out of their homes, which were then wrecked. This would mean that more than 17,000 people were evicted. In the following year, 6000 families were ejected from their homes and their land. The figures would increase in 1848 to 10,000 families. Then the official record shows that 16,500 families (that is, more than 87,000 people) in 1849, 20,000 families in 1850 and 13,000 in 1851 were evicted. These figures do not include those who simply abandoned their land, made an arrangement with their landlord to emigrate or, by entering the workhouse, lost it.

The Bishop of Meath claimed that he saw a cabin pulled down over the heads of people dying of cholera. Among the ruins, he administered the sacraments for the dying in the midst of an equinoctial gale and in torrents of rain. The bishop declared that the roof-wrecking mechanism or scaffolding, 'a machine of ropes and pulleys', was used for the more solid buildings.

'It was found that two of these machines enabled a sheriff to evict as many families in a day as could be got through by a crowbar brigade of fifty men,' he said. 'It was not an unusual occurrence to see forty or fifty houses levelled in one day, and orders given that no tenants or occupier should give them even a night's shelter.'

In Kilrush in County Clare, in a period of eighteen months, 12,000 had left their land due to clearances. 'Of those who survive,' said the *Limerick Chronicle* in September 1849, 'masses are plainly marked for the grave. Of the 32,000 people on the relief lists of Kilrush union, I shall be astonished if one half live to see another summer.'

The evictions were later popularly depicted as running along the Catholic–Protestant faultline, with the landlords on the Protestant side and Catholics on the other. In fact, many Catholic landlords were energetic evictors also. On top of that, the so-called 'middleman tenant', who now, under considerable economic pressure himself, evicted under-tenants, was always able to shift blame to the landlord, who was indeed often gouging him. A Dr John O'Neill, a middleman in North Cork, wrote, 'To the class of smallholders on the farm I have already made large allowances, and yet I feel they require further assistance, which I would willingly bestow on them if I had it in my power. Unless they are befriended by [the over-landlord] Sir Riggs Falkiner, I fear they will go to the wall.'

Evictions increased after the Irish Poor Law Extension Act in June 1847. It signified that the famine was over, and that no future financial aid would be descending from the Treasury. Repayable grants, however, would be extended to many embattled local Poor Law unions. But in real terms, any future help for the Irish must come from the Poor Rate paid by landlords, a sum paid by anyone owning or leasing property valued at £4 or more per annum. The new act created disquiet, and worse, in the hearts of larger landowners.

The evictions in Ireland were unpopular in Britain, and were condemned by Trevelyan. They were seen as a means for landlords to place the burden of their tenants onto the state, a further proof of landlord selfishness. Among individual landlords who came to the attention of Parliament, the Marquess of Sligo, having previously extended a great deal of rent tolerance to his tenantry, said in October 1848 that now he would need to evict ruthlessly since he was 'under the necessity of ejecting or being ejected'. Questions were asked in the House of Commons about the marquess having authorised evictions without appropriate notice being given to the local Board of Guardians, to whose work-houses and proposed soup kitchens many of the evictees would present themselves.

But some landlords would not evict. Lord Sligo chided his cousin and fellow Galway landowner, George Henry Moore, MP, who refused to throw his peasants off his land. Sligo said that without evictions Moore would end up like Sir Samuel O'Malley, on whose estate arrears of rent were such that the court of Chancery took over and evicted three-quarters of the tenants anyhow. Sligo said that in his heart's belief Sir Samuel 'had done more to injure and persecute and exterminate the tenants than any man in Mayo'.

Thus, went the argument, immediate and surgical evic-tion was the lesser of two evils. To what extent the evicting landlords were influenced by political economy, or a belief in the great scythe of Providence, or by Malthusian theory, we do not know. Nor do we know to what extent Sligo's inversion of thinking – the evictor as the more merciful culler – was the result of a profoundly swallowed moral unease.

The Edgeworth family of Edgeworthtown, County Long-ford, were sworn non-evictors. Maria Edgeworth, eighty years of age in 1848, was a renowned novelist (author of *Castle Rackrent, The Modern Griselda, The Absentee*) and the most eminent of the Edgeworth clan. In 1849, she died of heart trouble and was mourned by her tenantry. She, like many of the Irish gentry, was very interested in properly arranged emigration. Lord Lansdowne of County Kerry, at just over thirty a young treasurer in Lord John Russell's cabinet, financed a program of well-coordinated emigration, with the majority of his tenants arriving safely at their destinations.

In the diocese of Derry, the Catholic bishop and ninety of his priests passed a series of resolutions in July 1848. They thanked County Derry's largest proprietors, the London Companies, for their humane treatment. But they attacked the many evicting landlords of nearby Donegal.

Perhaps the most famous evictor was Major Denis Mahon of Strokestown in County Roscommon in Ireland's midlands. (Strokestown and Mahon's house are today the site of the Irish Famine Museum.) In 1845, Major Mahon inherited the 200-year-old Mahon estate. The property had more than 13,000 tenants on its 27,000 acres. He employed his cousin, John Ross Mahon, as his agent, and John Ross recommended that Major Mahon evict tenants so that the small farms could be amalgamated into larger ones. On these, solid tenant-farmer Protestants brought in from Scotland could grow grain. For beginning to implement these schemes, Major Mahon paid with his life, for his evictions were an engine of fury as well as of agricultural progress.

To turn his land over to these more profitable and modern forms of agriculture and grazing, he needed space presently taken up by unproductive tenants incapable of paying rent. He began by evicting 1000 people. But, like other landlords, he knew he could never fully rid his land of them unless they vanished totally, far from the need of his control and compassion, and far from the Irish workhouses, for whose upkeep he had to meet part of the cost. He wanted a depopulated landscape. So he spent £4000 to charter ill-provided ships to take the evicted tenants to Quebec in the summer of 1847. Mahon's four relatively small vessels were the *Naomi*, the *Virginius*, *Erin's Queen* and *John Munn*.

One of the evicted families was that of James Sheridan. On 5 June 1847, the Sheridan family boarded Mahon's first chartered ship, the *Naomi*, in Liverpool (to which city Mahon had transported them as deck cargo). Death seemed daily omnipresent on the *Naomi* – 196 people died aboard. Waking in the unspeakable steerage, in which nearly 700 were crowded in an infectious stew, people found the dead beside them. They were committed, unabsolved, into the sea. Only six of the eleven members of the Sheridan family survived the voyage. On landing, survivors were placed on the infamous quarantine island of Grosse Ile in the St Lawrence River. The Sheridan father, James, his daughter, Bridget, and a son, John, all died at sea or in quarantine in the island. Mary Connor Sheridan, the mother, died in the hospital at Grosse Ile in the last week of August 1847. The remaining six Sheridan children, aged between ten and twenty, were sent to the Catholic orphanage in Quebec.

The Mahon arrivals in general were considered to be in such appalling condition that the Canadian Parliament complained to Westminster about it. A half of those who survived the sea voyage died on Grosse Ile in that summer of 1847; more than 600 children were orphaned there. The ships on which Mahon's evictees travelled had the highest death rate of any arriving in Canada throughout the summer of 1847, with 511 in total.

Mahon also turned out on the roads 600 families who refused to leave for North America. But he did not do all of it with impunity. On All Souls Day, 2 November 1847, while many of his 'assisted migrants' were still expiring in quarantine on Grosse Ile in the now freezing-over St Lawrence, Major Mahon was ambushed on his way home from a meeting of the local Board of Guardians and shot dead. Three weeks later, the Reverend John Lloyd was killed nearby. The chief reason for the killing of the Reverend Lloyd was that he ran, in the words of a priest, a school that was a 'factory where numbers of famine Protestants are manufactured'. That is, according to the allegation, Lloyd – like a number of evangelicals in Ireland – had used the opportunity of the famine to tempt people to convert to Protestantism on the promise of food, land or both.

Men were arrested for Mahon's murder, stood trial and were either executed or transported. The two men hanged for the killing were James Commins, a local accurate shot, and Patrick Hasty, owner of a *shebeen*, or unlicensed saloon. Such was the fury the evictions had brought forth that at Hasty's funeral, tenantry and former tenantry fought for the honour of carrying his coffin. The local parish priest, the Reverend Michael McDermott, declared that Mahon was Nero and that his evictions had led to his murder.

After Mahon's murder, the authorities declared Roscommon a 'disturbed area', and many landowners fled with their families. New and more severe 'outrage' legislation was passed and British surveillance of the Irish, and fear of false accusation among the populace, increased (as the journalist from the *Illustrated London News* described in Chapter 9). The end of evictions and forced emigrations would have been a better start on producing good order, but the phenomenon continued in a robust form. In Ballykilcline near Strokestown, on land managed for Queen Victoria, there had been a long-running rent strike. The tenants had shown their soli-. darity against the land agents by employing a young lawyer from Dublin, of the kind who would these days be called a 'human rights advocate'. Nonetheless, with famine's onset, hundreds of farmers were evicted and 'emigrated', the active verb taking on a colour of passivity and acceptance on the part of the emigrated. But at least the Crown paid the tenants' way to New York.

If the best-known evictor was Denis Mahon, the most scandalous was Lord Palmerston, Henry John Temple, long-term foreign secretary in a series of both Whig and Tory governments, and ultimately prime minister of Great Britain in 1855, at the age of seventy. At the time of the famine, he was still foreign secretary under Lord John Russell. 'Tenant-right,' he declared, 'is landlord wrong.' He owned lands in Sligo, where his neighbours, Sir Robert and Lady Gore-Booth, also resorted to eviction.

According to the parish priest of Lissadell, Sligo, however, Sir Robert Gore-Booth seems to have had concern for his evicted people. The priest asserted that the emigration of peasants from Gore-Booth's land was voluntary, and that the Gore-Booths had made arrangements for their former tenants once they arrived in New Brunswick in Canada. Many declared that no other group of Irish immigrants was so well provided for, both on the emigrant ships and once they arrived in the province. The masters of the vessels that Gore-Booth chartered were instructed, on reaching port, to contact a certain Irish timber merchant in St John, New Brunswick, who had undertaken to give jobs to many of the former tenants. Some were to be sent inland to Frederickton, and others were to be made comfortable in St John itself, lodging at the Gore-Booths' expense. Yet once the Gore-Booth tenants reached St John, the New Brunswick immigration officers said that even Gore-Booth should be condemned for 'shovelling out' his helpless and his sick. Very many of the passengers were a burden on the town council and the government of the province. Still, all this was a faint whisper of the rage that would break out when Palmerston's tenants began to arrive.

In the summer of 1847, Palmerston, as absentee landlord, ordered or approved of the eviction and involuntary emigration of 2000 tenants. They had been selected by Lord Palmerston's agent, Joseph Kincaid, who picked 'those who were the poorest'. Kincaid believed that the emigration would advantage the colonies and that he had the welfare of the cottiers in mind. In fact, like most agents evicting on behalf of landlords, he had probably made selections for forced emigration of the troublemakers first – men who were insubordinate, recalcitrant with rent and sympathetic to the sentiments of Ribbonmen. After that, the evicting process would have moved on to the more innocuous.

Later, in 1851, Kincaid would claim to have given

between £3 and £5 to each of 150 tenant families he evicted in Roscommon on another estate he managed. But it does not seem the Palmerston evictees left with any such largesse. In the summer of 1847, his tenants were sent off in nine ill-provided shiploads to Canada. The *Eliza Liddell*, carrying women, children and the aged, was Palmerston's first vessel to arrive at St John, and its passengers became an immediate charge on the New Brunswick community. On another, the *Lord Ashburton*, which landed its people at Grosse Ile, 107 people had died on the voyage, 174 of the passengers were near-naked and 87 of them had to be clothed at public expense 'for decency's sake'. The *Aeolus* arrived late in the season, when the St Lawrence was already clogged with ice so that, as a destination, Quebec was out of the question. Hence its passengers were landed – when the first snows had already fallen – at the overcrowded St John quarantine station on Partridge Island. The quarantine station doctor asked if anyone was so tame as not to feel indignant at this outrage, and certainly the rest of the New Brunswick community was in a fury at Lord Palmerston's opportunism and callousness. The Common Council of the city of St John wrote to him stating that they 'deeply regret that one of Her Majesty's ministers, the Rt. Hon. Lord Palmerston . . . should have exposed such a numerous and distressed portion of his tenantry to the severity and privations of a New Brunswick winter . . . unprovided with the common means of support, with broken down constitutions and almost in a state of nudity.' They received no response to this protest. Lord Palmerston might have been too busy putting all the pressure he could on the Americans to open their ports to ships such as the ones that had carried his tenants. In any case, many of the survivors of Palmerston's evictions and those of other landlords walked away from St John to the American border and across into Maine, some of them dying on this last winter leg of their journey.

From some members of Parliament arose the cry that the government open proceedings for manslaughter against a landlord named Blake and his sons, who had begun evictions without even observing the legal process. Home Secretary Sir George Grey declared that it was impossible to read about these evictees without feelings of considerable pain, but then fantastically argued that if the tenant was treated unjustly by his landlord, he 'would have a right of civil action', that is, the right to bring a court case against him. Prime Minister Russell expressed far less qualified rage: 'The murders of poor cottiers and tenants are horrible to bear, and if we put down assassins, we ought to put down the lynch law of the landlord.' Russell also had to face and deal with Lord Palmerston and another cabinet minister who was an Irish landlord – Lord Clanri-carde, the postmaster-general. If Lord Russell reprimanded them, history does not tell of it.

A great number of those evicted in the winter of 1846–7 found the means to get only as far as Glasgow or Liverpool, travelling on the freezing decks of ships crossing the Irish Sea. Lord Brougham, an amiable progressive – indeed, too progressive to be widely liked – who had, in the 1830s, been involved in the campaign to end slavery, was aware of the arrival of these people. In the process of attacking the Earl of Lucan and other evicting landlords in the Commons in February 1847, and chastising them for evicting in the middle of the most bitter winter in memory, he noted with alarm a flood of penniless Irish appearing on the British mainland. In the five days before Brougham uttered his protest, 5200 Irish paupers had landed in England, Wales and Scotland. They had no possessions and were in an advanced state of starvation, even while famine fever and cholera raged among them. The growing host of the Irish who arrived in Liverpool were from Mayo, Lord Brougham observed, and, given the behaviour of Mayo landlords such as the Earl of Lucan, their numbers were sure to increase. Brougham did not mention another problem faced by the Irish newcomers – being from Mayo, they would be unaccustomed to urban life, at a loss in the cities of Britain and easy to write off as subhuman.

In answering Lord Brougham, the Marquess of Westmeath eroded this sentimentality by saying that a great number of the people had not been evicted but had arrived without relinquishing their land – that is, had simply walked away from it. This created a legal trouble for the landlords, said the marquess, and inhibited their ability to obtain the abandoned land without complication. Obviously legal miscreancy on the part of those who fled muted the compassion the House felt for them.

Between 13 January and 1 November 1847, 278,000 Irish poured into Liverpool, 80,000 into Glasgow and some thousands more into Manchester. Throughout mainland Britain, nineteen relief officers and thirty Catholic priests caught cholera from them and died.

*

From 1849, when the police started keeping records of evictions, a further 250,000 persons (on top of those evicted in 1846–8) were formally and permanently evicted – the evictions thus continuing until 1854, well after the end of the famine. The most sweeping clearances and evictions recorded from 1849–54 occurred in Clare, Mayo, Galway and Kerry – that is, in the hardest-hit south-western and western counties that made up the collective regions of Munster and Connacht. The concentration of evictions was quite possibly the same in what had been some of the high days of the eviction process – between 1846 and the end of 1848. And the figures may be incomplete, since tenants sometimes feared eviction and clearance so much that they would unroof their own cabins, on condition that they were allowed to take away the timber and thatch, which they would not have been free to do had they been formally evicted.

By the late summer of 1847, some Irish were suddenly willing to emigrate of their own accord, proving anxious to flee a country they now considered accursed. In evictions, women's grip on their doorposts could only have been loosened by the main force of dragoons and policemen. That so many should now go by their own volition was astonishing. Most of the people making for the ports desired to reach the fabled United States. The ships they boarded were of varying quality, but such was the impetus to escape that people were willing to sign on for dangerous autumn or even winter sailings. Some tenants who wanted to escape left in the middle of the night without telling anyone. On the public works, a name would be called out but no one would respond – this time not because of death, starvation or fever, but because the owner of the name had gone to look for a ship. Most of those who were thinking of America were people who were not at the bottom of the pit and had some funds left at least to find a place on one of those untrustworthy vessels known as 'coffin ships'. Few people from County Mayo and other western counties could afford even that.

In the ports, people were cheated out of their remaining funds by being sold false tickets or nautical instruments they were assured they would need at sea. Nor did the Americans look forward to the mass arrival of fever-stricken Irish. In early 1847, two new Passenger Acts were passed by Congress, raising the minimum fare from Ireland to America to £7 and regulating the numbers who could be carried on ships. But ships' captains seemed to be able to get around the regulations. Through Castle Garden clearing station, just off lower New York, 850,000 Irish would enter that city alone in the next four years. Obviously not every one of them had paid £7 to get there; nor had the Irish accumulating in the streets of Boston or Baltimore, or moving down over the border from Canada.

Early in April 1848, Home Secretary Sir George Grey proposed a bill that would not only prohibit evictions without proper notice to the local Board of Guardians, but would also prevent the pulling-down of huts and houses. Although this bill quickly passed the Commons, it was attacked strenuously in the Lords, especially by Irish peers such as Lord Monteagle. Monteagle, Thomas Spring Rice, former chancellor of the exchequer, was an interesting case. He saw no benefit in limiting the landlord's right to evict, but his main reason for opposing the bill was that he was an apostle of the benefits of emigration and he was in the process of introducing much of his tenantry to it, clearing them off his scattered properties in Shanagolden in Limerick on the banks of the Shannon, and pulling down their houses after they departed.

However, a number of positive signs attest his humanity. When the Office of Public Works was in arrears in his area during the famine, Monteagle advanced £4500 of his own money to keep them functioning, and, according to the letters he received from his apparently grateful former tenants after emigration, he had also tailored their rents during the dark years of the late 1840s. Monteagle estate ledgers show that rent-free accommodation and even pensions were allocated to widows among the tenants. Monteagle's wife, Lady Theodosia, collaborated with him and did a great deal of what could be called the legwork among their tenants.

The British had put in place a scheme by which the money from the sale of Crown lands in Australia was used to pay bounties to ships' captains for delivery of emigrants to the Australian colonies. To guarantee the health of emigrants on such a long journey, the shipowners were paid for each healthy passenger they landed in the Australian colonies. This was the scheme of which, to a large degree, Monteagle availed himself in order to accomplish a humane, if paternalistic, deportation of his peasantry. He had first made use of it in 1838. It was suspended in 1840 because of a depression in the Australian colonies, but it was renewed in 1847. Monteagle proposed an arrangement by which the tenantry were forgiven arrears, could sell up their effects and receive a grant of money if they quit their land. Should the shipping owners and immigration agents require a deposit, as in some cases – dependent on family size and health – they did, Monteagle advanced it, the emigrants pledging to repay it out of wages earned in Australia. Monteagle not only put his former tenants on well-founded ships, but organised for their reception in Sydney and Melbourne.

The criteria for emigration under this scheme were well-defined and not everyone could be accepted. Just the same, throughout the remaining famine years and beyond, Monteagle immigrants, now settled in Australia, were able to send back money to enable further emigration, or to support those relatives who could not emigrate.

This does not mean there was not anger and resistance to Monteagle's plans. A Patrick Trehy refused an offer of £25 to help his family emigrate. When he was evicted, he and a number of his family took advantage of the sum offered and went to Australia, no doubt harbouring bitter thoughts. Yet altogether, by comparison with Palmerston and others, Monteagle's behaviour, admittedly combined with a desire to clear and agriculturally improve his land, did him considerable honour. A James Fitzgerald wrote to him from Melbourne in 1853, in a letter not uncharacteristic of others written to him by former tenants, in which he said, 'Your benevolent and very kind letter dated January reached me safely and I can only say I cannot sufficiently thank Your Lordship for the great interest shown in our humble affairs.' Fitzgerald went on to discuss paying off the £5 he owed Monteagle for the extra sum payable for the passage of his family, but then asked, 'Permit me to call attention to the enclosed letter of credit for £15 . . . to defray first the cost of sending out John Dinnene . . . concerning whom all particulars can be obtained from the Rev Father Michael McMahon, Parish Priest of Kilcolman.' It would be preposterous to think of an evictee of Lords Palmerston or Brougham putting such trust in their former landlord's hands.

Monteagle's sense of appropriateness was expressed again in 1849, when what now would be called a public relations tour of Ireland was planned for Queen Victoria. He condemned it as a deceit 'which was intended to give the lie to the appalling condition of the emaciated inhabitants of this country'. Nor was he the only member of the establishment to think so.

In Ireland and Ethiopia, at least, the amount of famine emigration sparked a further, increased emigration in the post-famine era, since emigrants knew that, on arrival, they would be greeted by their relatives who had earlier escaped the famine and its politics, and would find accommodation, jobs and the company of a familiar community of earlier emigrants.

Through death and emigration, the population of Connacht in the west of Ireland fell by nearly one in four by 1851, and that of Munster in the south and south-west by 22 per cent, while Ulster's fell by 16 per cent and Leinster's, the eastern region that included Dublin, by 15 per cent. The very mass of this sudden exit would create an overseas population of Irish who urged their siblings and parents to come and join them in some new land and sent money to help them on their way.

Between 1851 and 1861, a further 19 per cent from Munster and 10 per cent from Connacht and even more – 13 per cent – from Leinster, left the countryside of 'Ireland of the Sorrows' thinner in people, and more desolate. In 1879–81 another series of bad potato crops, low prices and poor grain harvests also produced chronic hunger, but no mortality on a mass scale. Yet there was a large increase in emigration. The Irish were not willing to risk the possibility of further famine.

So Ireland became the only nation in northern Europe to decline in population, to the extent that the all-Ireland population of 1841 declined from 8 million to a little over 5 million by 1881 and a little over 4 million by 1946. Though there had been considerable emigration from Ethiopia and Eritrea since the 1970s, and although a similar set of factors caused relatives of earlier emigrants to leave and settle in many countries on earth, it did not produce a decline in population comparable to Ireland's. In 2003, the UN estimated the Ethiopian population to be 71.5 million (with an average life expectancy of 45 years). A 2009 estimate was 80 million, twice the number registered in the Derg's imperfect census of 1984.

By the time normal life returned to Ireland in 1853 and 1854, the Irish population was two million fewer than in 1845. This made for a shortage of labour and a rise in wages. Families did not any more farm the small plots named 'conacre' in return for which they gave their labour to their landlord. The former owners of small farms targeted by the Gregory clause were, in large number, dead or had fled or – if they remained – were agricultural labourers. Since farms were larger, barley, oats, wheat and other grains were grown in unprecedented quantity, and that and the continually reducing numbers of

Irish remaining at home kept prices reasonable. So people did not depend on the potato as their major staple any more. The Lumper potato was, in any case, replaced by smaller crops of tastier ones, and ultimately bigger potato harvests occurred in the late nineteenth and early twentieth centuries, after Louis Pasteur and Alexis Millardet had discovered at the Pasteur Institute in Paris in 1882 that bluestone (copper sulphate) solution could be sprayed on plants as a great preventative of fungal attacks on potato, grape, and other susceptible crops.

No such change in the land system occurred in Bengal. Whereas in Ireland by 1851 two million people had vanished – one in four people – the no-less horrifying Bengal famine killed one in twelve, the Ethiopian one in thirty. In neither place did the land system change as obviously as in Ireland. Rice remained the staple in Bengal, teff and cattle the staples of Ethiopia.

12

Evictions and Movements, Mengistu-style

IN SEPTEMBER 1984 Ethiopia officially became a Marxist-Leninist state, with Mengistu Haile Mariam as secretary general of the newly formed Workers' Party of Ethiopia. His position of secretary general, like his past eminence within the state, gave him added energy to pursue policies already under development, of the kind that had been tried earlier in the century in Russia, at massive human cost. These were policies he certainly believed in as an ideologue, but that would also have value in his war against rebels.

The evictions that occurred in Ethiopia at the height of the mid 1980s famine went under the titles of resettlement and villagisation. They were forms of Soviet-style collectivisation and, even though some Ethiopian peasants reluctantly and under pressure of hunger volunteered, both resettlement and villagisation were, in general, massively opposed by them.

Resettlement was one of Mengistu's answers to the famine

and his other problems. Many outside observers argued that there was a sense in which the exhausted northern soil of Tigray and Wollo made resettlement from these regions an option for any responsible government. But, as run by the Derg, it was a debacle in which apparatchiks overrode the advice of experts in the Department of Agriculture. Under the pretext of resettlement, Mengistu was able to remove, as well as peasants, those he suspected of helping the revolution of the Tigrayan People's Liberation Front (TPLF). He could use resettlement areas as rehabilitation centres for politically undesirable people. Administered not by experts in the field but by the chief of Mengistu's secret police, Legesse Asfaw, resettlement would leave the Tigrayan rebels alone in a vacated landscape, one in which all their support had been stripped away.

Part of Mengistu's desire for collectivisation and resettlement was frankly stated in these terms in a document produced by the Derg's Council of Ministers. 'Almost all of you here realise that we have security problems . . . the people are like the sea and the guerrillas are like fish swimming in that sea. Without the sea there will be no fish. We have to drain the sea.'

A further objective of resettlement was the desire to integrate the various Ethiopian tribes and nationalities. The fact that many Ethiopians favoured their ethnic identity over their national Ethiopian one was a great problem in Mengistu's mind, as in the minds of the emperors before him. Over 60 per cent of Ethiopia's 1,119,683 square kilometres was occupied by nomads who had no revolutionary sense at all. Properly mixed up among other ethnic groups by resettlement, people would discover their common Ethiopian-ness. Also, Mengistu had an unquestioning Marxist belief, uninformed by much knowledge of what happened in the disastrous case of the Soviets, that the very act of resettlement would lead to the growth of abundant crops and new food surpluses. Finally, it could be used to remove the unemployed from the cities.

Within Mengistu's Ethiopia, resettlement, or at least concentration on a smaller scale, had been in progress for some time, since the mid 1970s. Between 1975 and 1981, thousands of young men who were guilty of political impulses had been picked up on the streets of the cities and taken to a sweltering area named Humera near the Sudanese border to work on collective farms and act as a defence force against the incursions of the Sudanese People's Liberation Army. Most of those sent to Humera, or to Hamer Koko in Kafa province, which was in the southern corner of Ethiopia between Sudan and Kenya, died of hunger or disease. Those who found their way back to Addis were rounded up and returned to their camps in the wilderness.

Similarly, Dawit Wolde Giorgis had himself once tried to resettle 40,000 Ogadenian nomads in the Harar province. These were pastoralists who crossed from Ethiopia to Somalia and back again according to habit, rainfall, and available pasture. The reason for their resettlement was to improve their sense of Ethiopian national identity. Giorgis moved these people from the dry lowlands to a more tropical region, where, for the first time in their lives, they beheld and were terrified by crocodiles. He heard an elderly nomad woman proclaim, 'In thirst or in hunger, oh Allah, content am I to suffer and die in the land and under the skies of my ancestors.

There is nothing like home.' Subsequently, as dawn revealed one morning, all the nomads disappeared from the resettlement site. No such swift and easy departure would be available under Mengistu's resettlement.

No one was to be resettled from the Ethiopian-held parts of Eritrea in the far north. If the process had begun there, the populace would have fled north *en masse*, into the sectors controlled by the Eritrean People's Liberation Front, the Ethiopian rebels fighting for an independent Eritrea.

Resettlement would not only bring great pain but would reduce the amount of food being produced in the time of famine, and thus drive up prices while gouging the resettled Ethiopians.

The rationale for Mengistu's other great plan for upheaval, villagisation – the drawing together of country people into newly built and gratuitously placed larger villages, which had not existed until now – was, according to the publicly proposed objective, to provide people more easily with schools and medicine and markets. Again, villagisation resembled the sort of collectivisation that occurred in the first decade of the Bolshevik revolution in Russia, and which there had created the catastrophic famine of the early 1920s. The Ethiopians hated it because it took and kept most of them a long way from their farms, as well as their churches and mosques, on whose succour they depended in bitter times. But for Mengistu it also had the benefit of clearing the countryside so that rebels were bereft of support and stood out in a vacated landscape. The hated new villages into which people were moved were called *safaratabia* – fake or artificial hamlets.

*

Wolde Selassie Ghebremarian was a Coptic priest from the north of the country who was affected by Mengistu's series of forced resettlements. He had been living in an area held by the TPLF. The region's cattle had been struck by disease in 1984, and the government spread a message that it would vaccinate all cattle free of charge at Adowa, an historic town in the north of Tigray. So the farmers rounded up 750 head of cattle and started out on the road. Wolde and the rest left their families behind in their village – in his case, a wife and three children. The group arrived in Adowa on 6 December 1984, took their stock to the cattle market and were at once surrounded by soldiers.

'We shouted, who was going to take care of our cattle? . . . They answered that it would be no loss if we lost our cattle, the government was going to resettle us and would replace our cattle in the new settlement.' This proposition did nothing for the people the men had left behind.

Locked up with other candidates for resettlement in a holding camp in Adowa, each farmer was fed two pieces of bread a day. The group saw the soldiers who guarded them feeding themselves out of bags of emergency grain marked with the logo of the European Economic Commission and the governments of Canada and West Germany. After eleven days, Soviet pilots transported Wolde and the others by helicopter south from Adowa to Makale – trucks would not have got through because the TPLF controlled the countryside – where a great holding camp for eventual resettlement was situated. (Another was at Debre Birhan, north-east of Addis in that city's home province, Showa.) One of the survivors said that an uncountable number died at Makale of exposure and disease. Wolde and his fellow cattle owners lived under guard in an open field without shelter. The night's dead became visible at dawn. Those who escaped at night were killed, 'sometimes as many as a hundred each night'.

Next, a relay of Soviet-made Antonov transports moved Wolde and thousands more to Bole Airport in Addis Ababa. These planes were unpressurised and were designed to carry fifty paratroopers, but 300–350 of the candidates for resettlement were crammed aboard each flight, the soldiers forcing aboard even the sick. At Bole Airport, those capable of standing came off the plane, then troops carried out the dead bodies and those incapable of movement, and the fire brigade hosed the pools of vomit and piss from the floor of the plane. Each peasant was now given one cup of water and then squeezed onto buses for the journey to Wollega province to the west of the country. Ninety-five per cent of the country's buses would be used to accomplish the great clearances from north to south, from east to west.

Many more died during this next journey of two days or longer, in an atmosphere in which survivors said there was not enough room to breathe and where people were forced to relieve themselves on the floor. Wolde and the others finished their journey at the town of Asosa, humid jungle country in the lowlands near the Sudanese border. As another Wollo farmer would say, 'For five days and nights we travelled by moonlight, darkness and daylight, and then they dumped us into the grass.'

*

Life in the artificially created villages would be testing and fatal for some, but living in their traditional villages before that had frequently been harsh too, because of military barbarism, the racial hatred that often spurred it, and the confiscation and destruction of food.

'They destroyed our house and burned the Koran,' claimed one Oromo man. 'I have beautiful daughters that were raped. The Amharas did this.'

Such outrages against women were regularly reported. 'The militia told the men to go to some place and the women to another. No Muslim men were allowed to be with their wives. Then five militia took each woman.'

The soldiers particularly liked to rape the wives of Coptic priests. Teenage boys were taken for the army, but younger boys were often shot or forced to dance around the bodies of their mothers.

Most of the refugees to Somalia and the Sudan claimed to have been arrested at various times and held to ransom by the army. The amounts involved were up to one hundred Ethiopian dollars, a relatively small amount, except for a farmer's wife.

Villages suspected of supporting the Oromo Liberation Front were destroyed, and to the Oromo and other targets, the Amharic and the army were simultaneous entities. Yet, despite the blaming of the Amharic ethnic group, the government militias also contained Christian Oromo. 'Three years ago,' observed another Ethiopian refugee in the Sudan, 'we were bombed because we were suspected of supporting the OLF. Before that we were bombed because we were suspected of supporting the Somalis.' Even in the beginning of the famine, the army and government militias were still doing their terrible work.

The army's activities made the situation worse, according to refugees: 'The Derg is one of the reasons people are hungry . . . I can't even remember all the people who have had their crops burnt. The government always comes during harvest. The army took five hundred cows and oxen from my village, they burned people's houses, and took honey, butter, and anything made of leather . . . they didn't bother to carry the grain; they just burned it. The militia, their farmers from the area, they take our tools so they can use them . . . the army burned my grain in 1983 and they took twenty-four tons of honey.'

In 1984, said one refugee, the government had arrived at night, had burned his house and taken three cows. The military killed young people who might join the Tigrayan rebels, so that each village had to develop an armed guard, who kept watch and warned the people when the army was on the way. Another farmer refugee claimed that the Derg bombed local markets so that merchants would not go to them any more. It was because of the Derg that they were in Sudan, he said. Even with droughts, he claimed, he would have been able to trade and make a living. But not with the army.

According to the Tigrayan refugees, who came from the far north, from places like the ancient town of Axum, many escaped from the trucks when the army came to get them, but the good thing about the TPLF, they said, was that they did not prevent people from going back to their area to feeding centres, if they chose to. After all, apart from the danger of them being captured for resettlement, though that happened rarely in food distribution centres, it was appropriate to the TPLF to have their sympathisers fed under the aegis of Mengistu.

Axum was the pre-Christian capital of Ethiopia, and its temples and its black granite obelisks remain today. These were the tallest pieces of stone ever quarried and erected in the ancient world. Ethiopian legend says that when the Queen of Sheba made her journey to Jerusalem, she was impregnated by King Solomon and bore him a boy who, in later years, stole the ark and brought it to Axum. Not that this meant much to the deprived people of northern Tigray. One of the columns of Tigrayan famine refugees from the region of Axum was attacked by the Ethiopian air force, who were said to have killed 80 to 100 people.

To be villagised or resettled, some surmised, might make people less vulnerable to such attacks. But many others knew that, once moved, they would be permanently under the thumb of the same regime that permitted the army to run wild and that, as well, however inadequate it might be to feed them at the present, they would lose control of their land forever.

In the manner of other governments and other famines, Mengistu believed that the people of the north, in their resistance to resettlement and villagisation, had brought their troubles on themselves. Chief of security Legesse Asfaw travelled to the towns of Makale in Tigray and Dessie in Wollo, both of them centres of the famine, and urged the hungry into making a move, promising that their salvation lay in the new resettlement location, where they would be given tools and food and shelter. The hungry he addressed did their best to repeat Asfaw slogans: 'Down with imperialism! Down with capitalism! We shall overcome nature! Long live Mengistu!'

It was not only Ethiopian cadres who believed in these two great goals of Derg policy – resettlement and villagisation. There were some outsiders who believed in resettlement as an idealistic if imperfect process, and a solution to Ethiopia's pain. With good intentions, some Western voluntary agencies, such as Band Aid, the relief body founded by musicians Bob Geldof and Midge Ure, helped to support the process with food. Band Aid believed that resettlement was necessary, but at the same time that it should not occur with coercion. Coercion, however, by hunger or the state, was the essence of the process.

Mengistu's original resettlement plan in November 1984 was that 300,000 families should be moved, but he quickly adjusted it to 500,000. 'As I looked up to the sky, it appeared to me too light,' went a song from Wollo. 'It seems they have taken Allah too for resettlement.' The resettlement sites were to be near Asosa in Wollega province, Gambella in Illubabor, Pawe in Gojjam and Mettima in Gondar – all these regions being in the west or south-west. Resettlement sites, said Dawit Wolde Giorgis after his defection to the west, were in many ways the equivalent of the gulags of Russia. For resettlement often occurred and was maintained under the barrel of a gun. Like the priest Wolde Selassie, mentioned above, farmers who came to market towns to buy grain and salt or to sell animals and cheese, cattle or honey were captured and forced into lorries by soldiers with quotas to fill.

One man was rounded up on his way to get treatment at a hospital. Some Tigrayan peasants said they had to leave for the resettlement sites after the military deliberately poisoned large areas of their land with insecticides, while over 80 per cent of the Wollo people interviewed later in refugee camps in the Sudan said that they had been rounded up while attending mandatory government meetings. There would be no registration of such people, no records of who was sent to which camp, and so, as had happened in the Bengali round-ups, families were often separated with no chance of knowing where their relocated family members were. Among the Tigrayans in the resettlement camps, the average family was only two, which seemed to bespeak either that many had died of hunger or disease, or else families had been split. The latter was not a universal case: sometimes families were resettled together. One refugee claimed that when he went on his own to collect a rumoured ration, he was told that he must bring his whole family. 'When I returned with my family, they took us to the airport.' One farmer who lived near the ancient city of Axum declared that after he had heard about food relief for the twelfth time, 'We decided not to let the soldiers eat all the food so we went to Axum', where, of course, they were rounded up.

But those left behind in their home province starved in great numbers in a desolate and partially depopulated landscape, from which in many cases those on whom they depended had been removed. Often these abandoned trekked to the nearest relief depot.

Patterns of resettlement life developed. Party cadres and militia members led out the resettled each day to hoe the earth – a crisis of pride for the northern farmers. 'We became oxen in Asosa,' lamented a Wollo man transplanted to the west. 'We became tractors. The cadres told us, If you have finished your flour, eat soil and come to work.'

Asosa resettlement camp, further to the north of Gambella, lay between tributaries of the Blue Nile. Asfaw decided that here he would mix up the Wollo people and the Amharics, the latter considering themselves the true Ethiopians. He hoped that the influence of the Amharics would make the others more loyal. In fact, the mixture created camp conflicts. The Wollo people, meanwhile, claimed they were hungrier in Asosa than they had ever been in Wollo. 'I lost two children in Asosa. In Wollo I knew there would be drought, but the majority of the hunger is in Asosa. I can eat my one month's ration in two weeks.'

Tens of thousands of Tigrayans were transported by plane to Gambella in Wollega province, towards the Sudanese border. The resettlement area was located within what was called the Gambella National Park, where animals the highlanders had never seen before were sometimes visible around the Baro River – venomous snakes, hippopotamuses and elephants. 'We were living with lions,' one survivor declared, even though the psychological impact seems to have been greater than the casualty level. With a tendency that the Irish showed – to remember past times of relative hardship as a golden age – a farmer would say, 'At home we kept our meal times. No one died of hunger. But in Gambella the hunger brought disease, and we died.'

Gambella was tropical and sparsely populated, chiefly by Anuak farmers and fishermen who worked the waterways of the Baro, and who themselves would soon be subjected to villagisation. There was also a pastoral population of Nuers, who were darker, a Central African people who crossed the Ethiopian–Sudanese border as they chose in search of pasture. These locals of Gambella were said to have resented the sudden appearance of a new population descending from the sky onto their land. The highlanders were lighter-skinned and thus somehow suspect in the eyes of the Nuers, and the lowland Anuaks had always suspected such highland, northern people with a regional and ingrained passion.

As for the idea of escape from resettlement areas, 500 people were executed while trying to escape Gambella, and about 1000 perished while trying to walk back to their homes in the north. Even so, 5000 managed to get home again and hide – some of them joining the TPLF, since they were barred from joining the local Peasant Association and from getting any of their land back. As well, 10,000 taken to Gambella managed to cross the border to refugee camps in the Sudan.

The journey to the Sudan from a region such as Gambella took between fifteen and thirty days of walking in unfamiliar country. Those who tried to escape would often take their elders with them, at the elders' own urgent request, but in the hard and panicked conditions along the track, the tired, and those stricken with fever, were left beside the way. Some of these groups of escapees were attacked by armed militias from across the Sudanese border, and the younger women were sometimes abducted, along with any boys who might be suitable as soldiers. When ambushed by men emerging from the bush, the escapees did not know which army was attacking them, or which splinter group of the Sudanese People's Liberation Army, itself fighting for the oppressed southern Sudanese people, and in need of finance. Thus, some such groups traded escapees back to the Ethiopians in return for money or ammunition. Indeed, elements of the Sudanese rebels were tolerated within the Ethiopian border, as long as they acted as bounty hunters.

Many escapes were abortive. One farmer said that he and his family twice attempted to flee and were caught. They were beaten by cadres and imprisoned in a lock-up full of 'dust and insects'. They were not fed for the first five days of their detention. 'During the day we dug latrines. They beat us with whips, fifty lashes twice a day for one month.'

Escaping from Asosa was easier because the journey to the Sudanese border was only three to eight days. People tried to travel in large groups for fear of lions and hyenas, and, arriving in Oromo villages, they found that inhabitants were willing to help them along their way just to get them out of town.

There were stories that officials chose the resettlement sites cursorily and from the windows of helicopters. And in the country selected, in the midst of the national famine, under the severe care of Mengistu's Marxist cadres and militias – in country unfamiliar as to climate and soil, and in which there were often no buildings, no implements nor anything else necessary for proper habitation or agriculture – people were to remake their lives. A third of the best producers of food in the country had been removed from their accustomed land. One of them spoke for hundreds of thousands when he said that he wanted to die 'in the land where his umbilicus was buried'. Many of those like him would, in one way or another but also from the effects of malnutrition, never leave this place of exile.

At resettlement sites, the local peasantry had already been put to work building *tuqals* to house the incoming settlers, who began to arrive by the thousands in February 1985. The arrivals were nonetheless to find camps lacking in genuine buildings, agricultural tools or hospitals. Churches or mosques were not permitted. The newcomers were organised into work brigades by party officials. From the first arrivals in the camps, the cadres had chosen the militias to police the population – if necessary they were to act as enforcers, perhaps a lesser version of the Jewish *kapos* in the Nazi system.

The resettlement camps themselves contributed notably to the starvation rate. According to refugees, in a site of 500 people, thirteen or fourteen people died each day. In another resettlement village of 6000 people, twenty to twenty-five deaths occurred every day. In a resettlement site known as Amba 9, it is claimed that 1500 people out of 7000 died in the first two and a half months. These figures came from those who abominated the regime to the extent that they had been willing to seek refuge in other countries, but if they are half-true, they show that, far from enlarging the lives of those resettled or villagised, the camps and villages managed to kill a proportion.

An Ethiopian farmer originally from the north of the country but resettled by military force to the south, uttered a typical complaint: 'This is why we are starving. One day we are told to farm for the militias and on another day for the regional Peasant Association chairman, and on the other day or week (until finished) we plough for the Woreda Peasant Association representative, etc., etc. And on it goes.'

The food so produced did well enough to support party cadres, and was often shipped away, so for the individual displaced farmer in Mengistu Haile Mariam's tyrannical Ethiopia, the reality was that while he worked for others, 'our [own] crops will be infested with weeds, and sometimes our teff will be reduced because it was not cut and harvested and collected when it was ready'. In the midst of food production, the resettled farmers and family members they had with them began to starve and to depend on foreign aid for survival.

The conditions of labour on the collective land controlled by the Peasant Associations and militia were severe. 'If a woman gave birth, they wouldn't give her a ration until she started working again,' an Ethiopian refugee later said. 'If you were sick one day,' said another, 'and didn't get a paper to excuse you from work, the militia was sent to beat you.'

In western Ethiopia near Goba, the villagisation program was implemented simultaneously with government military sweeps that displaced people, in many cases from relatively flat, fertile lands, which the government then turned into state farms.

As part of villagisation, every farmer's equipment was confiscated by the cadres, which caused many who were villagised in Harar province in the east to cross into Somalia. All animals belonged ultimately to the Peasant Association. 'All our animals are registered, even chickens. They register crops, too: the only thing they didn't register was our clothes. They took all our property, our livestock and our crops.'

The Anuak, a more Central African-looking people from the south, were themselves forcibly villagised. They told stories of houses being pulled down in old villages while women inside were giving birth. A number of Anuak people who fled to the Sudan, declared when interviewed by Cultural Survival, an American non-profit human rights group, that they had been hungry before villagisation, but now they starved as they cut trees and slashed grass. Anuak were pushed off their land to make room for resettlement and this disrupted their normal food supply, and in any case the militia confiscated the Anuak gardens prior to their being villagised. As in Ireland with the Indian maize, the Anuak found that once their normal harvest had been shipped away by truck they had to live on unfamiliar wheat. 'Wheat is strange to Anuak; we cannot pound it. Fishing was prohibited in the river. Those who fished risked being beaten.'

The Anuak lost their cattle because they were no longer allowed them. The government also curbed hunting. One of those interviewed escaped to the Sudan in order to avoid being arrested on suspicion of hunting. The Anuak of course had begun to flee in reaction to villagisation much earlier than the famine, though the famine accentuated their movements.

When Anuak men got married they gave their wife a large bead, valued at $1.50, and two cows. The government began to forbid this practice and to collect the beads by force. Those who refused to hand them over were beaten. Clothing was standardised by the Derg and Anuak women were required to cover their breasts.

There was also conflict between Anuak and Tigrayans when they were villagised together as a means of enhancing their nationalism. 'Our people don't like these highlanders and clash with them . . . They rob the mangoes planted by the area people . . . first they settled the highland people into the burial grounds of our ancestors, then they took the land of our ancestors away from us and moved us into the grave-yard also,' remarked one Anuak.

Anuak and Tigrayans were sometimes forced into the same huts and coerced marriages took place between them. The Gambella People's Liberation Movement arose in the Anuaks' ancestral area to attempt to protect their people and undermine the designs of government. But the movement attacked a resettlement camp and one of the buildings burned was a clinic. This brought a terrible vengeance down on the Anuak in the settlement and villagisation areas. The government armed the resettled people from Wollo to kill the Anuak, and massacre was added to the misery of the newly villagised.

The number of Ethiopian refugees created by politics, famine, resettlement and villagisation between 1975 and 1980 was breathtaking. Nearly 800,000 fled to Somalia, 50,000 to Djibouti, 750,000 from the north-western regions of Tigray and Gondar, and from Wollega and Illubabor in the south.

At the end of February 1985, the *belg* rains came and peasants saw hope and resisted settlement all the more, and so stronger and stronger methods had to be used to move them. Escapees from the holding camps were now executed by firing squads, and so too were recaptured escapees from Asosa and Gambella. By the beginning of 1986, 600,000 people had been resettled, a number that fell well beneath Mengistu's hoped-for quota of 1.5 million.

Between resettlement and villagisation, six million people were ultimately forced to be where they did not choose to be, to farm unproductively, to labour for Peasant Associations in which they lacked faith, and to contribute hundreds of thousands to the some two million excess deaths of Mengistu's famine.

13

Resistance

THE MATTER OF the 'rural outrages' of the Irish peasantry as a form of resistance to their fate has already been dealt with in part. Ireland's ingratitude remained puzzling to the British government, indicating to it an innate turbulence in the Irish. In fact, the so-called rural outrages were based on the reality that, in the name of political economy, throughout the period of the famine, grain and other produce, including livestock, were exported out of Ireland. Any attack on the integrity of these exports was not only a violation of God's commands against theft but an interference with the free market. Charles Trevelyan and others seem to have been surprised when the sight of British troops guarding the shipping of the harvest along country roads, or by way of the canal system of Ireland, generated rage among the Irish people, and the crime of stealing 'Trevelyan's corn'.

In the needy years of 1845–6, a compact region of

neighbouring counties – Limerick, Clare, Tipperary, Roscommon, Longford and Leitrim – accounted for 60 per cent of the crimes. The shooting of Major Mahon was considered a most extreme form of rural outrage. But there were sufficient lesser attacks on landlords, such as houghing cattle – that is, severing tendons in their legs – breaking down landlords' doors, rick-burning, and generally threatening them, that there was talk of passing in the Commons new coercion laws aimed at suppressing crimes of discontent. The taking of or administering unlawful oaths as a matter of forming secret societies, and societies of men to raise wages, were both considered a form of Ribbonism.

There was a middle- and upper-class revolt as well. In both the Irish and the Bengali famines, a belief that food was being exported from the stricken areas had a powerful influence on people. In Ireland, a group named the Young Irelanders split off from Daniel O'Connell's Repeal Party, which wanted Ireland to separate from England and repeal the Act of Union between Ireland and England, but by peaceful persuasion. Young Ireland, on the other hand, proposed an armed uprising and stopping by force the export of any of the harvest from Ireland.

The leader of Young Ireland was William Smith O'Brien, a middle-aged Irish landlord and member of Parliament, who had been uncorrupted by offers of cabinet positions from the major Westminster parties. William Smith O'Brien had become aware at the beginning of 1846, in the late winter, that in Clare, which was his home county, as in Cork, Waterford and Kilkenny, coroners' courts were returning verdicts of death by starvation on an increasing number of corpses. He informed the House of Commons on 17 April 1846. Certainly, said Smith O'Brien, forestalling criticism of himself as a landlord, call on the resident landlords of Ireland to give help to the poor. But why should absentee landlords (such as Lord Palmerston), living in part abroad, be allowed to evade paying the rates for local relief? Smith O'Brien also warned – as would prove to be the case – that the workhouses were not adequate or appropriate to deal with the disaster that was developing. He knew well that there would be further suffering throughout the summer of 1846 while people waited for the new potato harvest.

It was a brave speech by a man who commuted between his property in County Clare and the House of Commons regularly, and who thus knew the situation on the ground. But whatever such Irishmen said was treated as suspect by those who had never seen Ireland at all, or at least had not seen it in the present crisis. Convinced now that he must take more radical action, he went on strike from committee duty, and so was treated to the rare honour of being imprisoned in small rooms between the House of Commons and the House of Lords.

O'Brien came to the conclusion that Ireland's woes could be remedied only by an uprising of the people, who had been provoked by the scandal of the shipping-off of the harvest. His lieutenant, Thomas Francis Meagher, son of the first Catholic mayor of Waterford in centuries, was a young, dandified orator of great presence, handsomeness and powers of rhetoric. He possessed, probably like William Smith O'Brien, a rather romantic idea of rebellion. Young Ireland saw rebellion as a spontaneous thing, a matter more of the sword than of the carbine. 'Abhor the sword – stigmatise the sword?' he challenged his contemporaries in Dublin.

'No, my Lord, for at its blow a giant nation started from the waters of the Atlantic and by its redeeming magic, and in the quivering of its crimson light, the crippled colony sprang into the attitude of a proud Republic [the United States, that is] – prosperous, limitless and invincible.'

One of Meagher's persistent lines concerned the export from Ireland of food its land had produced. In 1847, at a meeting of the Young Irelanders at the Rotunda in Dublin, the young Meagher lifted a fistful of papers. This was, he said, a statement of Irish exports from 1 August 1846 to January 1847. From the statements, he promised, people would perceive 'that England seizes on our food while death seizes on our people'. He then gave a summary of the number of barrels of pork, flitches of bacon, firkins of butter, hogsheads of ham, barrels of oats and so on, which were being exported. And, as one Young Irelander put it, the potato was destroyed while fields quivered with golden grain. 'It was not for you. To your lips it was forbidden fruit.'

Indeed, the export would have made a difference to the starving Irish if even some of it had been released as emergency rations to the populace, but that would have outraged the principles of free trade. In England, however, not everyone subscribed to those principles, and voices were raised against Irish exports, notably that of Sir George Poulet Scrope, an eminent political economist and passionate opponent of Malthus.

John Mitchel, the Presbyterian Unitarian minister's son, and Thomas Meagher both declared that food exports from Ireland hugely exceeded imports, but there is a later counterclaim by some historians that, by 1847, the opposite was true. Since the British government did not keep accurate aggregate figures of the trade between Ireland and Britain, the question might never be settled. But, as well as of grain, there was also a massive export of other foodstuffs from Ireland, as Meagher had pointed out. A table for one day, 20 December 1846, shows seven ships arriving in Liverpool containing 800 pigs and 139 sheep, along with hundreds of bags of wheat and oatmeal, eggs, lard and other foodstuffs. Ships full of Irish famine refugees tied up beside vessels laden with provender from Ireland. The *New York Herald* of 5 July 1847 said that arrivals of wheat in their port from Ireland had been 'very considerable'.

In 1848, Meagher went to France, where Alphonse de Lamartine, a poet, had been elected president after a bloodless coup in which soldiers made common cause with the workers. The Young Irelanders hoped for a similar revolution in Ireland – spontaneous, driven by moral force and the obviousness of the justice of their arguments. But they would find out that the Crown had no intention of being overturned by such means.

The signs for Young Ireland were, at first, promising. In the midst of famine, during the spring and early summer of 1848, Meagher was able to hold huge, seditious meetings on top of such sites as the mountain of Slievenamon in Tipperary. With people screaming for justice, many of them middle-class townspeople, Young Ireland saw revolution within grasp. But when the government unexpectedly issued warrants for the arrest of the Young Irelanders, they escaped from Dublin with Smith O'Brien, the parliamentarian and baronet's son, leading them. As they moved through Kilkenny and then the Tipperary collieries, they gathered thousands to hear them speak, but every evening the local priest would visit these men and women engorged with rage and avowedly willing to rise, and talk them out of it, under the threat of being denied the sacraments. In every area the Young Irelanders visited it was the same, but at last 200 brave souls joined them.

At Ballingarry, Tipperary, the Young Irelanders attempted to ambush a party of police. After an initial assault by Smith O'Brien's party, the police ran up a laneway and entered the two-storey house of a woman known to history as Widow McCormack. The Young Irelanders besieged the police, who were so ambiguous in their nationalism that many of them stuck out their hands from windows to shake hands with Smith O'Brien, whom they respected. After many sallies by the rebels, priests arrived and anointed those of the besiegers who had fallen. In the end, the Young Irelanders had to take to the countryside.

The rising was written off by the press as the 'Battle of Widow McCormack's Cabbage Patch'. Smith O'Brien, Meagher and two others were found guilty of treason, and by special legislation were sent to Van Diemen's Land. Mitchel had already been transported for fourteen years to Bermuda, but then transferred to Van Diemen's Land. Others were transported for sedition or escaped to America.

From Van Diemen's Land, a number of them escaped with the help of supporters. Tammany Hall, the Democrat machine in New York, even sent an agent to help rescue Mitchel. Meagher and Mitchel became notable Americans who never ceased to put the famine at the heart of their oratory.

Meagher would become a Union general and die while he was acting governor of Montana; Mitchel became a leading Confederate newspaper editor. Smith O'Brien was pardoned in 1854 and returned to Ireland in 1856, where he became a beloved deliverer of occasional long letters published to the Irish people. The price he had paid over an ill-advised cause had earned him the respect of all Irish nationalists.

In the regions of Bengal, commissioners and district officers reported hunger marches being organised by communists in late December 1942. There were countless crimes against property, and looting of paddy from warehouses, including those containing supplies for feeding the army. But in late 1943–4, there was an increasing lack of protest as people became hungrier and more diseased. Revolution is not the metier of the starving.

The famine had further political impact. As its news spread across India in 1944, and as the Congress leaders emerged from prison, the famine fortified their criticism of British policy in India. The complacency of Viceroy Linlithgow was, of course, condemned. So was the refusal of the British government to permit more food imports into India through the reallocation of shipping. Because Archibald Wavell had become the new viceroy at the last stage of the famine, his more kindly interventions were not weighed as heavily as Britain's general failures.

At a local level when the famine eased, Bengali women joined men in political demonstrations based on the Tebhaga movement, which would reach its height in 1946–7. Tebhaga protesters, who consisted of the families of sharecroppers, *bargadars* – people who had not suffered the extremes of famine the landless labourers and their families had, but had experienced want sufficiently now to try to amend their situation – demanded two-thirds of their families' produce for themselves, leaving one-third for the landlord, instead of the established arrangement of a fifty-fifty split. The argument of the *bargardars* was that the landlord made the least contribution to farm improvements and labour.

What had happened up to this point, too, was that the tenants were traditionally required to stack the harvest at the owner's property, and share with him the straw and other by-products. The tenants now refused to observe this tradition. They argued that the harvest should be stacked at the tenants' compounds, where land agents would not rig the figures to enlarge the landowner's portion of the crop share, and where the landlord would not get any share from the by-products.

The landholders refused to accept the terms, called in the police and had many of the Tebhaga activists put in gaol. But the movement made such progress in some regions that the peasants declared their zone as Tebhaga *elaka*, liberated areas, and Tebhaga committees were set up to govern local areas.

The famine – along with traditional grievances against landlords – was a motivator of the movement. Tebhaga had originally been organised by Kisan Sabha, the peasant wing of the Communist Party, with which the Muslim League had a sympathetic relationship, but was followed, too, by many people whose chief ideology was simple justice. Such was their thirst for equity and their sense of grievance that the movement became an uprising, and angry torchings of the houses of the opulent caused some landlords to flee their land. The Tebhaga movement hit nineteen districts of Bengal but was intensely felt in coastal areas such as southern Parganas and Khulna, and as far inland as the river provinces to the west of Assam in the north, and Rangpur and Jalpaiguri. That is, it occurred in areas both in the east and the west, and among Muslims and Hindus.

Though the famine might have been one of the spurs of the movement, it continued after Indian independence. A bill was introduced into the Indian Legislative Assembly in early 1947 to satisfy some of the sharecroppers' demands.

Ireland's Parliament had been abolished in 1800, after the uprising of the United Irishmen. This was a continual cause of complaint from Irish nationalists and a perceived factor in the severity of the famine: the Irish complained that, had they had their own parliament and not been ruled from Westminster, the famine's impact would have been less severe. Their lawmakers would have convened in Dublin and been capable of bringing to their parliament reports of the famine, which they had observed firsthand in their own constituencies. These personal observations were something neither the British cabinet nor Trevelyan chose to make.

In the same way, Eritrea had had its own parliament until Emperor Haile Selassie, attempting to draw the loyalty of the province exclusively to himself, abolished it in 1961. The Eritreans saw themselves as a separate people, and the Eritrean rebellion began immediately after the abolition, though at first, like the planning of the United Irish uprising of 1798, it was the preserve of intellectuals and elites. The Eritreans resented the loss of their own legislature not least because, during the less-than-kindly fifty-year Italian occupation of their country, and then afterwards, they prided themselves on adopting Western technology. They argued that under their own government, with its emphasis on education, their province was far more sophisticated and well-supplied with schools and clinics, and their citizens so much more accustomed to independent thought, that now the emperor was punishing them for all that by abolishing their progressive parliament. In the early 1970s, they would also be outraged by the emperor's chosen ignorance regarding the famine, and by the general backwardness of his government, which let it happen.

In 1961, a long, punitive thirty-year occupation of the Eritrean capital, Asmara, by the Ethiopian army began. First the emperor and then Mengistu counted the crushing of the Eritrean rebels a national priority, and spent money on the conflict that would have been better devoted to feeding their starving. The rebellion that overthrew the emperor had, at first, created hope of peace in Eritrea, but within the Derg, as we have seen, there was a lethal tussle which the hawks, led by Mengistu, won. The military budget in 1984, just as the famine reached its height, consumed 60 per cent of national income, and Mengistu's Ethiopian army was 300,000 strong.

After the fall of the emperor and an early taste of an increasingly intransigent Derg, seven Tigrayan university students in Addis Ababa formed the Tigrayan People's Liberation Front.

It was the behaviour of the Ethiopian army in Tigray that gave overall impetus to the rebel movement. In 1975, the Eritrean People's Liberation Front and the Tigrayan People's Liberation Front formed an alliance, even though they had different aims – the Eritreans seeking independence, the TPLF fighting for an Ethiopia in which they would be represented and treated with justice and equity. In response to the brutality of cadres and the army, the Oromo Liberation Front was also founded and operated in the south-east in the area of Harar, and then, in the 1980s, in Wollega province in the west as well. To add to the mix, in the east an Afar Liberation Front was founded, in answer to the Derg's attempts to make the Afar into collective villagers. Wherever these rebel groups operated, Mengistu denied food relief – in any case, the first food priority was the army. Rightly, wrongly or unknowingly, Western aid agencies supplied the Ethiopian army for their battles against insurgents.

By the time the famine of the 1980s began, the Eritrean and the Tigrayan rebels were more than guerrilla groups. They were fully equipped conventional armies, each lacking only an air force. Though helped by some outside parties, by the Saudis, Palestinians and even, at one stage, the Israelis, their main source of *matériel* was weapons and ammunition captured from the Ethiopian army. During the war, I visited the Eritrean rebels in the highlands twice: once to write an essay for the *New York Times* magazine, then to make a documentary for London Weekend Television. I saw a range of weapons, from T-55 tanks to 88mm heavy artillery and the racks of rockets known as Stalin's Organs, all with Russian instructions attached in Cyrillic script, and all formerly

Mengistu's arms. The rebels wore camouflage fatigues captured from Ethiopian depots and troops. All these had been paid for by Ethiopia, even at the famine's peak, and surrendered up in turn by an Ethiopian army that proved itself inadequate for the task Mengistu set it.

Dawit Wolde Giorgis and other authors, such as the political scientist Roy Pateman, give a picture of how badly the Eritreans were treated by the Ethiopian army and thus how its actions swelled the ranks of the rebels. Before being made head of the RRC, Giorgis had served as governor of Eritrea under the Derg from 1979–83. He found himself in command of a country of ruined schools and bridges. The town of Decamere, south of Asmara, had once been called 'the second Rome' for its restaurants and coffee shops, but was now a roofless collection of hovels. Eritrea was a countryside empty of young men, since they had all been arrested, driven by government extremism into hiding, or into the ranks of the rebels. According to his account, as people came to trust Giorgis a little in Asmara – a fair imitation of an Italian town itself, with its opera house and wide boulevards – Christian women dressed in long *shemmas*, their hair braided and tattooed Coptic crosses on their foreheads, crowded round him asking where their husbands were and whether they had been shot by the Ethiopian army. Giorgis found that many of the missing people had been imprisoned outside Asmara, at the site of a trade fair held by the emperor in 1967. The Expo '67 site was not a conventional prison: behind its high-wire walls torture was the accustomed mode, and Eritrean males, shot through the back of the neck in true Lubyanka style for their supposed and sometimes real association with the rebels, were buried in the grounds among eucalyptus trees. Giorgis says that he broke the news to 270 women that their menfolk were dead, and he heard their traditional ululating cry, something like keening, which they produced in different keys for births, weddings and deaths. He was surprised that many of them thanked him because they were able now to wear their widows' weeds and devote themselves to mourning.

Giorgis decided to offer an amnesty for rebels to turn themselves in. But Mengistu and the Derg clamped down on such policies. Even in the midst of famine and the hungry years that followed the famine, Mengistu would not tolerate such appeasements and their resultant freeing of funds to deal with the famine. While Giorgis argued that there was no military solution, and that to seek one would be to add to the hunger of both Eritreans and Ethiopians, frontally taking on the rebels remained the Derg's and Mengistu's military policy.

In the port of Massawa down on the Red Sea, a harbour very important to Ethiopian interests – without such ports, Ethiopia would become landlocked – Giorgis organised a peace festival for 1982. His enemies in the Derg declared that this was 'Eritreanism', a further sop to Eritrean feeling. Mengistu himself flew into Asmara for talks with Giorgis, who claims to have told him the Eritrean conflict required tolerance and patience. The way to defeat the EPLF, said Giorgis, was by way of an economic and social campaign, and by a more peaceable demeanour on the part of the Ethiopian military. Mengistu could not accept anything like this, and before the famine struck Giorgis lost his governorship and came home to take over the RRC.

Major offensives were launched into Tigray and its

borderlands between 1980 and 1985, and there were three even larger offensives in Eritrea to go with the early ones. During the sixth offensive against Tigray, in August 1980, the army destroyed grain stores, enforced the collection of taxes and contributions, and caused 80,000 farmers to abandon their land. The seventh offensive began in February 1983 and was aimed at Shire in western Tigray, an area that normally produced a bounty of grain. More than 100,000 residents and 375,000 migrant labourers, who had arrived to help with the harvest, were forced to flee. Many of these would ultimately arrive in the Korem famine shelter to the east, and the Ibenat shelter towards Gondar. Their appearance put under stress the resources of all agencies then in the field.

When the famine was in its early phase, recruiting from millions of Ethiopian peasants and the forced conscription of boys in high school and the resettlement areas continued apace, as Mengistu and his Russian military advisers prepared for a great assault, and a final solution to the Eritrean situation.

The Red Star campaign of 1985 involved a heavy bill paid to President Brezhnev's USSR for sophisticated military equipment, all at a time when the relief agencies of the West were supplying Ethiopia with emergency food. Mengistu raised 120,000 Ethiopian soldiers to crush Eritrea. It is hard to watch film of the Addis Ababa parades of these uniformed men and boys: the flash of hard light off their massed bayonets; the thunder of their stamping military boots, so different from the rubber sandals Eritrean infantry men and women wore. For one knows that these Ethiopians, fed by relief agencies working to a greater or lesser extent under a blind-eye policy, were on their way to a military catastrophe, and that all the equipment in evidence represents an utter waste.

For this supposedly final campaign, it was Mengistu himself who planned the strategy and deployment of his forces. When, on the so-called Nakfa front (named after a highland Eritrean town), the rebels, while giving ground, also inflicted massive casualties, Mengistu assassinated a number of generals.

Nonetheless, there had been early and considerable advances for the Ethiopian army, though some of them were partly based on the pliability of the rebel command and of its leader, Issayas Afeworki. The highlands that ran throughout the middle of Eritrea were the natural habitat for the rebel army, who did not mind retreating to survive. The rebels were well-organised and robust in morale. Every night, fleeing through mountain passes, their fellow Eritreans joined them, telling horror stories about the massacres committed by the advancing Ethiopian troops.

The overwhelming Ethiopian forces pushed them back to Nakfa, which became the town on whose capture Mengistu staked the entire Red Star campaign. Indeed, its fall would have been a crisis for the rebels. By the time Nakfa was fully besieged, there were nearly 200,000 Ethiopian troops surrounding it, with 15–17,000 Eritreans as its garrison. They lived in the ruins of the bombed town, whose jacaranda trees were the only surviving signs of normality along the ruined avenues. Ethiopian bombers were overhead continually, and the damage they did not do was concluded by the artillery. But one of the reasons Nakfa did not fall was that Mengistu, self-appointed chief of staff, had ordered his front-line troops to halt their advance so that the Third Infantry Division, his former unit, would have the honour of taking the town. The honour would never be achieved. By the time the Third Infantry Division arrived, it was struck by Eritrean forces equipped with captured weapons they understood better how to use than had the Ethiopian conscripts. Soviet military advisers accompanying the Ethiopian army had counselled the methods used by Marshall Zhukov and others in the Red Army on the Eastern Front in 1944 and 1945 – using overwhelming force in frontal attacks. None of this worked against the mobile and superbly trained Eritrean rebel army, who were skilled in flanking movements and in ambush.

In a counter-attack, the Eritrean rebels routed the Third Division and killed its commander. They drove the Ethiopian army back a mile, killing 11,000 soldiers, inflicting thousands more casualties and capturing great numbers. While Nakfa was simply another town to the Ethiopian soldiers, it was a symbol of survival to the Eritreans, and now trench-lines, deep bunkers and strong points were built by both armies across the highlands. After three weeks of useless campaigning, Mengistu returned to Addis, which his troops had left – cheering from the backs of trucks, saluting from the turrets of Russian tanks – only a month before. The Eritrean success was the most complete act of defiance yet offered to an Ethiopian government.

No one in Addis or in the Derg mentioned the defeat. A deputy minister of information named Bealu Girma wrote a *roman à clef* about the campaign, entitled *Oramai*. When published it sold quickly but was soon suppressed, and two months after its publication Girma disappeared. For Mengistu and the Derg, Nakfa was a defeat that dared not speak its name, as was the famine, now just petering out for the mass of the peasantry and the resettled into mere continuing seasons of chronic hunger.

Two years later, after all that useless expenditure, Nakfa was still in rebel hands. I spent the better part of a week there, sheltering with an Eritrean guide among bureaucrats and soldiers in an eight-foot-deep bunker with an L-shaped entrance. The city remained under siege, but the Eritreans had driven back the Ethiopians to right and left, and both sides were holding trenchlines. The Eritreans also operated in mobile groups beyond the Ethiopian lines, destroying columns of supply trucks and, at one stage, mounting a raid on the Ethiopian warplanes parked at Asmara Airport. Thanks to Mengistu, the rebels were still in possession of their highlands and were defending them with what is known in the arms trade as 'sophisticated weaponry', for which Mengistu had paid his not-so-pretty penny.

It was a triumph of bluster and good luck that Mengistu was able to receive so much famine aid while wasting so much substance on an unnecessary war.

In Mengistu's last days, when the famine had ended and while subsistence farmers were still chronically hungry, he did not cease pursuing his profligate military policy, sending off his Antonov bombers and helicopter gunships to attack cities that had fallen into the hands of the rebels.

Farmers could not plant or harvest for fear of attack from above, and normal daytime trade could not take place. In this way, the dictator hoped to impose a new famine on the rebel areas, and without the operations of the Eritreans' and Tigrayans' aid agencies – the Eritrean Relief Association (ERA) and the Relief Society of Tigray (REST) – might have succeeded.

Makale, the capital of Tigray province, now belonging to the rebels, would be twice bombed at massive cost, and Massawa, the port on the Eritrean Red Sea coast, was pulverised by Mengistu's bombers. In 1993, at the time of the Eritrean referendum of separation from Ethiopia, I saw Eritrean survivors of Massawa's bombing still living in ruins. In a small ticket office on the Massawa railway station, amidst burnt-out freight trucks and bomb craters, I met a man in his twenties with his young wife and three children. Both the man's arms had been blown off in one of the bombing raids and he wore a black plastic prosthesis on both. The raids of 1991 also burned 25,000 tonnes of food aid and destroyed the port installations. Near the war's end, an Eritrean woman cried, 'Whenever Mengistu realises he is defeated, he kills people with airplanes.' Mengistu used napalm, phosphorus and cluster bombs against Hawzen in Tigray, killing 1800 people. In his last days, he managed to replace his losses of equipment in a deal with Israel over the black-skinned Falasha Ethiopian Jews, who claimed to be descended from King Solomon and the Queen of Sheba and who numbered 15,000. In the Israelis' concern for the Falashas, and their desire to bring them safely to Israel, they supplied Mengistu with cluster bombs and other equipment, and in return the

Falashas arrived in Israel on relays of planes. Cluster bombs from a number of sources had been commonly used in the war, and would explode in mid-air and disperse over a wide area other smaller bombs, from which the ERA trucks hid by day. They had a ferocious impact not only upon the bodies of those hit but upon the minds of survivors. These bombs were among those dropped on the port of Massawa once the rebels had captured it, in a pounding aimed to prevent the port's use for aid shipments. No great fuss or complaint, on the scale of the Eritreans' and Tigrayans' earlier supposed attacks on convoys, was made about this destruction.

Up to the very eve of his fall, Mengistu depicted his enemies as dangerous Arabist fronts, even though the majority of both the Eritrean and Tigrayan rebels were Coptic Christians. The rebels were pawns of other Arab states! he cried, and their success would turn the Red Sea into an utterly Arab lake! This was a rhetorical ploy with which he and his ministers abroad had considerable success.

Mengistu's punishment was coming. The Eritreans had made a great military advance in 1988, when the EPLA took all but a handful of urban centres and captured or killed 18,000 hapless young Ethiopian troops. It was in that context that a massacre of Eritreans at the town of She'eb to the north-west of Massawa occurred, carried out by the Ethiopian army, and thus in part by Ethiopian conscripts previously recruited from high schools and the streets of cities and villages. The She'eb massacre in 1988 motivated the EPLF even more, for some of the victims had been crushed to death by tanks. This was not an isolated incident, however. Reprisal massacres had been common in Eritrea since the mid 1970s.

Massacres occurred in Tigray and the Ogaden as well. But those in Tigray and Eritrea, together with a further threat of famine in 1986–7, fuelled the inevitability of Mengistu's fall from power.

The final Eritrean rebel encirclement of Asmara occurred when the port city of Massawa fell to the rebels in February 1990. According to a Human Rights Watch report of 1991, a number of Eritrean hostages were used as human shields by Mengistu's forces, in an attempt to hold onto the port. As Asmara itself fell to the Eritreans in 1991, and as the Tigrayan tanks advanced on the city of Addis Ababa, Mengistu fled and caught a plane into exile in Zimbabwe. His Ethiopian trial for war crimes would begin in 1994 and at last find him guilty, *in absentia*, in 2006.

With the end of the conflict, the infield operations of those remarkable agencies, ERA and REST, were scaled down. As for the results of the famine and the rebellions, the way the new Eritrean and Ethiopian governments, led by former schoolmates Issayas Afeworki and Meles Zenawi, came to betray the goodwill of the people who had brought them to power is the subject for another book.

14

Relief: Ireland

IN IRELAND IN November 1845, a Relief Commission was created to administer the sale of the Indian maize Peel had ordered from the United States. Peel genuinely thought this supply of maize would see the Irish through the summer, and thus that he had dealt with the crisis, for no one expected the blight to come back.

The Indian maize was to be distributed to central depots that would be established in various parts of Ireland under the direction of the officers of the army commissariat, with sub-depots under the charge of the constabulary and coast-guard. When the supplies in the local market were deficient, meal was sold from these depots at reasonable prices to local relief committees for re-sale to the public. The officers of the central depots were to receive and collate reports from the local relief committees, which were made up of members of the local gentry, Church of Ireland ministers, lawyers and other worthies. The overall Relief Commission contained such figures as Thomas Redington, the undersecretary of the Irish Executive, Sir Randolph Routh of the army commissariat and Colonel Harry Jones of the Board of Works.

They began to wonder where to turn to for relief funds. They saw there would be a need for further government intervention above the Indian maize Peel had bought. But they knew it was against the principles of government and of political economy for Westminster to spend money directly on feeding the Irish.

By January 1846 the first of the Indian corn from North America, the same that in the southern United States produced the food called hominy, began to reach Irish ports, Cork first of all. All up, the shipments were estimated as sufficient to feed 1 million people for forty days. But it would still take some months of organisation before the first corn was distributed, stored and ready for sale.

Unlike the corn grown in Ireland, the Indian corn was so hard to crack that it should rightly have been chopped in steel mills, but there were no such mills in Ireland. It was very difficult to cook and, if not properly done, could cause bowel disorders. Sir Randolph Routh, the old quartermaster appointed as the chairman of the relief commissioners, issued a pamphlet on how the Indian maize should be prepared by the officers at the depots. It had to be kept in kilns for eight hours, dried for forty-eight hours, ground, allowed to stand for seventy hours and then left for another twenty-four before it was placed in sacks. This difficulty of its preparation and the inappropriateness of the food to the necessity derived from a belief that would be evident in the Bengal famine as well: relief food must be made troublesome and unsavoury to ensure that people did not lightly have recourse to it. It was tested with the inmates of some of the workhouses, who refused to touch it. But everyone knew that the hungry of Ireland would need to sooner or later.

Come 15 May, the date assigned for the first sale of meal, many women queued up outside the warehouses to buy their pound of Indian meal, their pennies – acquired by labour or by selling clothes or furniture or the family pig – in hand. The maize was sold to the Irish at cost price at first, and later for a little more than that. Some relief committees bought up supplies for unofficial distribution to those who could not afford it, even at its moderate price.

The Irish had various names for the corn – *min dèirce*, beggar's meal, Indian buck, or, as previously described, 'Peel's brimstone'. The first to have recourse to it were the people of the extreme west and south-west of the country. They needed something to eat, but the reality was that, though the maize might relieve hunger, it was of little nutritional value. One commentator declared that the distribution of raw meal to starving, weak and homeless beggars was as useful as giving them river sand.

Yet, despite all the suspicion of 'yellow male', and the difficulty in preparing it, the maize, minimal as it was in quantity, probably saved a number of lives in that grim time and thereafter.

In London, Trevelyan, execrated in history for being a man of ideology, was pragmatic to the extent that in December 1845 he permitted a scheme of public works to be put in place, run and supervised by the Irish Board of Works. The public works were scheduled to begin in March 1846. Local relief committees were to apply for funds to run works in their areas, which would give employment to the hungry. The British Treasury would grant 50 per cent of the cost of road improvements and other public works, the rest having to come from local grand juries – that is, the local gentry and better-off tenants who were eligible to sit on such juries. In Ireland the grand juries did more than sit at trials – they were also involved in road repair, fever hospitals and other civil institutions, and during the famine their members would make up the relief committees and the Boards of Guardians.

Trevelyan regretted the generosity of his public works scheme almost as soon as it was put in place. Many of the projects were designed to improve facilities around a particular landlord's property. Others were merely make-work projects. Local relief committees were accused of issuing tickets of employment in 'an irregular manner'. As well as that, a system of measuring how much work a person did in the day had not been put in place. And then there were not enough surveyors and other qualified people to supervise the work. Famine roads, which begin nowhere and lead nowhere, are often seen as a symbol of the futility and indignity of the relief works, but they were also a windfall to corrupt supervisors, who could create fictitious workers and pocket their wages.

The fact that in the summer of 1846 there had been far fewer Irishmen turning up in England to work on the English harvest was taken as a sign by Trevelyan that the Irish were finding it too easy to earn money on the scheme. He was also concerned that it was taking men away from working on the Irish harvest. He did not take account of the fact that the smaller number of Irishmen coming to Britain might have been based on physical weakness brought on by the last winter of want, and by the necessity of getting money immediately.

After the works had lasted through the summer, the further failure of the potatoes made it necessary to continue them. Over the winter of 1846–7, Trevelyan urged that the pay on the works be dropped. That winter would be one of northern Europe's worst, and in it the bare-footed went to labour. Two million people were dependent on this relief by now, either directly or indirectly. Some dropped dead while crushing stone, many of them with rocks or shovels in hand. The public works became a venue of death, often from relapsing fever. The Irish generally spent all their winters indoors and were not used to exposing themselves for hour upon hour, day upon day, to the ferocious Atlantic-brewed weather of the Irish outdoors.

The scheme was also imperfect in that it rewarded those who laboured hardest, and so discriminated against the weak. Many families nonetheless knew that this work was their only chance in that bitter winter, which accounted for the fact that the labourers referred to what they built as 'male [meal] roads' or 'stirabout [porridge] drains'. Men, women and children presented themselves in bleak landscapes for a daily wage of ninepence or tenpence, deliberately set low to stop the Irish from exploiting it. Due to a lack of small coin and of pay clerks, the handing out of the weekly wages would often not end until midnight on Saturday, a further test of the endurance of labourers.

Captain Henry O'Brien, a retired artilleryman who was an official of the Board of Works in East Clare, wrote to Trevelyan on the day after Christmas 1847, worried about all the reported corruption and inefficiency on the works, but aware that, for all their faults, they were necessary for the survival of many people. He declared, 'The labourers worked for their wages, but seeing clearly that what they are doing on the public roads is of no clear value, their heart, they say, is not in it. Naturally quick in feeling and acute in intellect, they have no lively interest in the completion of a task which, though it keeps them from starvation, is manifestly unproductive.' He told Trevelyan that he took pains to ensure that only the destitute were employed on the roads, and possibly needed to assure Trevelyan that this was so as a means of proving that he was not a soft-hearted exaggerator.

An engineer employed on the works described 'the poor enfeebled labourer' lying on the side of the bog he has been employed to drain, or by the road debris, 'giving his dying blessing to the bestowers of tardy relief'. Some parliamentarians' idea for legislation to employ Irish labour on railway construction was voted down in part because it would benefit certain landowners over others. It became politically impossible, too, for the prime minister to implement a scheme to distribute £50,000 worth of seed to tenants.

In February 1847, it was announced in the House of Commons that 15,000 people were dying each day in Ireland. Nonetheless, subsequently, because of corruption and its administrative flaws, the public works scheme was abandoned, at Trevelyan's suggestion, and there was a gradual dismissal of the people labouring on it. In March 1847, 734,000 people were employed on the scheme – approximately one in every three adult males. The Treasury imposed a 20 per cent reduction on 20 March 1847, to be followed by further, gradual reductions. By June, all works projects had ceased. Families who had depended on them waited for the next manifestation of public mercy.

Now a new system had to be established to prevent people who had previously been working on the roads from stampeding the workhouses of Ireland. The Poor Law system that had been operating in England had provided the impoverished with access to a workhouse, built to be forbidding in appearance, where they were fed in return for labour deliberately designed to be unattractive. Workhouse labour included bone-crushing to make fertiliser, sack-making, picking oakum to provide rope, corn-milling.

In 1838, a Poor Law was passed for Ireland, enabling the setting-up of workhouses under the care of Boards of Guardians. Each district where there was a workhouse was called a Poor Law Union. The Poor Law Unions of Ireland were based on the administrative units known as baronies. Eighty-two workhouses were built. The system was to be paid for by a tax known as the poor rate, levied on landowners and tenants. Because not all tenants could afford it, the poor rate was restricted to those who owned or leased land worth £4 or more per year.

A special problem faced the authorities when it came to the Irish workhouses. In England they were designed to be so intimidating, so associated with tedious and hard labour, that only those genuinely desperate would go anywhere near them. A Poor Law commissioner, a member of the overall management commission for the entire system, observed that in Ireland, 'The standard of their mode of living is unhappily so low that the establishment of one still lower is difficult.'

Yet the Irish abhorred and detested these institutions. And even as the famine progressed, anyone who could avoided the workhouse. Many had decided that whatever misfortune befell them, they would never go within its shadow, never pass through its neo-gothic standardised gatehouse. 'O King of Glory', went an Irish prayer:

Hear and answer us,
From bondage save us, and come to our aid,
And send us bread, as we cry in misery,
And may the workhouse be in ashes laid.

It was just as well these sentiments existed, since each workhouse serviced a region of tens of thousands and, in the most extreme cases, of up to 200,000 people.

The chief method to stop the tens of thousands displaced from the cold comfort of road works from, nonetheless, being forced to descend on the workhouses was the February 1847 Temporary Relief Act, commonly called the Soup Kitchen Act. It provided for an end to the sale of maize, the gradual scaling-down of public works and their replacement by soup kitchens, which were meant – at the time the act was passed – to operate for a limited period.

They were a departure – for the first time, food was to be served from premises outside the workhouse. The soup was to be free, however, and not dependent on any means test; the lists of those who needed to be fed were to be submitted to the relief committees by local figures such as priests. There was a hope that the new arrangement would make the Irish healthy enough to work through the summer and take in the harvest. The system was called 'outdoor relief' – although the relief was distributed sometimes indoors or under canvas. The overall body who was to administer the new arrangements was a Board of Temporary Relief, answerable to Trevelyan.

At the local level, the soup kitchens were to be run by newly appointed relief commissioners, who included the Poor Law guardians of the workhouse, leading churchmen, the three highest ratepayers and a local relief inspector. The kitchens were to be set out and put into operation at the expense of the poor rates, but until the autumn of 1847, government was willing to make advances against the security of the rates that would be collected. After that, the local relief commissioners would be dependent on their own resources. By then, in Trevelyan's view, the famine should be over. Trevelyan hoped so. The administrative stress was damaging his health, as were criticisms of his work from those who thought him too liberal, and those who thought him inhuman. He was becoming brusque with his colleagues.

Often farmers would send their wives and children to the workhouse and stay on their smallholdings themselves. But in June 1847, the passing of a further Poor Law Amendment

Act contained the infamous Gregory clause. The clause was framed by William Gregory, a landlord of Galway and MP for Dublin, and, though contained in a Relief Act, was the antithesis of relief. It required that anyone who tenanted more than a quarter acre of land had to give it up if he wanted to enter the workhouse or the fever hospital. The Gregory clause suited landlords, of course, but also the government's ideology, since only in the most desperate need would a farmer seek workhouse charity and thus be considered as having passed the ultimate test of genuine need while at the same time yielding up his land. It was intended both to thin out the numbers in the workhouse and to encourage emigration.

Many landlords used the Gregory clause, and the accompanying poverty of their cottiers, to clear their estates so that they could be employed for new, more profitable forms of agriculture, such as grazing and extensive grain-growing. It was taken for granted by a lot of landlords and their agents now that if any members of a family, even children, sought relief in the workhouse, their parents' cabin would be unroofed and burned down. Mercifully, the Poor Law commissioners in Dublin advised local Boards of Guardians around the country that dependants of men, but not the men themselves who held a rood – that is, a quarter-acre – of land, could receive relief without breaking the law. The reasoning was that women and children should not be allowed to die or to suffer acutely merely because the father of the family was so determined that he would not give up his miserable patch of earth. But the result was an inevitable splitting-up of families.

Gregory, asked by another member of the House of Commons whether the clause would destroy a class of small farmers of whom there were millions in Ireland, replied that he did not see of what use such small farmers could possibly be. Interestingly, Lady Gregory, forty-five years after her husband's death, living in depopulated Galway, became a host and patron to William Butler Yeats and adopted elevated views of the people of the west of Ireland, at least those who were still there.

Local relief committees wanted a definition of soup and a decision on whether it should include meat. The relief commissioners in Dublin told them there need not be meat, that soup was 'any food cooked in a boiler, and distributed in a liquid state, thick or thin and whether composed of meat, fish, vegetables, grain or meal'. The relief commissioners were at one with the government at Westminster in that they declared relief should be 'miserable and scanty'. One bowl of soup and one pound of biscuit, flour, grain or meal was to be the daily issue. If the soup had already been thick, only one quarter of the biscuit etc. was to be given. The Board of Health, however, recommended that the soup be solid rather than fluid, and the ingredients varied. They also recommended plenty of vegetables, since scurvy was still prevalent.

It was considered at an official level that the new program would take four to six weeks to become operative. Though food was to become ready for distribution as early as March 1847, this was a very hopeful timetable and the scheme was in place in very few areas by then. Between the winding down of the public works and the provision of soup lay a gap responsible for the deaths of many. But, reacting to the urgency, some local commissioners got their kitchens running very quickly. Indeed, some kitchens had already been set up by landlords. On the estate of Sir Lucius O'Brien (brother of the famous rebel Smith O'Brien), on the road which led from Newmarket-on-Fergus to Dromoland Castle (now, by irony, a five-star hotel and golf course), there were two ash trees where relief was handed out by the daughters of the O'Brien household. These ash trees were ever after to be known as the 'famine trees'. A similar plan was put in place by the aging novelist Maria Edgeworth in County Longford. The Society of Friends in Cincinatti, Ohio, had read of Maria Edgeworth's ministrations to 3000 starving people in her area, and consigned to her $180 worth of corn meal to be used in stirabout. The Friends had also entered the soup business in Ireland before outdoor relief became official. They set up a three-boiler soup-making plant in Cork City, and made and distributed 2500 quarts of a nourishing mix, which included meat, vegetables and barley.

In areas in the west, there was a problem in finding cauldrons for the cooking of soup, and there were other problems as well. In some places June arrived and still no kitchen was operating, even though the starving were desperate for it to open. Hence there were food riots throughout Ireland, and troops were sent for from their barracks to suppress them. Some soldiers were lenient and compassionate, both the Irish and men from the other areas of the United Kingdom. But they were under the orders of their officers, who in turn were under strict instructions themselves.

At the beginning of June, the guardians of the Galway

Union, who had responsibility for the workhouses in the area around the city, attributed the high level of mortality to the delay in opening the soup kitchens. In the Roscommon Union no soup kitchen had opened by the end of May and the local government inspector of the kitchens provided relief out of his own pocket. When, finally, a soup kitchen opened on 15 June in the Skibbereen Union, a region of the most widespread death, priests were criticised by the authorities for trying to force onto the required lists the name of every person they could who was entitled to outdoor relief. Yet the soup was meant to be available free for the starving, and even though the government's idea of true need always differed from that of people on the ground, its issue was not dependent on any means test – an indication that the Westminster government believed now that death was widespread in Ireland, and that perhaps even the majority of the Irish needed outdoor relief.

The organisation of the soup kitchens was often a triumph of administrative skills on the part of local Boards of Guardians, and the kitchens ended up feeding three million people – well over a third of the population. The problem remained the soup's poor nutritional content, which, despite the Board of Health's recommendations, was sometimes so low in vegetables that it allowed the onset of scurvy.

A famed London chef named Alexis Soyer, who worked at the Reform Club, frequented by Whig politicians, had helped to run a London soup kitchen in 1845 at the time the first potato failure had brought hardship to the English, even though the potato did not dominate the diet of the poor in England to the same extent as it did in Ireland. He found it a technical and culinary challenge to devise means to produce food for great numbers of people and then successfully distribute it. He designed a new boiler for the purpose and published a number of recipes for cheap soup, with no meat component, but nutritious and costing three-quarters of a penny per quart. Some doubted the value of Soyer's soup, one critic suggesting that he feed it and nothing else for two weeks to members of the Reform Club and see what condition they ended up in.

On behalf of the Whig government, Soyer went to Ireland to establish a 'model' soup kitchen, which opened on 5 April 1847 in a large tent located outside the Royal Barracks in Dublin. It was a highly publicised affair, which both the English and Irish press attended, and notable guests were each given a helping of the soup. After the respectable had left, a hundred paupers from the Dublin Mendicity Institution were ushered into the tent and served. Part of the model of the soup kitchen was that people would enter the tent or other premises by way of a zig-zag entrance in which they waited in single line. A bell signalled when a certain number of paupers in the queue could enter, and those who did not fit in waited outside for the next bell. The bowls and spoons on the table were attached by chains, and a prayer was said before there was any eating. Each person received a quart of soup, and a quarter pound of bread for consumption outside the soup kitchen. The sittings were each supposed to take no longer than six minutes. Soyer's soup kitchen also made sufficient soup to supply other relief centres within Dublin, so that between 6 April and 11 August 1847 an average of 8750 persons were fed daily on his soup.

In the middle of April 1847, Soyer made ready to return to London, and left Ireland in a fury of publicity. In an irony of the parlous times, public dinners were held in his honour and the citizens of Dublin gave him a snuffbox in appreciation of his making cheap soup 'palatable'. The provision of free soup at such a cheap price – barely more than a farthing and a half, a farthing being a quarter of a penny – suited very well the economies of the time.

The transfer from relief in wages to relief in cooked food was not universally popular, especially as the soup varied so much in quality. In Clonmel, Tipperary, a member of the grand jury described the local soup as 'totally unfit for human food'. For the same reason, in a number of areas the soup kitchens were attacked by the hungry and a few were destroyed. In Kells in County Meath, in an event known as the 'Stirabout Rebellion', an angry crowd gathered around the soup kitchen and refused to allow anyone to receive their ration, on the grounds that they did not like the indignity of receiving a useless fluid. In County Limerick a number of soup kitchens were destroyed because people thought they were being fobbed off with a food that would not sustain them or in any way sate their hunger. In the city of Limerick itself, the soup boilers in one kitchen were 'smashed to atoms' and a meeting of the relief commissioners was broken into and all the documents destroyed. When the ringleader was arrested, a crowd attacked the local barracks with stones, and the frightened police fired shots into the mass of people. In Corafin in County Clare, on the edge of the desolate area known as the Burren, the soup kitchen was destroyed by a number of people who demanded uncooked food in place of the soup.

From now on, therefore, as far as Treasury was concerned, famine relief was to be a matter for Irish poor ratepayers and charity from within Britain and without, in part from the forerunners of today's non-government organisations or relief agencies – the British Relief Association and the Society of Friends, for example, who would carry much of the weight. Through the soup kitchens, the government and Trevelyan had tried to deal with hunger head-on, though at someone else's expense. But the idea of dispensing food for free as outdoor relief, that is, relief given outside the walls of the workhouses, the latter being considered the only proper venues for the issue of free food, offended Trevelyan's principles.

In fact, even before the Soup Kitchen Act was passed, the Poor Law guardians and local relief bodies in many places were already feeding people soup, partly financed by discreet amounts of money given to them by the lord lieutenant in Dublin. Before the Soup Act, Westminster ordered that this be stopped, because it was outdoor relief. But in many areas the committees and guardians persisted – for example, in Castletown, Queen's County, where landholders 'above immediate want' were said to have been able to subscribe something to the poor rate. There were also unofficially run soup kitchens in many parts of Dublin, where things operated in a 'regular and orderly manner', and up in rural Roscommon. As early as 1846, the guardians of the Fermoy Union were handing out a breakfast of stirabout to 4–500 people. The guardians throughout Kilkenny were able to feed 2000 people in much the same way. The Skibbereen guardians described the distress in their union as heartbreaking and helped the Church of Ireland's Reverend Caulfield. In 1846, Caulfield had come from his parish of Clane in Kildare to assist by opening a soup kitchen, in which over 1000 people were fed a pint of soup each day. Some soup kitchens were operated by landlords 'having their house surrounded from morning to night by hundreds of homeless, half-naked, famishing creatures'. The kitchens of the Quakers were already operating and putting bowls of soup in people's hands without asking any payment of them. It is impossible to estimate the lives saved by these personal acts of energetic compassion, or how high the death rate would have been without them.

After their early reconnaissance of Ireland and the effects of the famine, a Dublin-based Quaker Relief Committee was founded. It received £4800 from Irish Quakers, £35,500 from English Quakers and £4000 from non-Quakers in both countries. The donations received from the United States much exceeded these amounts. It happened that by the end of 1846, the Quakers in England and Ireland had made contact with the American Quakers, who now raised a massive relief amount. One of the first organisers of aid from the United States was Irish-born Quaker Jacob Harvey. He estimated that during 1847, Irish immigrants in America, overwhelmingly working-class people or servants, remitted $1 million, the equivalent of £250,000, to aid for Ireland. Protestant churches and New York synagogues also contributed donations.

A number of Quakers from England and Ireland now travelled to the west of Ireland to oversee the distribution of food relief. Meanwhile, in Dublin another central committee was formed by citizens. It included both the Protestant and Catholic archbishops of the city. Donations, however, tended to fall as 1846 progressed, because of the hope of a more plentiful harvest at the end of the summer.

The reappearance of blight in the late summer and autumn of 1846 brought the relief efforts back into being with, among other organisations, the British Association for the Relief of Distress in Ireland and Scotland appearing. The British Relief Association was founded by Jewish banker and philanthropist Lionel de Rothschild at the beginning of 1847. Its board members began their first meeting by each contributing £1000 of relief. A sixth of the money raised by the organisation would be used for the famine in the Scottish highlands, and the rest was for Ireland. The association appointed the Polish putative nobleman and former explorer of Australia Count Paul Strzelecki to act as their agent in Ireland.

The central relief committee of the Society of Friends continued its aid, and a new general central relief committee was formed in Dublin in December 1846, once it was apparent that no end to the suffering was in sight. At that stage, before his ultimate transportation to Australia, William Smith O'Brien sat on the latter committee. Donations from all over the world again began to arrive. Toronto sent

£3472, Buenos Aires £441, South Africa £470 and Delhi a further £296 from private Irish soldiers serving in the army. Most of the money raised – £20,835 – went to allay want in Connacht in the west, and must have helped sustain lives. But many committees began to wind up their activities at the end of 1847, as did relief committees elsewhere in the world, when the harvest came forth unblighted. Even the Society of Friends scaled down its efforts, though it continued to give indirect relief in the form of seeds and capital equipment such as spades and fishing tackle. Apart from that, their resources were exhausted, they said.

In 1848, the blight appeared again. The British Treasury secretly offered the Quakers £100 if they would resume their relief operations. They refused to accept it, on the basis that far more radical measures were needed.

Because of the British Relief Association's close contacts with Charles Trevelyan, it was often seen as an arm of government relief. But there were a number of ideological conflicts between Strzelecki and Trevelyan, especially over the issue of feeding some 200,000 children through the schools in the west, a plan of Strzelecki's which Trevelyan saw as too profligate. The association, subject to Trevelyan's influence at the board level, closed its operations in the summer of 1848. In September that year, a disheartened Strzelecki left dismal Ireland, refusing to accept payment for the work he had done, though still pursuing a campaign to be recognised and compensated as the first discoverer of gold in Australia.

However, Joseph Bewley, the Dublin Quaker merchant, established a further relief committee in Dublin and the Friends in London went into action again. From English

Quakers they received an extraordinary £35,000. But the donations received from the United States far exceeded these amounts, as Jacob Harvey again organised a massive relief operation.

Joseph Bewley himself, like Harvey in New York, would be among the victims of the famine, in that they died premature deaths and, according to the opinions of contemporaries, in both cases from overwork. Many of the Friends were punished for their efforts: Jonathan Pim, a Dublin merchant, suffered acutely from exhaustion, even though he would recover to serve in the House of Commons as a Liberal. As well as Bewley and Harvey, another merchant, William Todhunter, also died – again, according to his physician, of exhaustion – while about a dozen other Quaker workers were struck down by famine epidemics.

Pope Pius IX had sent a donation of Roman $1000. Later, under pressure from British emissaries and from his own conservative conscience, he would condemn and prohibit any Catholic uprising. But in March 1847, he issued an encyclical to the Catholic community worldwide, requesting Catholics to set aside three days of prayer for Ireland and to make donations. This had an impact among the Catholics of Britain as much as it did in remote Australia, Venezuela and South Africa, and donations flowed in, though not entirely from those Irish-born or of Irish descent. In Australia, where Irish convicts, former convicts and free immigrants made up nearly a third of the population, funds were raised with some urgency. In the more distant parts of the colonies, in what would become Queensland, there was an Irish Famine Relief Organisation. The Choctaw nation of America sent its mite as well. Privately raised aid came from Britain, from Newcastle, Gateshead, Hull, Birmingham, Leeds, Huddersfield, Wolverhampton and York.

To the chagrin of Lord John Russell, prime minister of Great Britain, the United States intervened more and more with relief. The American government's motives were not entirely pure. The British government believed that US relief exports and their free issue to the hungry of Ireland would help drive up prices for American produce in general in Britain, and indeed even for those Irish whom the proffered American grain did not reach. The general Irish Relief Committee in New York declared that the miseries of Ireland were the direct cause of America's increasing wealth. 'What is death to Ireland has but augmented fortune to America.' American merchants were fattening on the starvation of other people, it said.

In February 1847, Congress was approached to permit the Boston Relief Committee to be provided with a sloop of war, the *Jamestown*, and the frigate *Macedonian*, to transport supplies to Ireland. Congress agreed, a gesture all the more remarkable because American forces were committed to war against the Mexicans. Manned by volunteers, who slept in hammocks on deck to maximise room for supplies, the *Jamestown* left Massachusetts on 28 March. After fifteen days and three hours, it arrived in Cork. Captain Forbes of the *Jamestown* argued that if the supplies could cross the Atlantic in fifteen days, there should be no greater delay in getting them into the hands of the poor. The ship, said a newspaper in Cork, took a shorter time to bring its supplies than it would take to get 'an intelligible answer' from the Board of Works or to understand one of the acts of Parliament aimed at relief. A Liverpool philanthropist, William Rathbone, had agreed to help to oversee the impartial distribution of this relief.

It seems that in Ireland, relief, with its concentration on emergency food, might have been better targeted than in some modern famines. Nonetheless, there were complaints about relief assessors travelling the country by fine coach and staying at the best inns, phenomena seen now in the gleaming vehicles and accommodation at the best hotels, which has been associated with aid workers of the International Committee of the Red Cross and other bodies.

Sometimes the aid offered to the hungry was, in the minds of the givers, ordained by God. But its intention lay in affecting drastic change in those subjected to the charity. The phenomenon of 'souperism' – conversion to Protestantism for the sake of food and advantage – grew in large part from the founding in 1830 of the Protestant Colonisation Society, whose objective was to create Protestant colonies in the Catholic recesses of Ireland. This society, too, would offer soup and other favours, but at a particular cost.

By the early 1830s, it had already succeeded in founding its colonies of Protestants in County Donegal and Kildare. The evangelical Reverend Edward Nagle established a colony even in remote Achill Island in County Mayo, and another on the Dingle Peninsula in Kerry – in both cases country beyond which lay the Atlantic, a fact that might have emphasised the Protestant Colonisation Society's sense that they had created mighty fortresses there against the general barbarism of the west of Ireland. The missions were founded with the support of local landowners, who were devout members of the Church of Ireland (the Anglican church, that is). Landowners' wives were particularly enthusiastic contributors to the projects. Those from the Catholic masses who were converted by the society were ostracised and subjected to 'exclusive dealing', an early form of the boycott, which involved refusing to sell goods or to give any succour to any convert to Protestantism.

When the famine began, a further conversion movement came into being, the Society for the Irish Church Mission, which worked in Connemara in western Galway. This group were also willing to offer generous support, and in trying as well to bring about conversions, they believed they were liberating the Irish not only to a pure appreciation of the deity but also to a Protestant culture associated with habits of industry, social progress and inventiveness.

At the height of the famine, a priest in Ballinakill near Clifden on the Galway coast described proselytisers going from cabin to cabin 'proffering food and money and clothing to the naked and starving on condition of their becoming members of their conventicles'. Priests in the west inveighed against the evangelicals from the pulpit, but their words could not bear away the reality of starvation. Many of the conversions were temporary, provoked by want. Yet 'souper-ism' would come to hold a much greater place in the Irish imagination than the ultimate figures justified. Part of the reason was the fervent, vitriolic and memorable oratory directed against the opportunistic proselytisers by the Catholic clergy. The bulk of Church of Ireland ministers themselves also mocked the work of the 'colonisers', and their trading of food for faith.

As for Catholic clergymen, Sir Randolph Routh, the chairman of the relief commissioners, found that during the famine the vast majority of priests were behaving 'most liberally, and most meritoriously', and cooperating well with their Church of Ireland colleagues. Some bishops were criticised, however, for not being demanding enough in seeking help for their people, and there were even some priests who went ahead with grand renovations or new building of churches during the most bitter years.

15

Relief: Bengal

THE QUESTION MUST be asked: why did Bengal suffer from a lack of administration and hence of mechanisms to distribute food? The centre of government in the regions was the British district officer, who was also the district magistrate and collector of revenue. His job was to keep order according to the government's strictures. When Burma fell in 1942, the demands made on him were entirely to do with the coming Japanese invasion. His first task was to create a civil defence to prepare for the heavy air raids that were likely in the front line area. He was required to requisition supplies, land and buildings for the retreating British and Indian armies, and for military airfields. He had also to look after Indian refugees from Burma who turned up, trembling, alarmed and hungry. They had reached the town of Chittagong, far inland on the Karnaphuli River, by way of Assam and told tales of Japanese atrocities. At the level of the British and the Indian ruling class, even as far away as the capital, Calcutta, people were panicking. The Japanese advance through Burma had been so swift that there was a sense of inevitable capture. A witness who appeared before the Famine Commission described the all-absorbing tension in Calcutta, the emptiness of streets (the starving had not yet arrived), the abandoned houses and shops. The families of government servants were ordered out of the coastal regions, and few people did not believe that by the next cold season, the Japanese would hold Calcutta.

Exposed far out on his limb, the district officer was meant to calm some of the misgivings the refugee stories evoked in the general population, while simultaneously going about the business of denying them their boats and vehicles. He also had instructions to address the local inflation of currency, and all the turmoil of a beaten army streaming through the region to take up defensive positions to the west. By June 1942, Chittagong was in front of the first line of defence, and the district officer was ready to abandon it as soon as the port and its installations were destroyed. The permanent harbour works were prepared for demolition.

In a sixty-mile line south of the town, district officers and their administration kept working in front of the positions taken up by the British armies, and were thus in no-man's land. One wrote that he never knew whether he was going to wake up the next morning to find a Japanese soldier bringing in his morning tea.

So the efforts of the district officer were devoted to military issues and were not as exercised by the coming food crisis. Meanwhile, the only official in the Bengal village was the *chowkidar* (watchman), who did duty as a policeman and to whom all deaths were to be reported. He was poorly paid and often illiterate, and he lacked the authority of the village officials of the *ryotwari* areas, the areas in which village taxes were raised, and in which the officials were respected, or at least eminent, members of the community.

Thus few people except the inhabitants themselves – and those local wealthier families who often preyed on them – had any concept of what was happening on a village level, or whom to call on to set up a local machine for relieving the famine. In Bengal in particular, putting in place a system of distribution was a great challenge to any relief effort.

The Famine Commission would later stress the necessity of boat traffic and 'the meagreness' of the roads. Throughout the greater part of the province, roads had to be raised above flood level and a large number of bridges were needed to span the smaller rivers and canals. But the larger rivers defeated engineers, or else bridges to span them were considered too expensive. In many districts, therefore, the chief means of communications were by 'country boats' and the occasional river steamer.

In December 1942, when the series of Japanese attacks on Calcutta had caused panic in the city, a large number of foodgrain shops closed as their owners left for the country-side. The government of Bengal felt it was now necessary to requisition stocks from the warehouses of wholesale dealers, and from that moment, said the Famine Commission, 'the ordinary trade machinery' could not be relied upon to feed even Calcutta. The authorities thought there would be food riots because of dealers holding on to grain, and therefore sent out police to seize stocks that were withheld from sale. But they could acquire only 17,000 tons over five months. Profiteering Bengali politicians started to issue grain-trading licences to their friends, so that they too could engage in hoarding until the price favoured them. The government of India itself had earlier taken off price controls of wheat throughout the country – another admission that trying to keep prices low was not working.

As in other famines, there was also the problem of more affluent people in the richer areas becoming immune to the presence of victims and blinded to their needs. There are tales from the Irish famine of people walking past the dying on the street to attend lectures on the abolition of American slavery. The Indian writer T. G. Narayan was honest enough to say that 'in sheer self-defence' hearts hardened towards the destitutes in Calcutta and their suffering failed to register.

John Muehl, a young American serving in the Royal Medical Corps, visited Calcutta at the time that refugees to the city were expiring on its pavements. Since he had come from the front in Burma, at first he saw Calcutta as a city of luxuries. Then he became sickened by the deaths in the streets that occurred 'side by side with cocktail parties, hors d'oeuvres, seven-course dinners and padlocked garbage cans'. On his first evening in the city, he dined at the famous Firpo's restaurant, and on the way back had to step among the dead and dying. The elegant food became 'like lead' in his stomach, and before he had reached his room at the Grand Hotel he was sick. But the longer he was in town, the more indifferent he became. He admits, too, to the callousness Narayan mentioned, once finding himself eating a chocolate bar as he stepped by a dying woman.

After a ruinous cyclone in 1940, the *Times* of India, a Bombay English-language newspaper of record, had founded an Indian Relief fund. In 1943, the fund was revivified and, from a central office in Calcutta, began asking the readers of the *Times*, whose readership included British civil servants and business and professional people, as well as the Indian privileged classes, for donations. Contributions came in from every region – Bombay, Madras and the colony of Ceylon (Sri Lanka) – and within a few weeks amounted to £14,000.

Other charitable organisations set up relief kitchens throughout the city. The Bengal Central Relief Committee, established by the government of Bengal under the chairmanship of the governor, was responsible for some of them. The others were contributed by the Hindu Mahasabha, a communal organisation that had broken away from the Congress Party; the Marwari Relief Committee, Marwari being a cultural group from Rajasthan; the Bharat Sevashram, a self-help cultural organisation of citizens and monks; the Friends' Ambulance Unit, a Quaker group; and Rotary. These organisations attempted to provide each destitute with a daily free meal of about 750 calories, a target they could, with sustained effort, manage to reach, but which was insufficient to ensure life.

A great deal of informal aid was given by soldiers of the British and Indian armies at military camps and along the roadsides. Sometimes the food was not entirely appropriate to the needs of the hungry – jam, or pudding, or other foods likely to upset now-delicate digestions. Sometimes what was given flowed from simple compassion, though in other instances there might be a *quid pro quo* involving sex.

The average Bengali consumed 140 kilograms of rice in one year, but in bare subsistence rural farming families this fell to 90 kilos a head each year. The famine-relief diet, supplied in the form of gruel, or *khichri*, amounted to thirty kilos of grain per person per year. In the popular view, emergency food to make *khichri* was in many cases pilfered by officials and sold on the black market. The hungry also stole what rice they could from the stores of the relief kitchens, in part because the *khichri* was so unappetising – made out of, among other things, gourd, pumpkin, cucumber, kernel of banana trees and wild vegetables. Its smell was appalling and the colour blackish. This gruel did not contain even half the calories needed for an adult. A serving typically contained eight ounces of grain, mostly millet, a food unfamiliar to rice-eating Bengalis, to which was added these small amounts of vegetables, spices and sugar.

Nonetheless, the free meals were so sought-after that it was necessary for all kitchens in an area to issue the daily meal at the same hour, to prevent recipients moving from one to another. In November 1943, the kitchens fed an average of 2.1 million people a day. Doles of uncooked food were distributed to another quarter million. In the meantime, grain began to be sold at subsidised rates to about half a million. Obviously, millions starved beyond the reach of this mercy.

*

During April and May 1943, when corpses were beginning to appear in the villages of Bengal, the provincial Bengal government began a propaganda campaign to convince the people there was no serious shortage of rice. Their intentions were good – to stop local hoarding and to temper the purchases of grain by better-off families. Even now, had the total amount of rice in Bengal been equally distributed throughout the population, though everyone would have endured some hunger, no one would have starved to death. The acting governor of Bengal, Sir Thomas Rutherford, declared, 'It is this price racket based on scarcity that has been killing people as much as scarcity itself.'

By May 1943, in Midnapore and Parganas in West Bengal, babies and nursing mothers were scraping by on the milk powder distributed under the cyclone-relief program the year before. Voluntary groups were setting up soup kitchens in the towns of Chittagong and Noakhali in East Bengal, but they could not buy enough food to operate properly.

Many had died of starvation before the third all-India Food Conference assembled in New Delhi on 5 July 1943 and established a new Basic Plan. The free-trade idea was abandoned, a Foodgrains Policy Committee was set up and the export of rice from India was prohibited. Only small amounts of rice had been exported, in any case. Though an original Basic Plan adopted at the beginning of the year had allocated 217,000 tons of rice to Bengal, the revised plan now allotted a mere 15,000 tons, but along with 340,000 tons of wheat, 46,000 tons of chickpeas and 40,000 tons of millet. At the beginning of August, in an attempt to make hoarders sell, Bengal set maximum rice prices at six to eight times the pre-war rate and offered to buy at these rates all the rice that was offered. But again they could purchase very little, for hoarders were still holding rice in warehouses in the hope of even greater profit.

Now, from the very evidence of the dead on Calcutta's streets, the government of Bengal told their district administrative offices to sell food grain (if they had a chance of getting it) at a subsidised price, to begin public work for wages, to hand out free gruel, to give small gifts of cash in emergencies, to make loans so people could buy cattle and to devote themselves to relief as their primary work. An overall famine commissioner was appointed in September 1943. Engineers supervised the Bengali-government-initiated public works, in return for which a small wage was paid. Many on the works showed mercy to pregnant women, to whom they paid a digger's wage without requiring them to work.

In America in late November 1943, a group of influential people formed the Emergency Committee for Indian Famine Relief. Members included Pearl S. Buck, the American Nobel Prize-winning novelist; Clare Boothe Luce, writer and wife of the founder of *Time* magazine; and Henry F. Grady, who was to be the first ambassador to independent India. The main objectives of the organisation were not only to raise funds for famine relief but also to pressure government authorities to allocate ships and transport planes to the task of moving food to Bengal. The committee was unsuccessful in its attempts to persuade the US government to divert shipping, however.

In early December, the Quaker organisation the American Friends Service Committee dispatched the first American relief supplies to Bengal – 20,000 cases of evaporated milk. The American Red Cross sent the same, with two million multivitamin tablets. James G. Vail, an official from the American Friends Service Committee, was appointed to go to India on behalf of all the American agencies and supervise the distribution. At first he had a budget of $100,000, but donations quickly fell away. Vail faced the usual problem of finding trucks to transport the American aid, or negotiating with other agencies to distribute it.

Still, concerned Americans saw hope in a new international organisation. Forty-four nations, including India, gathered at the White House on 9 November 1943 to sign an agreement that created the United Nations Relief and Rehabilitation Administration (UNRRA). Roosevelt raised the hopes of those concerned with India when he said that it was the task of UNRRA to operate in areas of food shortage. It was to be UNRRA who would assure a fair distribution of available supplies among all liberated people in the world, and address death by starvation or exposure. The India League of America, the combined relief committees, and the Post-war World Council, set up to be in place when peace came, made appeals to UNRRA for the starving in Bengal. These pleas ran up against bureaucrats, who interpreted the meaning of the UNRRA charter along the lines that only areas liberated from the enemy were eligible for aid. Dean Acheson, at the time undersecretary of state, stood by this interpretation. The British delegate to UNRRA, Minister for Food John J. Llewellin, supported Mr Acheson's position and called a press conference to prove that nothing needed to be done in India and that the UNRRA agreement did not apply to it. Sir Girja

Bajpai, agent general for India in Washington, quietly supported Acheson and Llewellin. And so Bengal received no UNRRA aid.

Throughout the Bengal crisis, many kept wondering why the authorities ignored the *Manual of Practical Instructions Regarding Famine Relief Administration* published in 1904. The manual, based on inquiries into earlier famines, declared what the emperor of Ethiopia and Mengistu would later know. 'The first danger signal is the unusual wandering of paupers.' Another signal, said the manual, is a contraction of credit followed by feverish activity in the grain trade, and an increase in crime. If the infirm, other than paupers, begin to take to the road in great numbers, it is almost certain that 'gratuitous relief' is called for.

Once hunger and starvation struck, the provincial administration was not equipped to deal with it quickly and with effect. The 'famine code' laid down in the manual that supplies would be automatically attracted to where they were needed. But since it was never invoked by the viceroy, Linlithgow, no regulations existed for such a distribution. And, given events, there were not many citizens able to help with the distribution, even had it been available.

Relief, as it developed, came mainly in the form of agricultural loans. Such aid would develop returns too slowly to save the lives of many artisans, barbers and day-labourers. In February 1944, 30 million rupees were made available for loan by government. In summary, a total of 74 million was spent on relief in Bengal, including on agricultural loans; 30 million rupees on gratuitous relief; and 14 and a half million for test works on the way to introducing a scheme of famine labour. The sum represents an expenditure of approximately 35 cents per capita over eighteen months.

In his first address to the Indian Parliament on 17 February 1944, the new viceroy, Archibald Wavell, did not address the question of Indian independence but indicated that while India still had some problems, the food situation would improve greatly in 1944. Some thought him overly optimistic. For one thing, Bengal under Chief Minister Nazimuddin was still inefficient and slow, as much so as under his predecessor. Wavell had ordered the government of Bengal to set up and operate by 31 January 1944 at least 1000 retail outlets for the distribution of ration foodstuffs. Food rationing was introduced to the city of Calcutta on the last day of January 1944, though it would take until early May for it to spread throughout the greater Calcutta region.

The number of starving and sick destitutes in Calcutta had been estimated to be at least 100,000 in October 1943, and now the new viceroy Wavell demanded that the government of Bengal move them out of Calcutta and into feeding camps, where they could be given medical attention. The Bengal Destitute Persons (Repatriation and Relief) Ordnance was passed by the provincial government at the end of the month. Many critics said that it would be better to truck the destitutes home instead of sending them to the food depots and camps built outside Calcutta, and even Wavell wondered if his intervention would do any good. There had now been a promising, if small, autumn crop and the winter crop to be harvested later in the year had, wherever it was planted, looked excellent and better than other years. In the meantime, Wavell ordered the army to transport food to rural areas, to give medical assistance, to provide shelters and to transport migrants back to their villages.

General Claude Auchinleck had by now been given one of Wavell's former duties and was commander-in-chief in India. Auchinleck made arrangements at once to carry out the viceroy's orders. The army moved only 55,000 through their relief camps, but others left Calcutta on their own, attracted away by reports of the setting-up of relief kitchens in country areas.

From August 1943, Air Raid Protection (ARP) doctors and emergency hospitals had been placed at the disposal of the public-health authorities for handling destitutes who collapsed in the streets of Calcutta. By the end of November, within a month of Wavell launching the army into the fight against famine, the military services had ordered sixty-eight medical officers to public-health assignments in Bengal. The Indian Medical Service also detailed several of its medical officers to the province. But up to February 1944, only 160 civilian doctors – about a quarter of the number sought – had been recruited from throughout India to serve in Bengal. There were also sixteen military hospitals in place, with a mere 2100 beds. Fifty mobile medical units were staffed with health technicians. They inaugurated programs of mass inoculations against smallpox and cholera, improved village sanitation, disinfected water supplies and treated malaria cases. The number of vaccinations against smallpox jumped 73,000 in October 1943, to 464,000 in December, to 4.3 million by April 1944. Of course, this was a mere fragment of the Bengali population, but it can be argued that it was the most Wavell and Auchinleck could do with their resources.

While in Bengal people were being felled by cholera and malaria, from their bases in Burma the Japanese crossed the border on 22 March 1944, to try to capture the allied airfields in north-west India. There were initial reverses, but British and Indian defenders fought the Japanese troops to a stand-still around the frontier towns of Imphal and Kohima. There followed weeks of intense and brutal conflict. Additional troops and supplies were rushed to the battle area, further imperilling India's transportation system. Many doctors went back from the areas of want to their units in the front line.

The Japanese threat rebuffed, doctors returned to the famine areas. By the following October 1944, 32 million had been inoculated against smallpox and 18 million against cholera. The military medical units were very well supplied, equipped and maintained, but the civilian hospitals were not. Malaria was a particular problem, because the Japanese had captured the quinine-supplying parts of the world, and there were only small stocks remaining. Still, the well-off wanted protection, so shipments of synthetic anti-malarials such as mepacrine and quinacrine, and of the remaining quinine itself, had to be transported under armed guard.

As described, doctors encountered great peasant resistance to being inoculated against cholera and smallpox, even as polluted water continued to take its toll. There were wildfire rumours that inoculations were toxic. Before the crisis, water had come from tube wells, fed from above and then running almost horizontally before emerging from an embankment. The earlier breakdown of the pipes in the wells, and the impossibility of people outlaying money to repair them, had sent people to get their water from canals, heavily infected by bodies and waste. Inoculation, despite the popular resistance, was now saving people from the parlous condition of the water they drank.

Wavell found that getting food for Bengal from the great farming region of Punjab was very difficult. The government in Lahore declared that it had been one of the staunchest supporters of the war effort and that one out of every two Indian soldiers was a Punjabi volunteer, which entitled them to retain their supplies for the needs of their own people. They reiterated to Wavell their strong opposition both to price controls and to rationing of food stuffs. But Wavell made it clear that both were necessary. The Punjab chief minister, Sir Khizar Hyat Khan Tiwana, and Wavell got on well together and arrived at a compromise. Maximum prices for food grains were accepted by the provincial leaders but at a higher level than Wavell's government of India wanted. Also, the requisitioning of food grains would be less forceful and rationing adopted at a more leisurely pace than Wavell would have liked. Nonetheless, the foundations of a nationwide food-control structure were laid out in the Punjab in the final few days of November 1943.

After two weeks in New Delhi, Wavell took to the road again on a ten-day tour of Orissa, where there were pockets of famine, then to Assam and lastly to Bengal. Dacca he found appalling, with corpses strewing the streets. The Parganas district south of Calcutta looked a little better, but 'pretty grim'.

The Bengali ministers, he decided, had neither the intention nor the ability to cope with the food problem.

Military reconnaissance patrols were sent out on foot or by boat to search for corpses and the starving in each corner of houses and down every alley in the remotest villages. The reports of these patrols were sometimes sent back by carrier pigeons, and if there were many starving in a particular region, other troops would go out with food, bales of clothes and anti-cholera vaccine. And again there was talk of an excellent harvest.

On 24 June 1944, Wavell sent a personal appeal to Churchill and the government in London, and in return Secretary of State for India Amery wired New Delhi a promise to ship 200,000 tons of grain to Calcutta, in addition to the 250,000 promised earlier that year. Wavell was partially appeased. 'Still we are getting on. I have extracted 450,000 tons since the War Cabinet regretted that nothing could be done.'

There were other positive signs. From August 1944 onwards, under the new Basic Plan, large shipments of rice, wheat and millet were rushed to Bengal from other areas of India. This movement of grain was the opposite of Viceroy Linlithgow's policy. Two shiploads of Australian wheat also arrived. From Britain came medical supplies and dried milk. South Africa offered grain and milk powder. (The Japanese offered to send all the Burmese rice India needed, as long as the safety of their ships was guaranteed. Naturally this offer, which was in any case probably a mere ploy, was rejected.)

But grain not required for immediate consumption in Calcutta was piled up in godowns because the Bengal government did not have the resources to distribute it. Nor did it have the resources to transport grain out to the famine areas. Army officers with logistical training moved into Bengal's Department of Civil Supplies and organised the movement of these stores to distribution points in the *mofussil*. They more than doubled the food supply trucked to the towns and villages to 2000 tons per day. Army engineers constructed new bridges and culverts to help transport the relief grain. Troops still guarded river steamers and trains carrying supplies of food. Some police were tolerant of petty thieving by local men and women, but they arrested for trespass strangers who, searching for food, entered their area. Some magistrates even ordered these wandering people to be flogged.

With the coming of cold weather, when night temperatures fell into the Celsius teens, the people, without fat to protect them from the winds, shivered in their rotting famine rags. But by mid December the army had distributed 600 tons of warm clothing. One hundred tons were flown out to East Bengal by the US army air transport group. And by way of donations, relief kitchens were able to serve greater amounts, and expanded until they exceeded 6600 at the end of November. About half of these were financed and run by government; ten per cent by private relief organisations from outside India; and the remainder by Indian private agencies subsidised by government.

But for the millions of Bengalis who perished, none of it would be enough.

16

Relief: Ethiopia

In 1976, in the wake of Emperor Haile Selassie's famine, the United States Senate held hearings on the Ethiopian regime's request for military aid, and decided to use the threat of a reduction in food aid as a weapon against the Derg, to pay it back for its growing embrace of the Soviet Union. In the meantime, it continued to operate what is called a PL [Public Law] 480 program, sending Food for Peace through Catholic relief agencies and the World Food Program. As Mengistu moved further and emphatically into the Soviet camp, America went on donating food and funding development, but channelled them through UNICEF, United States non-government organisations (NGOs) and private voluntary organisations (PVOs) – essentially the same as NGOs. But in the early 1980s, for ideological reasons and because of their suspicion that Mengistu was misusing aid, the anti-Soviet West was at first more than willing to take him at his word when he went on denying that the famine was a pressing emergency on a major scale.

By mid 1984, reports were coming into Addis Ababa from the regions that at Relief and Rehabilitation Commission distribution centres and shelters – large buildings recently established to receive the needy – over 12,000 people a week were dying. This meant that thousands more were dying in the remoter country areas, in huts or on the streets. Many people were still wandering towards Eritrea or west to cross the border into the Sudan. But, according to overall figures, 60 per cent of those who set out looking for aid never reached their destinations.

By July 1984, the north-eastern Wollo province needed 7600 tonnes of food per month for its inhabitants, but received only 400, for which there was often no local transport for distribution. In the Wolaytta district in Wollo, nothing arrived. Sidamo in the south and the entirety of the southern Showa province, to the south of the capital, had no food reserves at all. Harar needed 5000 tonnes a month and got nothing; Showa 10,000 tonnes a month; and so on.

At the end of August 1984, Mengistu called an emergency meeting of the leaders of the Urban Dwellers' Associations of Addis. He told them there were rumours of drought circulating even within the ruling circles – but that these rumours were designed to subvert the revolution and create dissension. 'Imperialist CIA agents are trying to poison the minds of the people, to provoke unrest and spoil the celebration. You should be vigilant and dispel these rumours.'

Beyond the reach of Mengistu's oratory lay everywhere the sea of hunger. The severest rationing began around the

RRC distribution centres, which were meant to be temporary havens. Here, people built shanty towns or else lay in the open dying, most of them dressed in rags. For over a year, the food available for the millions of famine victims within reach of distribution food dumps had been wheat, vegetable oil and perhaps a little sugar. The adult relief quota had at first been 700 grams of grain and 20 grams of vegetable or butter oil per person, but this had been reduced to 500 grams per day in June 1984, and remained at that level for the rest of the famine in many of the RRC's centres. Children between the ages of four and fourteen received 350 grams of grain and 100 grams of supplement, dry skim milk or soya milk. Children under four were given 100 grams of supplement, but no grain. In the ever-enlarging settlements around the shelters, people would hand-grind their portions of grain into meal and, if water was available, make a porridge out of it. Where water was scarce they would roast the grain on tin over a fire and eat it dry. But people had to walk further and further from the shelters to find any wood.

Though an ideal adult ration is about 2000 calories, adequate for survival without physical exertion, at the height of the famine between March 1984 and December 1985 the food distributed, even with the help of foreign agencies, gave generally 1300 to 1700 calories a day. According to the World Health Organization, these were near fatal or fatal levels for adults under resting conditions and without illness.

The small amounts of food that did arrive before the major international effort of late 1984 and early 1985 had to be brought in from Massawa and Aseb, two ports on the Red Sea. This proved to be a problem because, as the warehouses in the ports began to fill up with sacks of flour and other foods, there were not always the trucks to bring it down the road to distribution points. The RRC had some 800 trucks, but inevitably some of them were under repair at any one time, so the amount they could deliver was not enough to sustain life. To make things easier, Aseb, closer to Addis, received 76 per cent of the shipped relief and Massawa, further north, 15 per cent. But, though Aseb was capable of unloading 150,000 tonnes a month, much of it was held up by Ethiopian bureaucracy and lack of trucks. The Ethiopian road system was, in any case, fatally limited. Before the revolution there were only 5.4 kilometres of road for every 1000 square kilometres. Showa, Addis Ababa's home province, and Eritrea, militarily and administratively important, contained 40 per cent of all the roads. Seven other provinces possessed the rest, in a country as big as France and Spain combined. There were vast regions that could not be reached and where, as a result, there were no distribution centres.

Dawit Wolde Giorgis, as head of the RRC, was in a strange position, required to walk a fine line between Mengistu's denial of famine and the dictator's contrary demand that the despicable West help without asking any awkward questions about Mengistu's own policies.

In New York on a further begging trip, Giorgis was asked about the cost of the coming Mengistu celebrations. He defended the government's record with evasions and lies. But he could not lie about Soviet assistance, which had been appallingly low. Fortunately for his stocks in the West, the Soviets suddenly did make an offer to send 24 helicopters, 12 transport aircraft and 700 trucks. He was able to report this gesture to the American press. Importantly, for infrastructure purposes, the East Germans donated twenty mechanics, and what had been an Ethiopian truck graveyard on the road from Addis Ababa to Massawa began roaring efficiently again.

In July 1984, British ITV showed the documentary *Seeds of Despair*. On the same night, the BBC showed a short film shot in Tigray. Both broadcasts created an immediate reaction of generosity among viewers, but they did not have the impact of the BBC News footage shown on 23 October 1984, shot in Korem in Tigray, in which broadcaster Michael Buerk said that the famine was 'biblical' in its scale. Bodies were heaped at the sides of the camp, Buerk said, and the footage showed: 'This mother and the baby born two months ago, wrapped together in death.' The next night there was a similar broadcast, this time from Makale. These broadcasts unleashed a tide of compassion. The Makale footage was shown by NBC in the United States and then around the world. Suddenly the UK Minister of Overseas Development, Timothy Raison, was summoning Giorgis. Maggie Thatcher, responding to calls from the public, was anxious to help – the RAF was willing to fly in food, whole squadrons being allocated to the task. Giorgis knew that this would enrage Mengistu and enlarge Thatcher's political repute. Giorgis, perhaps unwisely, bargained Raison down to two Hercules.

In New York, he was feted at the UN in a way that had not occurred on previous visits, and was promised much by Secretary-General Pérez de Cuéllar. In November 1984, Giorgis addressed the UN General Assembly. He met with de Cuéllar and made a personal appeal for more aid. The meeting reinforced Giorgis's impression that the famine was becoming a camera opportunity for Western leaders. As he would write, 'There were no quiet, private talks or agreements; it was all done with an eye to public opinion.' But one can wonder, given Mengistu's far fiercer politics, and the fact that Addis was plastered with his image, why either man should seem surprised that Western politicians and officials would behave as politicians and officials are wont to do, and pose for photographs.

The US election contest between Ronald Reagan and Walter Mondale was about to begin, and both the Democrats and the Republicans felt bound to promise a response to this 'new' crisis. The State Department now agreed to funnel its aid through Giorgis's RRC. The government's United States Agency for International Development (USAID) at first had decided to give the RRC 50,000 tonnes of food. But now an arrangement for 180,000 tonnes of assistance was signed. The Americans also wanted to send a US air force group, but ultimately settled for two commercial aircraft. Again, particularly at the State Department, there were camera opportunities.

Obviously in going to Ethiopia many agencies were following a political agenda. The anti-communist rhetoric of American officials who accompanied the arrival of the USAID supplies to Ethiopia sent Mengistu into paroxysms. Back home again, Giorgis tried to explain to the Americans how their manner and their utterances played into the hands of the hardliners around Mengistu's men, who wanted to expel them from the country. But the Americans explained that they were subject to US policy as much as he was to Mengistu's. They needed to satisfy the conservatives, who urged that all aid be ended and Red Ethiopia punished for its Soviet alliance.

In the West, many were now galvanised by the question of Ethiopia. Generous people, who had previously known nothing about the country and even now probably knew little about its politics, made astounding gestures. A couple in Scotland sold their home and donated the proceeds to aid. A farmer named Oliver Walston donated his harvest.

In November 1984, Bob Geldof and Midge Ure organised a group of thirty-eight famous British musicians to record the fundraising record 'Do They Know It's Christmas?' as the opening act of an aid agency, which would be known as Band Aid. He found a recording studio but it was available only for a day. Popstar Boy George, who had forgotten the date of the recording, urgently flew to London on Concorde and reached the studio in the last hour of recording. The record was mixed and released on 29 November. It immediately dominated the music industry and the UK charts. Geldof raised over $200 million through the record and a day-long internationally televised appeal, 'Live Aid', which took place simultaneously in London and Philadelphia and involved hundreds of leading musicians. In a similar vein to 'Do They Know It's Christmas?', American artists brought together by 'USA for Africa' recorded the single, 'We Are the World', in January 1985, and it was released in March, again to dramatic effect. Not to gainsay the generosity of so many in the West, it is true that they believed the problem of Ethiopia was drought and – until now – the world's ignorance of the drought. People did not understand that between their donations and the starving lay the intransigence of Mengistu, as well as the corrupt dealings of some Ethiopian officials, which led to some aid food being put up for sale in local markets.

The funds raised by Geldof were enormous and vitally significant in keeping up the aid momentum around the world, and shaming others into doing something. As much as $50 billion in pledges from governments and agencies is believed to have been instigated by the visibility the record gave to Ethiopia.

Canada was particularly generous. 'Take an Absent Friend to Lunch Today' was the fundraising slogan there. As a result, in Guelph, Ontario, Fred Benson gave his 107-acre farm to a Mennonite relief agency. Eskimos from Fort Smith in the Northwest Territories organised a concert for famine relief. The speaker of the Ontario legislature, John Turner, cancelled the Annual Speaker's Christmas party and donated the $10,000 saved to Ethiopian relief. Sweden, Australia and Canada had been a constant source of humanitarian assistance since 1974 and now held their own television fundraisers as well. In America, even the prisoners of New York State's Mount McGregor correctional facility contributed. The homeless of Los Angeles donated $175 in nickels and pennies. In the poorer parts of New York City, the schools tried to raise enough money to send a plane full of grain to Ethiopia. French tennis player Yannick Noah tried to initiate a national fundraising in France, but the response was muted. In Italy, by contrast, retired Italian soldiers who had taken part in the invasion of Ethiopia in 1935, Italians who had lived in Ethiopia, Italians who had married Ethiopians and Italian–Ethiopians in general helped to spur on fundraising momentum. And so it went.

The Ethiopian people remained ignorant of the world's response to their need, since only a few received the BBC News or the Voice of America, which recorded these events.

When Giorgis thanked the UN and other agencies for their help, but also noted that the international community had not taken heed of RRC figures earlier in the year, the *New York Times* declared, 'Ethiopians Blame the West for Famine'. A professor in New Jersey wrote to Giorgis, 'I find it interesting that the Soviet Union bears no responsibility [for its neglect of the famine] in your mind.'

Though they did not dare see what their master refused to see, the Derg ultimately let Giorgis put together a visiting delegation from the Council of Ministers, including the minister for the interior, who chaired the Famine Committee within the Derg. Giorgis's purpose was to strike out with them to threatened regions of the highlands, where the winter of 1984–5 was in progress and where exposure and pneumonia were killing people who had mere shreds of cloth to cover themselves with. At every relief station the delegation visited, they saw people spread about dying and dead in the outdoors, and the sick and the starving crammed by thousands into intensive-care shelters designed for mere hundreds, or else into the shambolic Ethiopian equivalent of fever wards.

There were 250 shelters in Ethiopia, and most of the sick lay in greater numbers outside them than inside.

At one of the shelters, a Derg minister asked a Save the Children volunteer to whom the delegation was introduced to explain the situation there, and the woman lost her temper. She said she was too busy to brief him and: 'It is ridiculous that we should have to tell you the problems of your own people! You should have been the ones to explain your needs to us.'

Some of the sick were full of a similar defiance, asking the Derg men where Mengistu was, pointing to the red flags which fluttered even around the shelters and distribution centres, and telling the ministers that that cloth should have been on the backs of the ragged sick and starving. The only strength of the terminally hungry was that they enjoyed free speech in a country in which it had been outlawed. All this was a revelation to the ministers, but they knew the tidings of it would be unwelcome to their master, and dangerous to carry to him.

To Mengistu's dissatisfaction, the airport was now full of foreign planes – the RAF, the German air force, as well as Jordanian, Swiss, and Soviet planes, all chartered by their governments. Addis Ababa was crowded by journalists, TV crews and aid volunteers, and very few of them were interested in Mengistu's forthcoming tenth birthday of revolution celebrations – the parades of military and ethnic groups, the state banquets and the speeches – except in so far as they offered a contrast to the famine beyond the city. And this after he had gone to so much trouble to make the celebrations function smoothly – ordering a round-up of dying prostitutes, beggars and street people and having them interned until after the holidays.

His festivities, Mengistu complained, were being mocked and denounced by the West, and Ethiopia had become a byword for African 'unsuccess'. The Ethiopian people had never been aware of the extent of the problem, Mengistu claimed. Now the world was trying to tell them all about it. In a meeting with his politburo, Mengistu raged against the foreign air forces parked at the airport, at the pernicious journalists, who had supposedly come to cover the celebrations but who now seemed interested only in the famine, and at the forty-eight voluntary agencies who were intruding on Ethiopia and whom he could not expel for fear that he would no longer be able to hold power without feeding at least his cities. He asked why it was not possible for them to send all their aid directly through the Ethiopian government, and let them distribute it. But given that he did not acknowledge the famine, how could he be trusted with the distribution of the aid? In any case, he would subvert much of the aid, and exploit and compromise at least some of the agencies.

In the meantime, visitors from all over the world, from Mother Teresa to the Kennedys to Jesse Jackson's wife, Mrs Jacqueline Jackson, came to see what was happening. Mother Teresa proposed a feeding centre in the desperate province of Bale, in the furthest south. She visited Mengistu, who seemed to give way to her on the project. But the building of the centre in the province was never permitted to occur. Giorgis asked the party secretary of Bale why there were no developments, and was told that he had orders from Addis to frustrate and discourage the project.

The schedules of visitors from the West were demanding in terms of time, and Giorgis complained that they took

RRC agents away from their work. Again, there was a certain irrationality in this: he had complained that the world was ignoring Ethiopia; now he was complaining that it was giving the country too much attention. He would have been naive if he thought that relief would come without any Western self-congratulation at all.

Visiting at Christmas 1984, Senator Ted Kennedy was allowed to go wherever he wanted. For once, says Giorgis, here was a politician who was not interested in a political pay-off. Among other locations, Ted Kennedy went to Bati in Wollo province, once a centre of traditional music but now a ruin full of the starving.

Giorgis was not so impressed with Bob Geldof. He was a city boy, said Giorgis, full of arrogance and vulgarity. Yet neither the regime nor the RRC rejected his input. Giorgis sent him to spend Christmas – in the spirit of the song he had produced – to Lalibela, the fourteenth-century church and monastery cut into the volcanic material of its region, where there was little to be observed. Marion Barry, mayor of Washington, arrived for a less than twenty-four-hour visit to Addis and saw nothing beyond it. According to Giorgis he seemed to want only chances to be photographed.

Harry Belafonte and his group, USA for Africa, came with a plane full of relief supplies. But instead of showing Belafonte famine victims, under pressure from Mengistu, the RRC directed him towards a mobile hospital unit run by Soviet doctors and technicians. The Russians chatted with Belafonte's group openly, took them around the hospital, showed them the facilities, and exchanged t-shirts with them. But the patients were not famine victims at all – most were casualties of the war against the TPLF. USA for Africa saw only carefully prepared and selected places. Sometimes party cadres posed as famine victims and sent the foreigners away with a firm sense that everything was under control. Belafonte visited Mengistu but, according to Giorgis, the meeting was uncontroversial on both sides.

The most meaningful visitor to the victims in the shelters and distribution centres would have been their leader, Mengistu. He did not visit the affected areas until so many outsiders had commented on it that he could no longer avoid it. Some time late in November 1994, he flew to Makale, walked around an area near the airport for a few minutes, then flew to Bati and stayed just long enough to have his picture taken. Mengistu spent about a total of thirty minutes in the afflicted areas.

In the meantime, Giorgis himself camped at Debre Birhan, only a hundred miles outside Addis, and found that people tried to stave off the highland cold by lying in shallow graves. Overnight there, thirty-one people died.

Makale, the capital of Tigray, was a front line between the Ethiopian army and the Tigrayan rebels. Here, 40–50,000 people had gathered at the shelters of the RRC and the Catholic Relief Service. Mengistu, after tactful approaches by the Italian ambassador, allowed Ethiopian pilots and Soviet aircraft, using fuel paid for by the Americans, to deliver the food required for them. As well, the RRC borrowed planes from the Ethiopian air force, but it had to pay for the fuel.

To get to the remoter areas, the RRC and agencies sent into the mountains muleteers with strings of as many as fifty donkeys, each loaded with half a quintal of grain. Later, the RRC, with the help of the UN representative in Ethiopia, Kurt Jansson – a controversial figure whom some would accuse of collaborating with Mengistu – devised a means of dropping sacks of grain in reinforced packaging from 100–150 feet. Still, much of it was scattered and spoiled on impact. Polish helicopters identified the target areas and prepared the local population for the drop beforehand. The Ethiopian air force transported grain and other materials to Addis. They too charged the RRC for the aviation fuel.

The RAF and Luftwaffe also flew relief to the drop targets. Grain was bagged and rebagged for strength in 25–35 kilo bundles and placed on wooden pallets. These were pushed out of planes that were often flying as low as ten metres. The effort was seen as symbolic by some. Only 11,000 tons of food were dropped in this international effort, but the exercise attracted the approval and interest of the world.

In the meantime, the relief shelters became what Giorgis would call 'meat markets'. Cameramen would search up and down the rows of famine victims, selecting only the most skeletal for filming and, in some cases, waiting for them to die before filming. Giorgis also complained that the voluntary agencies, some of them skilled and sensitive, others utterly insensitive, were squeezing him from one side, while the politburo squeezed him from the other. Many relief agencies brought in staff to do jobs that could equally be done by Ethiopians. Then, as in the Irish famine, religious-based agencies turned the area around the shelters into a mission, proselytising the weak. In March 1985, in the provinces of Sidamo and Showa, close to 700 places of worship built by Western sects were closed down.

Some of the party's provincial leaders fought foreign agencies with a fury that would have made Mengistu proud. The party chief in Gondar, Melaku Tefera, was angry with the Joint Distribution Committee, a US Jewish body that worked among the Falashas, the black Jews, who were peasants and artisans who lived in his province. When two US senators, Dennis DeConcini and Paul Trible, visited Gondar, Tefera endured them, but waited until they had left their hotel before turning up, accompanied by aides, to beat up the three Ethiopians who had accompanied the American delegation from Addis. Before they left Addis, the senators heard about the incident. They complained to the politburo about Tefera's action. The politburo called Giorgis and told him to inform the American delegation that they were liars and that their attempt to besmirch the image of the revolution had failed. Only the RRC apologised to the American senators.

The Ethiopians began closing their shelters in the spring and early summer of 1985. The argument was the people should be returned to their home areas or newly built villages to avail themselves of the *meher* rains of 1985 and so grow food. Tefera, on the orders of Legesse Asfaw, ordered the forced ejection by the army of 60,000 desperate people from the Ibinet shelter in south Gondar. News reports around the world expressed outrage, and the RRC was blamed as much as the government. The people from around the shelter were given fifteen days' rations for the road – not enough to save farming families, said the foreign agencies. Some were sick and likely to die on the road. The evictees were not given tools, seeds, medicine or other supplies.

Tefera then burned the area around the camp. Huts of grass and straw were destroyed by the thousand. Mengistu claimed later that it was a mistake of zeal on the part of local officials. Acting outside his appropriate role, Kurt Jansson held a press conference in which he announced that Mengistu admitted a mistake had been made, and this seemed to satisfy Western opinion.

There were other UN mysteries than Jansson. The executive secretary to the UN Economic Commission for Africa, Adebayo Adedeji, visited Ethiopia only once for a tour with Secretary-General Pérez de Cuéllar. Neither he nor his representatives attended donors' conferences on Ethiopia in 1984 and 1985.

Before, during and after the Mengistu famine, the Eritreans had their own aid agency. The Eritrean Relief Association (ERA) was founded in the early 1970s during the emperor's famine. With the tacit permission of the Sudanese government, it was able to transport food that landed at Port Sudan on the Red Sea coast across a desolate quarter of the republic of Sudan and into the highlands of Eritrea, where it was distributed throughout rebel-held parts of the region. In 1978, the Tigrayans founded a similar body, the Relief Society of Tigray (REST).

The reason these organisations were established was that the distribution of food aid to the non-rebel-held areas of their provinces was scarcely permitted, and in the rebel-held areas themselves hardly any aid at all trickled through. In 1985, when Ethiopia received 1.2 million tonnes of food relief, a mere 90,000 tonnes were distributed by the UN agencies cross-border into non-government-held areas of Tigray and Eritrea, even though a third to a half of the famine victims were found in such areas. Giorgis himself thought the government-held areas of Eritrea were being deliberately punished by the withholding of supplies.

Many traditional relief agencies maligned and resented ERA and REST because they reduced their areas of operation. The relief agencies also accused the rebels of attacking food convoys. In reply, ERA and REST argued – it seems with some justice – that under government coercion agency food-relief trucks were mixed in with Ethiopian military columns in such a way that the rebels could not know which was which.

In the areas they held, ERA and REST proved typically more adaptive in the way they managed to supply aid, and were efficient distributors of food. Both attracted more and more local support as it became clear that Mengistu was misusing food on a heroic scale and spending exorbitantly on his military.

In ERA's case, there was little wastage and pilfering. I observed myself the way ERA operated. The Sudan, at the time I first went to Eritrea, was a democratic nation led by Sadiq al-Mahdi. A traditional enemy of Ethiopia, Sudan was willing to allow the Eritrean People's Liberation Front

(EPLF) to run clinics for war wounded and warehouses for ERA operations in Port Sudan and in Suakin, an old Turkish-built port south of Port Sudan. Aid for Eritrea would arrive in Port Sudan and be stored there by ERA officials, then transported south and into Eritrea in Mercedes trucks from donor countries. The trucks were not allowed to fall apart but were serviced by ERA mechanics in garages in Port Sudan. The strain on the vehicles was enormous, for the aid had to be carried south across desert and then over empty riverbeds full of boulders and up the rough switchback roads of the mountains of Eritrea.

Trucks loaded with ERA food provided by aid agencies from the US, Australia, Canada and the Scandinavian countries began rolling out of their depot south of Port Sudan before noon, so that they would reach Eritrea by nightfall, when they would be safe from the Derg's daytime bombing raids. If they had not finished the journey to their appointed depot by dawn, they hid for the daylight hours in camouflaged bays dug into hillsides, and continued the following evening. Once the food was cached in every area, often in camouflaged warehouses dug into the sides of mountains, or else in bunkers in the torrid lowlands, ERA officials had to depend on distribution lists drawn up by the local village assemblies. In a warehouse bunker in a lowland village, under a roof that seemed to concentrate heat and amidst bags of flour and other aid, I saw, for example, a young ERA man in army fatigues working on his lists before making an evening distribution. In the bunker, among the food bags piled to the ceiling, there was very little space left over for his bed.

The distributions were done with some dignity – the

desperate scurry of hungry people around aid trucks captured on television in other emergencies was not a characteristic of the many food distributions I saw at night, or by day under cover, in Eritrea. Such well-ordered and systematic distributions could and should have taken place in Ethiopia.

Under the rebels' political contract, Muslims and Coptic Christians were fed the same ration. Such equity was not pure charity – it was essential for the unity of the rebel front. But nomads, whose nationality was less certain, were also fed. One night, after reaching a spot in which to sleep, in a dry riverbed, the party I was with was woken at dawn by nomads, who had slept in the riverbed too and were pounding mortars with pestles, grinding coffee, all around us. Within half an hour, even apart from the risk of bombing, the riverbed was uninhabitable because of heat. The nomads, members of a tribe named the Hadarab, their coffee drunk, withdrew to a food depot hidden among the trees where, safe from any overview by Antonov bombers, food distribution commenced. Perhaps the EPLF and ERA were trying by these means to give the nomads a sense of being Eritrean, but it did not matter what the motives were – it mattered that the social contract between the rebels and their people be observed and their countrymen not be allowed to starve.

Similarly, the connection between the Tigrayans and the people under their control became a social and political contract – food would be justly distributed by REST in return for loyalty. The rebel forces were also fed from part of this aid, just as Ethiopian forces were on aid Mengistu had commandeered. ERA and REST had stepped in to supply the succour that the emperor and then the Derg would not.

The political-contract approach did not operate under the same degree of moral pretension that characterised some Western aid, and yet it was more effective. Perhaps it should be the future of all government famine efforts, although a tyrannical government like that of Mengistu saw no need to recognise or honour such a contract with its own people.

For voluntary agencies throughout the world, Mengistu's famine and war raised the question of how far an NGO should go in cooperating with a tyrannous regime. Should a relief agency feed some of the people while fully knowing that food will be diverted and that their intended mercy will not be extended to troublesome regions, people or unpopular tribes?

It has been argued that aid agencies will collaborate rather than be expelled from a region considered favourable for their own fundraising. In Ethiopia, they had the lesson before them of Médecins Sans Frontières – Mengistu had expelled this agency for criticising his policies and his squandering of money on armaments.

Relief agencies compete for every compassionate dollar, are institutional, are afflicted with a corporatist outlook – all these are accusations that have become increasingly common. It is said by some that when aid workers gather for a drink in Asia or Africa, or anywhere else on earth, efficacy becomes a major topic of conversation, with some of them having become doubters of their own processes – efficacy agnostics. This is not to cast doubt on the goodwill of agencies or their volunteers. But after all this time, it is obvious that emergency and development aid from voluntary agencies have failed to develop Ethiopia beyond subsistence, beyond dependence and beyond the most primitive services of transport and health and education. Ethiopia remains a perpetual sick man, and cynics wonder if this situation does not greatly suit both those holding power in that country, and those agencies who want to operate in, and have news to impart about the place.

17

Other Catastrophes

IF MANY IN the British government approved of the sad but providential scythe that reduced the Irish population to a desirable level, in Ethiopia another version of Providence – Marxist theory as interpreted by Mengistu – was at work. But twentieth-century famines in Russia might be seen as even more nakedly driven by doctrine than Mengistu's famine.

The initiating principles for the Russian famine of 1921–2 were drought and abnormally heavy frost in 1920, but the regions that were most stricken were those in which armed squads had rampaged in previous years, requisitioning food to feed the cities and the army. In the Saratov province south of Moscow, where a brigade known for its brutality collected the requisition, the food levy left villagers stripped of any emergency supply at all. Methods used to gather more food still included holding children to ransom, and the whipping, torturing and execution of peasants. Requisition battalions would shoot dead any peasants who resisted them, using as justification the cry that those who were not willing to surrender their essential food were *kulaks* – bourgeois farmers driven by capitalistic motives. Some Red officials in the districts tried to temper the requisition process, and warned Moscow that no more could be squeezed out of the countryside. But no one listened.

One focus of the famine was the Volga region, where the steppes had turned to dust. The big industrial towns of the Don Basin to the south were stricken too. Then there was a second harvest failure in 1921, as in the previous year. Any growth that had occurred was destroyed in large part by rats and plagues of locusts. These alone were not sufficient to cause the famine. There had always been a store of communal grain for the village to fall back on. But it was either taken, or did not exist, because to escape further levies peasants had retreated to subsistence farming – producing just enough for their families to live on. In Samara province nearly two million people, three-quarters of the population, were suspected to be dying from hunger by the autumn of 1921, and the final number of dead was 700,000, there alone.

As people starved, the predictable typhus and cholera became common killers. Peasants ate grass, roof thatch, ground acorns, sawdust, moss and animal manure. They hunted rats and domestic pets. They devoured cigarette butts. Those with enough strength fled to the towns, if possible taking their scarecrow horses with them to exchange for bread. Vast crowds tried to catch trains to Moscow, but the government put limitations on travel to prevent the spread of famine diseases. The woman of Clonakilty reappeared in myriad form in the Volga region, and madness crept on and cannibalism began. So did it increasingly in other regions. A Russian from the steppes was convicted of eating several children, and in his confession declared that in his village everyone ate human flesh but pretended they didn't. There were several cafeterias in the village, he declared, and all of them served up the flesh of children.

That winter, people stacked the dead in barns as a food source. Corpses were even stolen from graveyards. If any of this was worse than Bengal or Ethiopia or Ireland, it has to be taken into account that the Russian peasant was already demoralised by the reality of Bolshevik collectivisation. It was often compassion for one's family, as well as the individual derangement of starvation, that drove people to cannibalism. One doctor who committed cannibalism wrote of 'the insuperable and uncomfortable craving' which people acquired for the flesh of the dead.

All the requisitions of food in the countryside did not save the middle class of the cities. At Moscow University, said one survivor, a professor hanged himself, Russia's foremost geologist took potassium cyanide, and as for the rest of the faculty, they were dying of influenza, pneumonia and cholera.

There was the familiar late acknowledgement of famine's existence by government. Maxim Gorky, however, wrote an appeal to the world, which began, 'Tragedy has come to the country of Tolstoy, Dostoevsky, Mendeleyev, Pavlov, Mussorgsky, Glinka and other world-prized men.' The All-Russian Public Committee to aid the hungry was founded as a result of Gorky's appeal to Lenin. Constantin Stanislavsky was a member, as was Alexandra Tolstoya, the writer's daughter, who had already suffered at the hands of the Cheka, the secret police. Prince Lvov, former Tsarist cabinet minister, collected aid in France. President Herbert Hoover offered to send the American Relief Administration (ARA) to Russia, on the conditions that it was allowed to operate independently of government and that US citizens be released from Soviet gaols. But Lenin was furious at the offer. Even the Gorky-instigated public committee was closed down for having received American aid. All its office holders except Gorky and one other were arrested by the Cheka and accused of counter-revolutionary activities. Gorky, admired universally, was urged by Lenin to go overseas for his health. Shocked by the way the authorities had handled the famine, Gorky left Russia.

The ARA did manage to operate in Russia and at the height of its activities was feeding ten million people a day. Its donations of seed made it possible for a new harvest to be planted, and the harvest of 1922–3 helped bring an end to the famine. The Bolsheviks – perhaps not entirely without some justification, but certainly with paranoia – accused the ARA of spying and of trying to discredit and overthrow the Soviet regime. So the central government interfered relentlessly with ARA's operations – again a pattern that would be seen in Mengistu's Ethiopia later in the century.

Seven million children would become the orphans of the famine. Some of them had been abandoned by their parents. They lived in railway stations, abandoned houses, building sites, dumps, cellars and sewers. Nearly all of them became child prostitutes.

If anything, ideologically induced famine would be more naked still with Stalin in the 1930s. There was a bad harvest in 1932. Stalin kept up grain exports from Russia throughout the famine years that followed. Cannibalism was common in this period as it had been in the early 1920s. But police and army and party officials were set the task of ensuring that the economic and political changes made by Stalin and the politburo in 1928 would stay intact. These had given priority to heavy industry at the expense of the production of food. Marxist theory overruled extremities of want. By December 1931, peasants were again eating dogs, horses, bark and rotting potatoes. An American Communist visited a village near Kharkov in the Ukraine. He found only one mad woman left alive, and rats feasting on the dead. Just the same, on 6 June 1932, Stalin and Molotov issued a joint statement to the effect that no deviation regarding amounts of food or delivery deadlines could be permitted. Stalin saw the famine as an affront to him and the Central Committee. He wrote, 'The Ukraine has been given more than it should get.' He suggested to one of the Central Committee who had reported on the famine that he was simply a good storyteller, 'fabricating such a fairytale about famine!' He urged that the man, Kaganovich, who had had a great deal to do with the planning that created the famine in the first place, should join the Writers' Union, where he could concoct stories and fools could read them. But other members of the Central Committee knew what was happening in Ukraine – the people in the countryside boarding trains for Kiev and arriving there as corpses. Stalin remained firm in denial, speaking of the 'glaring absurdities' of the news of the emergency.

No one knows how many died for the sake of feeding those who built smelters and tractors, but it may have been as high as 10 million, as Stalin himself seemed to believe. During World War II, he told Churchill that he had been forced by famine to destroy 10 million. It was fearful, he confessed, and the process lasted four years. But, 'It was absolutely necessary . . . it was no use arguing with them.' Naturally, at the time of the famine, there was an anti-government political reaction in the regions, which the state security police, the OGPU, repressed by its customary vigorous methods.

In northern China, drought was a great trigger for famine. The mountain regions to the west of the northern Great Plain were always treeless, barren and blighted by low rainfall. Elsewhere, however, flood was the destroyer.

There had been great works as early as 200 BC to protect areas against flood and to use water creatively. The Chengdu Plain in Szechuan to the south was irrigated and referred to as 'the garden of western China', and there were great flood-mitigation works in Shensi province, neighbouring Shansi and in Hunan.

In modern times, the crops the Chinese planted were diverse and included an array of wheat varieties: spring wheat, winter wheat-millet, another winter variation named *kaoliang*. Other crops were Szechuan and south-western rice, Yangtze rice and tea. The floods that regularly wiped away such lowland crops had caused famines throughout Chinese history, most notoriously on the banks of the Yellow River.

Under the old imperial regime, the conservancy of the Yellow River was under the control of only one bureaucrat, who reported directly to the Emperor. It was not enough.

Whenever the Huai River in eastern and central China flooded, there was a loss of food on a level that would affect the lives of tens of millions. In the 1920s, a scholar declared that from the point of view of famine distress, no area was in greater need of flood prevention than the Huai. Catastrophic floods occurred every few years in Hebei region, south of Beijing, as well.

A total of 435 famines across twenty provinces occurred between 1850 and 1932, and most were created by flood. For much of the nineteenth century, and even earlier in history, particularly under the incompetent and corrupt Manchus, Chinese provinces were ruled by warlords who were totally indifferent to the issue of food, drought or famine. Peasants did not attribute famines to mayhem and rapacity, but to the anger of the river gods. Perhaps the gods were also to blame for the locusts, which were a regular blight.

After the overthrow of the emperor in 1911, a sum equivalent to £3 million was devoted to flood mitigation in the entire country. But each provincial governor had charge of his section of the river and there was no unified control. This system, of course, contributed to the famine in the early 1920s.

A weak central government, both under the Manchus and the republic, spent its money on ammunition, artillery and aircraft. Epochs of resultant hunger in the countryside generated banditry. The bandits, former peasants or defeated members of warlords' forces, became unproductive raiders of other people's food, burning villages and towns.

In the nineteenth and twentieth century, many people left their homes and withdrew into the mountains, some to die because of the operation of bandits. As well as the predatory bandits, the army lived off the provinces in which they were garrisoned, and were considered just as bad as bandits. Domestic animals were seized to pull wagons loaded with ammunition and supplies for the army. Meanwhile, there was heavy and unpredictable taxation by various officials. Farming families were thus victims of plunder after plunder, exaction after exaction. In many provinces people turned to growing opium, though every acre producing the Lethean chemical was taxed as well, and provincial officials took a share of, or frequently control of, the opium traffic. The growing of opium, of course, further reduced the amount of land under food cultivation.

In the famine of 1921, the funds distributed by the central government in Peking (Beijing) were too small to lengthen life by more than a few days. Most philanthropic societies were restricted in what they could give, despite their wish to do more. The American Red Cross adopted a plan for employing able-bodied members of stricken families – an echo of Ireland. In return for a day's labour on public works, it was hoped that sufficient relief would be provided to support the labourer and his dependants. The wages paid on a piece-work basis were intentionally kept below the normal wage scale to prevent exploitation of the charity. The non-foreign China International Relief Commission was founded after the particularly massive famine in northern China in 1921, and its personnel resisted corruption and worked in the manner the Ethiopian Relief and Rehabilitation

Commission was meant to. It offered loans and investments rather than handouts.

Still in existence under the Communists, its efforts would not ultimately prevent a further, astonishing famine in 1958–61. According to government statistics, there were 15 million excess deaths in those three years, to which the government referred as the 'three years of natural disasters'. It powerfully resembled Stalin's famine of the early 1930s. Forced collectivisation and the preference for heavy industry over agricultural work, with millions of peasants taken from the land and relocated to the factories in a process named the Great Leap Forward – all this was the true cause of the famine. One contemporary wrote that in Xinyang in western China, people starved at the doors of the grain warehouses. As they died, they shouted for the Communist Party and Chairman Mao to save them. Indeed, had government granaries been opened, no one need have died.

'I went to one village and saw one hundred corpses,' wrote a witness in a generic famine passage that could stand for any of the famines narrated here, 'then another village and another one hundred corpses. No one paid attention to them . . . People said that dogs were eating the bodies. Not true, I said. The dogs have long ago been eaten by the people.'

The provincial mess halls for party officials absorbed and wasted supplies of food during this Chinese famine of the Great Leap Forward. Over 2 million tonnes of grain were requisitioned in some provinces and sent to feed the cities. In formerly agricultural areas, over-fervent party officials sucked up rural labour into small, backyard ironworks, massive irrigation and other labour-intensive work. Less food was planted, and calorie needs rose and were not answered because of the heavy labour that ambitious party officials, on probation with the party, demanded from conscripted peasant workers. The same earnestness had been shown by Mengistu's cadres in Ethiopia in their demands for labour from peasants whose food supplies were similarly on the decline. In both cases, the party seemed to offer the official a *lien* on the gratitude of his masters.

In the closed society of the Democratic People's Republic of North Korea, a famine that was triggered in 1995 first by drought and then by catastrophic floods – but also by the loss of manufacturing and other contracts with Russia – would go on to kill perhaps one million people. At least, that is the figure given by most experts, but being an expert on North Korea is a hard exercise.

Kim Jong Il, the North Korean leader, cited the floods as his reason to call for aid. He was, like Mengistu before him, suspicious of Western aid bodies, because he believed that aid was an extension of American politics. It is hard to agree in any form with Kim Jong Il, but the reality is that aid is coloured by politics, and the enthusiasm of religious aid organisations – as pure as their intentions might be – to take part in relief in such an extremely Stalinist, God-denying nation, could be seen as a proof that both ideology and the Cross followed the bags of emergency food. For these reasons, and because he could not let the West see that his governance had failed his people, Kim did not let international agencies carry out any research into the level of malnutrition in North Korea, the size of the threatened population, or the mortality rate among them.

There were complaints by agencies that food resulting from their aid went to the favoured and the army. As in Ethiopia earlier, the death rate certainly confirmed the fact that aid was not reaching all those who needed it. In fact, in 1997, to strengthen the support of the military for his regime, Kim frankly put in place a *songun*, or a 'military-first' policy.

Though the end date of the country's famine is generally given as 1998, some argue it has never ended. The famine cycle there is said to have become nearly intractable – the soil is eroded by over-farming in Stalin and Mengistu-style collectives, and people have been taken away from farming for the sort of great industrial surges favoured by Stalin and Mao. Acceptance of a two-meal-a-day policy has become one of the standards of loyalty to *juche*, the philosophy by which Kim Jong Il's edicts are the driving force in individual choice. But because of the highly secretive nature of the country, and despite the window that NGOs opened on it during the official famine, North Korea remains a place where another million or more could die, and news of it would remain as obscure a rumour as might a famine in a distant kingdom in the Middle Ages.

Meles Zenawi, the pragmatic Marxist leader of the Tigrayan rebels who became prime minister of Ethiopia in 1991, has, since then, been faced with many food emergencies, most of whose existence he has denied. It seems that there is a virus in Ethiopian government that transfers itself from regime to regime. Ethiopians who have left their country ask why the Ethiopian government fails to put in place permanent policies to reduce emergencies brought on by drought. And both domestic Ethiopia and Ethiopia dispersed point to the great agricultural companies of the world for charging high for seed and paying low for product.

Like the Irish, the chief and unqualified aid the Ethiopians overseas remitted home was money for their families, and that was enormous in scale, flowing from cab drivers and parking-station attendants, storekeepers and professionals all over the earth.

By 2008, the bulk of employment in Ethiopia was in its bureaucracy, and members of opposition parties had been imprisoned and tortured. In 2003, according to the *New York Times*, more than 12 million were at risk from famine in Ethiopia, half of them children under fifteen years. More recently UNICEF has said that 8 million Ethiopians are 'chronically food insecure', an unnecessary bureaucratic term, which conveys the reality that farming families do not produce enough to avoid being hungry and malnourished. At least 3.4 million of these were in immediate need of emergency food relief. Yet, like Mengistu, President Meles Zenawi told the National Assembly in March 2008 that reports of drought-induced deaths were false, denied that pastoralists in the south were losing livestock to drought, or that malnutrition was anything near the levels foreign aid workers claimed. Accusations were made, too, that Zenawi had stood in the way of the flow of relief by charging excessive fees for transportation, and limiting the means of distribution to a trucking company in which he was accused of having interests. Like Mengistu, he was vigilant to punish any aid agency who tried to take a political stance on freedom of expression and other rights. Photographs of the starving were banned, and aid workers in the field were told not to give interviews to foreign journalists.

In August 2008, Zenawi said that UNICEF's estimations of the numbers at risk were overblown. He was skilled at using the new cynicism about relief to his advantage. 'The more gruesome the picture, the better chance you have of getting your share of those resources.' In an interview, Zenawi assured those who questioned him that the Ogaden was being looked after adequately and with the same level of care as other provinces. 'I suspect we will always have pockets of hunger. The big question is whether we have enough in our own economy to be able to finance the safety net program. We have not reached that stage yet.'

When this interview was posted on an Ethiopian news site on the internet, the focus of Ethiopians who responded was chiefly on getting rid of Zenawi, although one Tigrayan read the criticism as part of the hatred of his ethnic group by Amharas in exile.

Zenawi's famine existed not only in the countryside but also among the slum dwellers of the city. As one woman said, 'We give birth to the children, but we can't grow them.' In 2008, malnourished children were being brought to feeding clinics. It was not uncommon for four-year-old children who weighed twenty pounds to appear at the field hospitals. They were weighed in a nylon harness attached to a scale and their arm circumference was measured. Those most under-nourished were kept in the clinic for up to a month, and the rest went home with a week's supply of Plumpy-nut, a nutritional paste. This high-protein mixture of peanut paste, vegetable oil, powdered milk, powdered sugar, vitamins and minerals was designed in 1999 by André Briend, a French scientist. It was manufactured in France and packed in silver foil designed to resist the effects of heat and distance. In the early twenty-first century, Plumpy-nut has become what the high-protein biscuit, otherwise known as BP-5, had been in late-twentieth-century food crises.

The poor of 2006 had to eat *injera* made of sorghum or rice instead of teff, and found these alternatives in many cases too harsh on the stomach, sometimes with fatal effects.

In 2002, Zenawi *had* acknowledged an Ethiopian crisis, in which 6 million people were in need of assistance, with another 2 to 3 million likely to be stricken in the coming months. Though fortunately averted by emergency aid, this threat had the potential to be worse than Mengistu's famine.

In that same year, half a million people were under threat of starvation in Mozambique. And in Malawi, where there had already been a terrible famine in 1949–50, 3.2 million people were threatened by famine. In the earlier Malawi crisis of 1949, men had taken to the roads, obsessed with getting food. 'People could not stay in one place,' said a witness. 'If they heard there was food somewhere they went to find it, no matter how far.' They travelled to the large towns of Ntcheu, Neno and Mwanza to work in the gardens of people who had plenty of food. Men who had come from elsewhere to marry in a particular region sometimes abandoned their wives and went back to their parents' home, supposedly to look for food – however, many, wanting to be free from encumbrances in this crisis, never came back again.

All the other debasements of that 1949–50 famine that occurred in Malawi arose again in Biafra in the newly independent Nigeria. In 1960, the country was a loose confederacy of ethnic groups: the Hausa and Fulani in the north, the Yoruba in the south-west and the Ibo in the south-east. The Ibo and the Hausas were enemies, and up to 30,000 Ibos were killed in conflict between the two groups. About 1 million panicked refugees from other parts of the country fled to their Ibo homeland in the east, where Colonel Emeka Ojukwu declared the independent republic of Biafra in May 1967. Two and a half years later, one million civilians had died in fighting with the Hausa and from famine. The Biafran famine was a media event as well as a tragedy – the first great famine to be covered by the new medium of television.

In Zimbabwe, as I write, there is a growing famine crisis. Because of the leader Robert Mugabe's new land policies, farms have fallen into disuse and the price of food, where it can be found in the markets and on the largely empty shelves of grocery stores, is rising every week, not simply by percentages but by multiples. In mismanaged Angola and Mauritania, in a relentless drought, an uncounted number of endangered people await help. In the landlocked state of Zambia, some hundreds of thousands are at risk, but the president has refused to accept genetically modified food, off-loaded from the West, to feed them. Agribusiness from the West is seen both as a plunderer of African seed varieties for use for its own commercial purposes, and as forcing genetically modified food strains upon native populations. This food, for which demand in the West is uncertain, is increasingly sent as food aid to Africa.

Darfur is a western province of the Sudan, situated in a pitiless desert that stretches away to and beyond the borders of Chad. Malnutrition levels, particularly among children, are very high there, but relief agencies find it hard to work under threats from the central government that they will be thrown out at any time. The flow of food from Khartoum, the capital, is so intruded upon by bureaucrats that one German agency shipped its food in via West Africa and the republic of Chad.

The Janjaweed Arab militias, armed by the central government, keep African farmers from cultivating their land and destroy before harvest whatever crops are planted. Reports of a collapse in cultivation of crops, due to people being driven off their land by the Janjaweed and Sudanese government soldiers, are universal throughout the province. Increasing numbers of Darfur people have fled to refugee camps, and in 2008 more than 3 million were dependent on food assistance.

The Global Acute Malnutrition index showed a rate of 21.3 per cent for malnutrition among children in 2007, but Khartoum blocked further testing and the Wali or administrator of north Darfur took on himself the right to censor any malnutrition studies before their release. In 2006, for lack of funding, the World Food program announced that it would cut the rations to Darfur from 1300 calories a day to 1050. This is half the minimum daily calories necessary to maintain health. The program said the problem was it had received just a third of the money it had requested from donor countries.

The Darfur rebels, for whose existence the government is persecuting an entire population, call themselves the Justice and Equality Movement – JEM. JEM was founded by former supporters, now disenchanted, of the Islamic leader of Sudan, Hassan al-Turabi, who is also leader of the opposition. In its pursuit of JEM the army is relentless. On BBC television, a Sudanese army deserter told of a standard military operation in Darfur, aimed not only on the plunder or destruction of crops, but involving orders from officers to kill adult women and rape and kill thirteen- and fourteen-year-old girls – all of them were, in the army's eyes, culpable of supporting rebel groups.

In the first decade of the twenty-first century, Darfur was an example of the way armies, militias, race and government policy combined to create what the experts call 'a humanitarian disaster'.

African famines, especially, have become more complex and difficult to deal with since now they often involve people suffering from AIDS. As well as that, the seasons are becoming more erratic as the climate warms. Arguments about relief and its efficacy continue. And in a modern world where the keeping of statistics is an obsession, the attempted secrecy of regimes, their power to permit relief to penetrate their country only to a certain degree, the existence of rebel groups and the appalling state of infrastructure guarantee that many die beyond view. It still remains impossible, therefore, to number the famine dead. Above all, there is no end to politicians who pursue, at the cost of all compassion and paying the price of human flesh, their denials, dogmas and ideologies.

Despite seasons of neediness continuing, famine did not return to Ireland after the 1840s, whereas it seems set for tragic repetitions in Ethiopia, and is not done with yet. Ideology might have played a large part in the Irish and Bengal famines. But, according to the distinguished economic historian Cormac Ó'Gráda, in Ethiopia and in many food crises of the present and recent past, it is oppression, war and 'civic mayhem' that have been the main reasons for famine mortality. 'Agency,' he says, 'is more important than a food production shortfall. Mars counts for more than Malthus.'

Surely, then, famine has not had its last ride.

Bibliography

BOOKS

Anderson, Mary B., *Do No Harm: How Aid Can Support Peace or War* (London, 1999)

van Apeldoorn, G. Jan, *Perspectives on Famine and Drought in Nigeria* (London, 1981)

Bhattacharya, Bhabani, *So Many Hungers* (London, 1947)

Bhattacharya, Bhabani, *He Who Rides a Tiger* (London, 1954)

Clay, Jason W. and Holcomb, Bonnie K., *Politics and the Ethiopian Famine, 1984–1985* (Cambridge, Mass., 1989)

Clay, Jason W; Steingraber, Sandra; Niggli, Peter, *Ethiopian Famine Policy and Peasant Agriculture* (Cambridge, Mass., 1988)

Climer, Kenton J., *Quest for Freedom: the United States and Indian Independence* (New York, 1995)

Daly, M. W., *Darfur's Sorrow: a History of Destruction and Genocide* (New York, 2007)

Das, Tarakchandra, *The Bengal Famine, 1943, as Revealed in a Survey of the Destitutes of Calcutta* (Calcutta, 1969)

Dreze, Jean and Sen, Amartya, *The Political Economy of Hunger, Volume 2* (London, 1990)

Edwards, Ruth Dudley, *An Atlas of Irish History* (London, 1986)

Edwards, Ruth Dudley and Williams, T. Desmond (eds) *The Great Famine, Studies in Irish History, 1845–52* (Dublin, 1994)

Famine Inquiry Commission, *Report on Bengal* (New Delhi, 1945)

Firebrace, James and Holland, Stuart, *Never Kneel Down: Drought, Development and Liberation in Eritrea* (Nottingham, 1984)

Fisher, H. H., *The Famine in Soviet Russia, 1919–1923* (London, 1927)

Flake, L. Gordon and Snyder, Scott, *Paved with Good Intentions: the NGO Experience in North Korea* (Westport, Conn., 2004)

French, Patrick, *Liberty or Death, India's Journey to Independence and Division* (London, 1997)

Ghebre-Medhin, Jordan, *Peasants and Nationalism in Eritrea: a Critique of Ethiopian Studies* (Trenton, N.J., 1989)

Giorgis, Wolde David, *Red Tears, War, Famine and Revolution in Ethiopia* (Trenton, N.J., 1989)

Goshal, Kumar, *The People of India* (New York, 1944)

Greenhough, Paul, *Prosperity and Misery in Modern Bengal: the Famine of 1942–44* (New Delhi, 1982)

Hancock, Graham, *Lords of Poverty: the Power, Prestige and Corruption of the International Aid Business* (London, 1989)

Hoare, Mary Anne, *Shamrock Leaves: Tales and Sketches of Ireland* (London, 1851)

Ikramullah, Begun Shaista Shurawardy, *The Biography of Huseyn Shaheed Suhrawardy* (Oxford, 1991)

Kapuściński, Ryszard, *The Emperor: Downfall of an Autocrat* (New York, 1983)

Kelleher, Margaret, *The Feminization of Famine: Expressions of the Inexpressible?* (Cork, 1997)

Keneally, Thomas, *The Great Shame* (Sydney, 1998)

John Killen (ed.) *The Famine Decade, Contemporary Accounts 1841–1851* (Belfast, 1995)

Kinealy, Christine, *A Death-Dealing Famine* (London, 1997)

Kinealy, Christine, *This Great Calamity: the Irish Famine 1845–1852* (Dublin, 1994)

Knight, Henry, *Food Administration in India, 1839–1947* (Stanford, Cal., 1954)

MacKay, Donald, *Flight from Famine: the Coming of the Irish to Canada* (Toronto, 1990)

Maren, Michael, *The Road to Hell: the Ravaging Effects of Foreign Aid and International Charity* (New York, 1997)

Mokyr, Joel, *Why Ireland Starved: a Quantitative and Analytical History of the Irish Economy, 1800–1850* (London, 1983)

Moon, Penderel, *Divide and Quit* (Berkeley, Cal., 1962)

Morash, Christopher (ed.), *The Hungry Voice: the Poetry of the Irish Famine* (Dublin, 1989)

O'Connor, John, *The Workhouses of Ireland: the Fate of Ireland's Poor* (Dublin, 1995)

Ó'Gráda, Cormac, *Black '47 and Beyond: the Great Irish Famine in History, Economy and Memory* (Princeton, 2000)

Ó'Gráda, Cormac, *The Great Irish Famine* (Dublin, 1989)

Ó'Gráda, Cormac, *Ireland before and after the Famine: Explorations in Economic History, 1800–1925* (Manchester, UK, 1993)

Pankhurst, Alula, *Resettlement and Famine in Ethiopia: the Villagers' Experience* (Manchester, c. 1992)

Pateman, Roy, *Eritrea: Even the Stones Are Burning* (Trenton, N.J., 1998)

Pike, Clarence Edward, *Famine* (Cornwall, Ontario, 1982)

Póirtéir, Cathal (ed.), *The Great Irish Famine* (Dublin, 1995)

Póirtéir, Cathal (ed.), *Famine Echoes* (Dublin, 1995)

Sen, Amartya, *Development as Freedom* (Oxford, 2001)

Sen, Amartya, *Poverty and Famines: an Essay on Entitlements and Deprivation* (Oxford, 1981)

Sen, Ela, *Darkening Days* (Calcutta, 1944)

Shell-Duncan, *Female Circumcision in Africa: Culture, Controversy, and Change* (New Brunswick, N.J., 2000)

Somerville, Alexander, *Letters from Ireland during the Famine of 1847* (Dublin, 1994)

Spear, Percival, *India: a Modern History* (Ann Arbor, 1961)

Stevenson, Richard, *Bengal Tiger and British Lion: an Account of the Bengal Famine of 1943* (Lincoln, Nebraska, 2005)

Tóibín, Colm and Ferriter, Diarmaid, *The Irish Famine* (London, 1999)

Uekert, Brenda K, *Rivers of Blood: a Comparative Study of Government Massacres* (Westport, Conn., 1995)

Valone, David A. and Kinealy, Christine (ed.), *Ireland's Great Hunger, Silence, Memory and Commemoration* (Boston, 2002)

Varnis, Steven L., *Reluctant Aid or Aiding the Reluctant: U.S. Food Policy and Ethiopian Famine Relief* (New Brunswick, N.J., 1990)

Vaughn, Megan, *The Story of an African Famine* (Cambridge, UK, 1997)

de Waal, Alex, *Famine Crimes, Politics and the Disaster Relief Industry in Africa* (Oxford, 1997)

Woodham-Smith, *The Great Hunger 1845–1849* (London, 1962)

Wrigley, G. A. and Mallory, Walter H., *China: Land of Famine* (New York, 1926)

ARTICLES

Beyene, Selam, 'Famine: Zenawi's Stealth Weapon of Genocide and Repression', *Ethiopian Review*, 15 June 2008

Bhattacharya, Malini, 'The Class Character of Sexuality: Peasant Women in Manik Bandopadhyay', *Social Science*, Volume 15, Number 164, January 1987

Cohen, Sarah, 'A Brief History of the Armenian Genocide', *Social Education*, Volume 69, 2005

Curtis, Patrice, 'Famine Household Coping Strategies: Their Usefulness for Understanding Household Response to Armed Conflict', Refugee Studies Programme Documentation Centre, 1993

Ethiopia Famine Food Field Guide, www.africa.upenn.edu/faminefood

Gade, William, 'Hyenas and Humans in the Horn of Africa', *Geographical Review*, Volume 96, 2006

Greenough, Paul, 'Indian Famines and Peasant Victims: the Case of Bengal in 1943–1944', *Modern Asian Studies*, Volume 14, Issue 2, April 1980

Heehs, Peter, 'India's Divided Loyalties?' *History Today*, Volume 45, July 1995

Kuma, Gupalakrishna, 'Ethiopian Famines, 1973–1985', World Institute for Development Economics, Working Paper 26, November 1987

Ladurie, E. L., 'Amenhorrhea during the famines of the 17th–20th centuries', *Annales de Demographie Historique*, October–December 1969

Lorgan, Christy Cannon, 'The Experience of Villagisation: Lessons from Ethiopia, Mozambique and Tanzania', Oxfam, Great Britain, January 1999

Ó'Gráda, Cormac, 'A Demography of Famine: an Indian Historical Perspective', *Journal of Development Studies*, December 1997

Ó'Gráda, Cormac, 'The Ripple that Drowns: 20th Century Famines in China and India as Economic History', *Economic History Review*, Volume 61, Issue 1, August 2008

Ó'Gráda, Cormac, 'The Great Famine in Folk Memory and in Song', personal copy in possession of author

Padmanathan, S. Y., 'The Great Bengal Famine', *Annual Review of Phytopathology II* (1973)

Sen, Amartya, 'Starvation and Exchange Entitlements: a General Approach and its Applications', *Cambridge Journal of Economics*, Volume 1, Issue 1, 1977

Snyder, Scott, 'American Religious NGOs in North Korea: a Paradoxical Relationship', *Ethics and International Affairs*, Vol. 21, 2007

Swedder, Richard A., '"What about Female Genital Mutilation?" And Why Understanding Culture Matters in the First Place', *Daedalus*, Volume 129, 2000

Tao, Dennis, 'China's Agricultural Crisis and Famine of 1958–1961: a Survey and Comparisons to Russian Famines', *Comparative Economic Studies*, Volume 50, 2008

Index

index

Thomas Keneally won the Booker Prize in 1982 with *Schindler's Ark*, later made into the Academy Award-winning film *Schindler's List* by Steven Spielberg. He has written ten works of nonfiction, including his recent memoir *Searching for Schindler*. His novels *The Chant of Jimmy Blacksmith*, *Gossip from the Forest*, and *Confederates* were all shortlisted for the Booker Prize, while *Bring Larks* and *Heroes and Three Cheers for the Parclete* won the Miles Franklin Award. He lives in Australia.

PublicAffairs is a publishing house founded in 1997. It is a tribute to the standards, values, and flair of three persons who have served as mentors to countless reporters, writers, editors, and book people of all kinds, including me.

I. F. STONE, proprietor of *I. F. Stone's Weekly*, combined a commitment to the First Amendment with entrepreneurial zeal and reporting skill and became one of the great independent journalists in American history. At the age of eighty, Izzy published *The Trial of Socrates*, which was a national bestseller. He wrote the book after he taught himself ancient Greek.

BENJAMIN C. BRADLEE was for nearly thirty years the charismatic editorial leader of *The Washington Post*. It was Ben who gave the *Post* the range and courage to pursue such historic issues as Watergate. He supported his reporters with a tenacity that made them fearless and it is no accident that so many became authors of influential, best-selling books.

ROBERT L. BERNSTEIN, the chief executive of Random House for more than a quarter century, guided one of the nation's premier publishing houses. Bob was personally responsible for many books of political dissent and argument that challenged tyranny around the globe. He is also the founder and longtime chair of Human Rights Watch, one of the most respected human rights organizations in the world.

.   .   .

For fifty years, the banner of Public Affairs Press was carried by its owner Morris B. Schnapper, who published Gandhi, Nasser, Toynbee, Truman, and about 1,500 other authors. In 1983, Schnapper was described by *The Washington Post* as "a redoubtable gadfly." His legacy will endure in the books to come.

Peter Osnos, *Founder and Editor-at-Large*